american
VIRGIN

WET

american VIRGIN WET

STEVEN T. SEAGLE WRITER

BECKY CLOONAN & CHRISTINE NORRIE PENCILLERS

BECKY CLOONAN & JIM RUGG INKERS

BRIAN MILLER COLORIST JARED K. FLETCHER LETTERER

JOSHUA MIDDLETON ORIGINAL SERIES COVERS

AMERICAN VIRGIN CREATED BY STEVEN T. SEAGLE AND BECKY CLOONAN

Karen Berger Senior VP-Executive Editor Shelly Bond Editor-original series Angela Rufino Assistant Editor-original series
Bob Harras Editor-collected edition Robbin Brosterman Senior Art Director Paul Levitz President & Publisher
Georg Brewer VP-Design & DC Direct Creative Richard Bruning Senior VP-Creative Director Patrick Caldon Executive VP-Finance & Operations
Chris Caramalis VP-Finance John Cunningham VP-Marketing Terri Cunningham VP-Managing Editor Alison Gill VP-Manufacturing
David Hyde VP-Publicity Hank Kanalz VP-General Manager, WildStorm Jim Lee Editorial Director-WildStorm
Paula Lowitt Senior VP-Business & Legal Affairs MaryEllen McLaughlin VP-Advertising & Custom Publishing
John Nee Senior VP-Business Development Gregory Noveck Senior VP-Creative Affairs Sue Pohja VP-Book Trade Sales
Steve Rotterdam Senior VP-Sales & Marketing Cheryl Rubin Senior VP-Brand Management
Jeff Trojan VP-Business Development, DC Direct Bob Wayne VP-Sales

Cover illustration by Joshua Middleton. Logo design by Steve Cook. Publication design by Amelia Grohman.

DC Comics, 1700 Broadway, New York, NY 10019. A Warner Bros. Entertainment Company.
Printed in Canada. First Printing. ISBN: 1-4012-1494-0 ISBN 13: 978-1-4012-1494-4

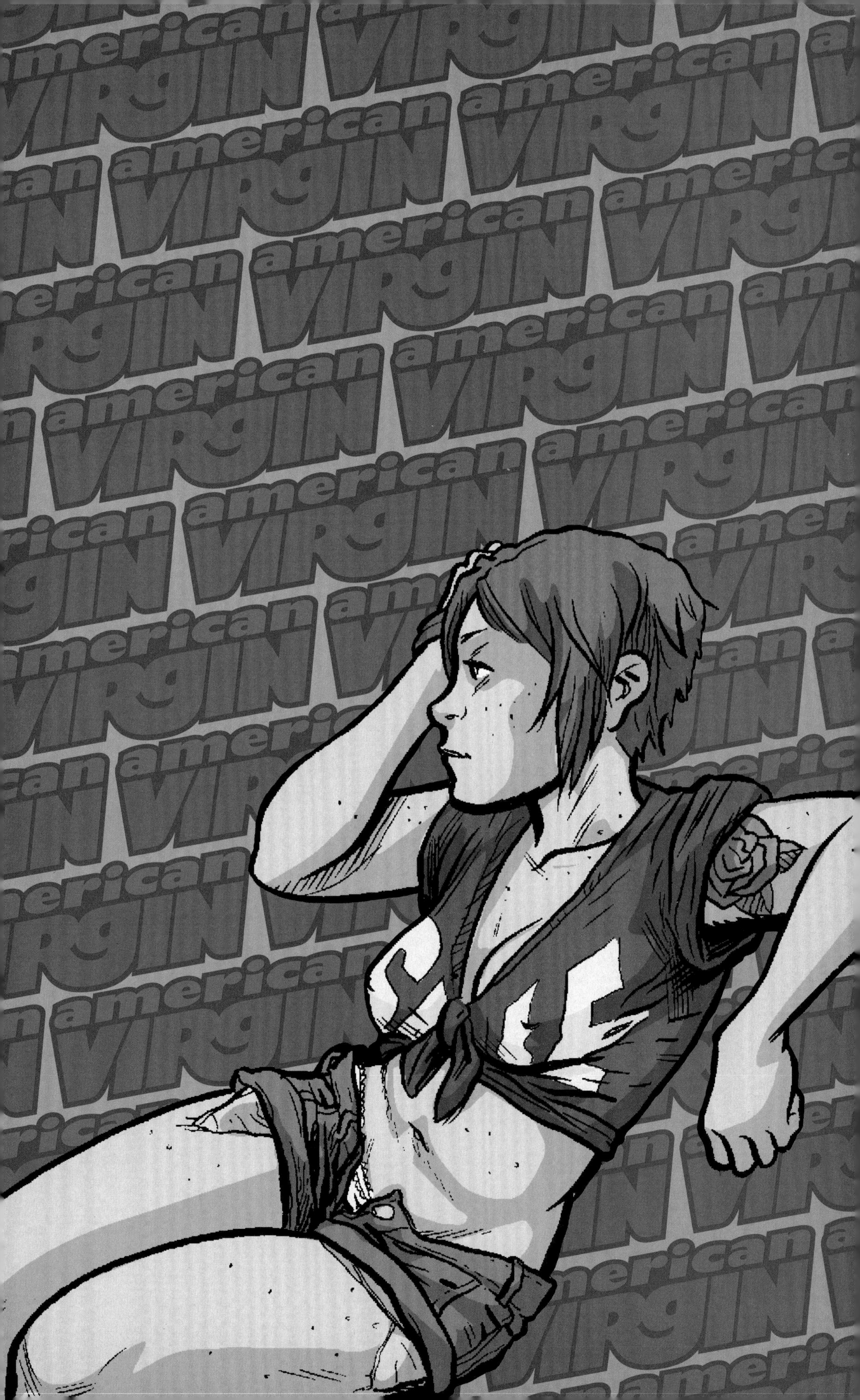
american VIRGIN

PREVIOUSLY IN AMERICAN VIRGIN...

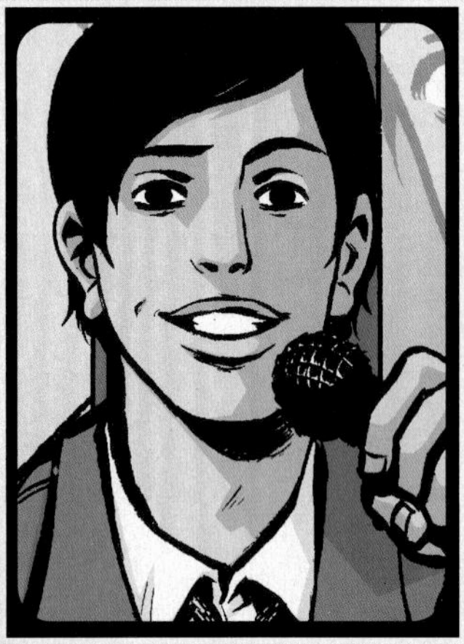

ADAM CHAMBERLAIN went from being the perfect young virginity advocate with the perfect young life...

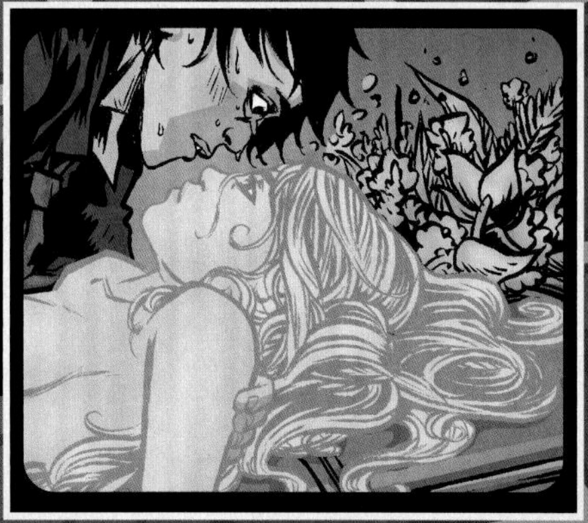

...to humping the coffin of his murdered ex-girlfriend and wearing a leather harness at a southern hemisphere gay-day in a little under a month.

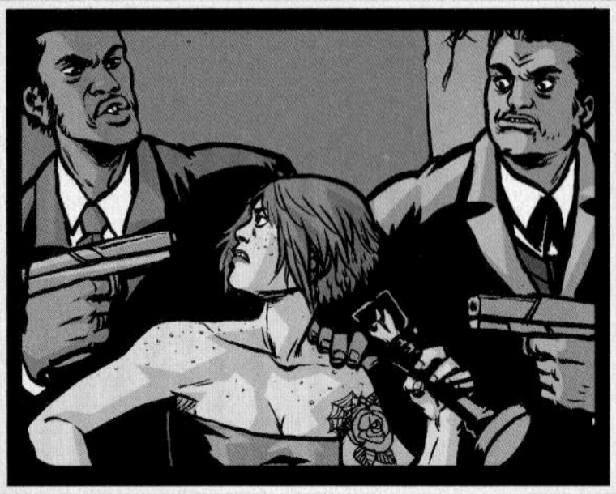

CYNDI STRUGG, Adam's trash-talking stepsister, accompanied Adam "down under" to help ease him through the gathering storm in his soul, but it just might be that CYNDI was running away from her own bullet-laden Miami past.

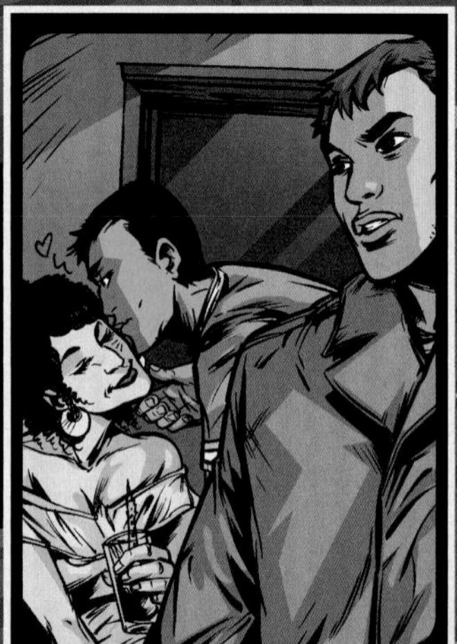

MEL, Adam's gun-for-hire guide, was forced to reveal a little piece of his past when the trio followed a lead on Adam's girlfriend's executioner right back into MEL's old Melbourne stomping grounds — the beach home of his inebriated ex CLAUDA and her Gay Olympics superstar brother DEACON.

Adam lived a "Hollywood" high life at the gala Christian Speakers conference spearheaded by his manager MOON...

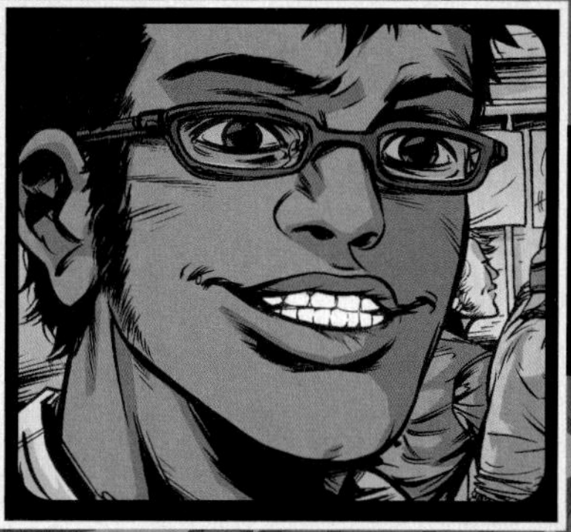

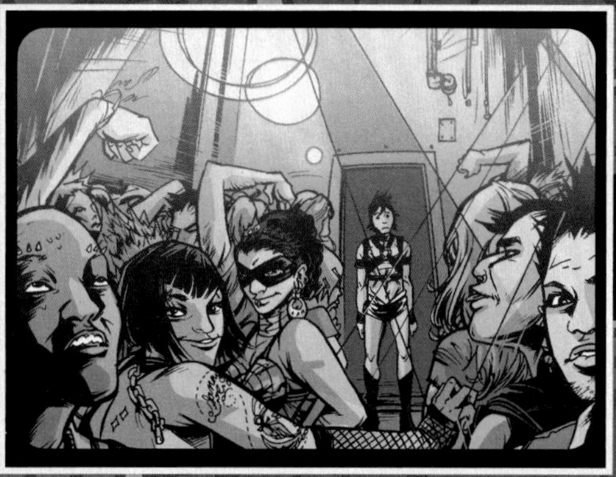

...but he quickly slid to the wrong kind of lights...

...cameras...

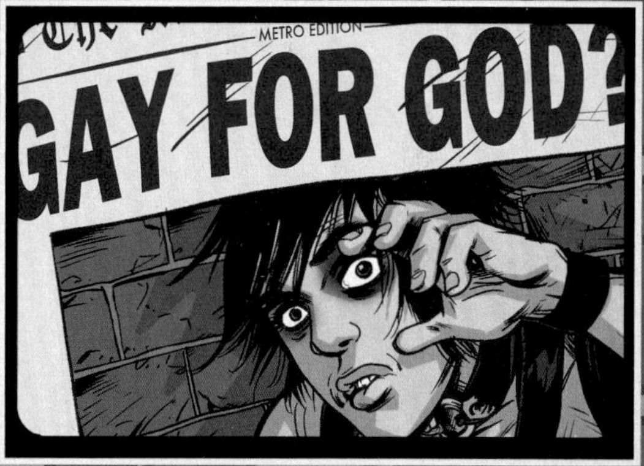
METRO EDITION
GAY FOR GOD?

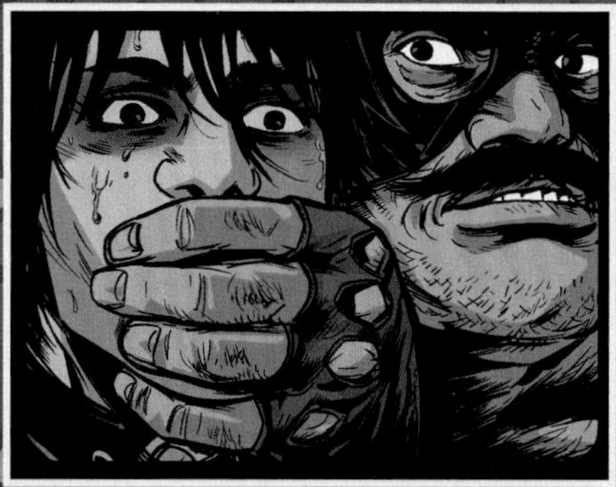

...and action.

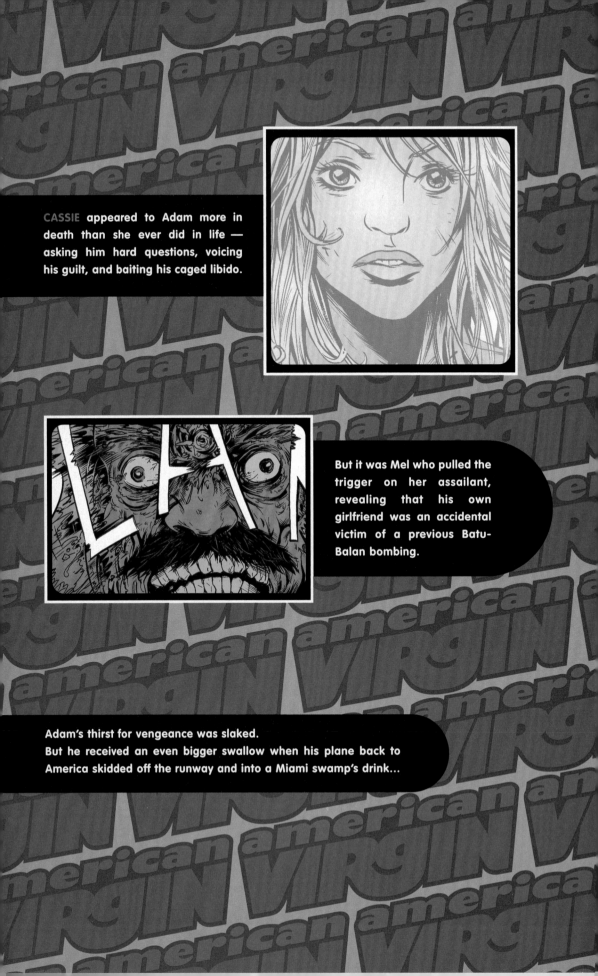

CASSIE appeared to Adam more in death than she ever did in life — asking him hard questions, voicing his guilt, and baiting his caged libido.

But it was Mel who pulled the trigger on her assailant, revealing that his own girlfriend was an accidental victim of a previous Batu-Balan bombing.

Adam's thirst for vengeance was slaked.
But he received an even bigger swallow when his plane back to America skidded off the runway and into a Miami swamp's drink...

CHAPTER ONE

Chapter art by Becky Cloonan and Christine Norrie

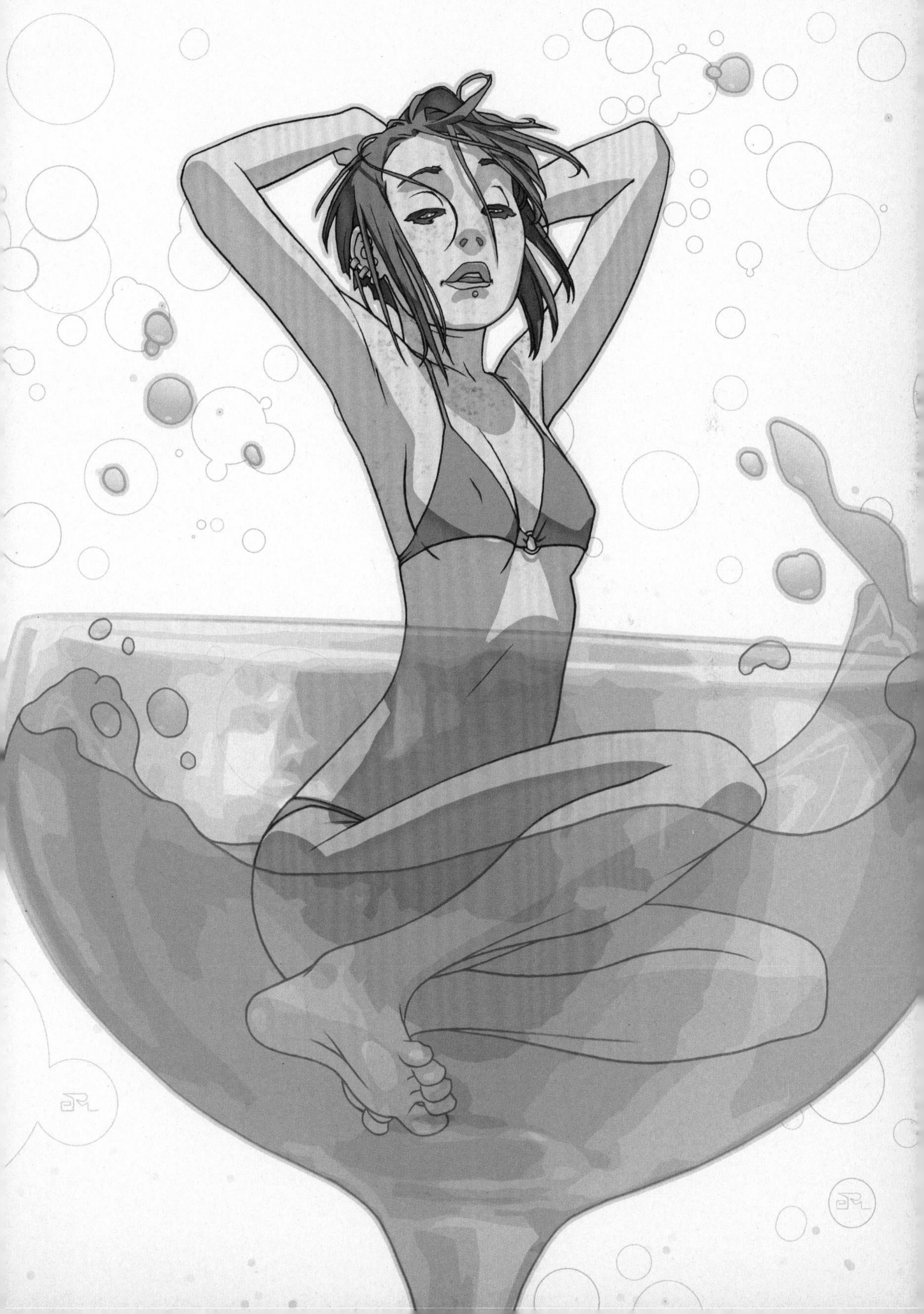

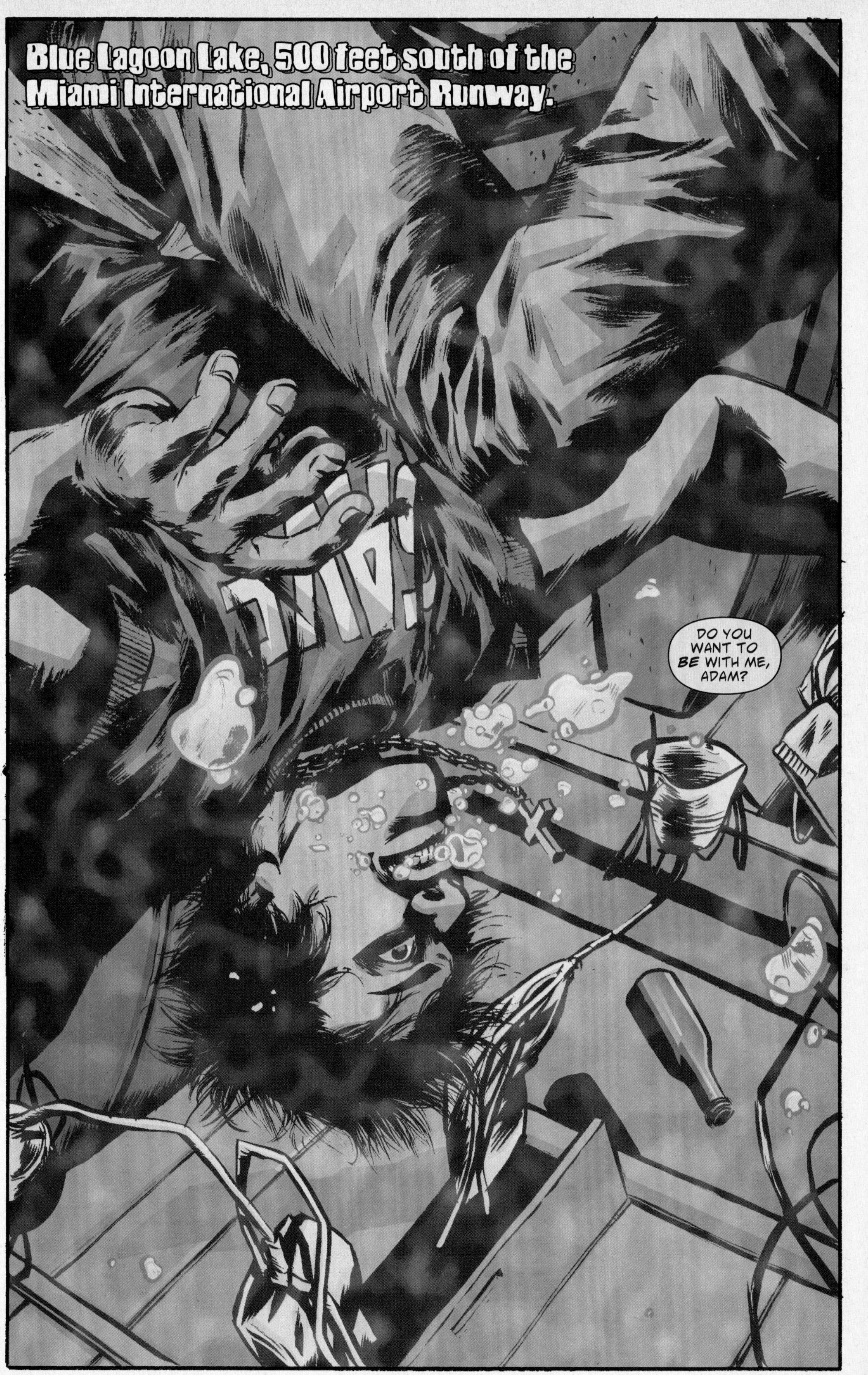
Blue Lagoon Lake, 500 feet south of the Miami International Airport Runway.
DO YOU WANT TO BE WITH ME, ADAM?

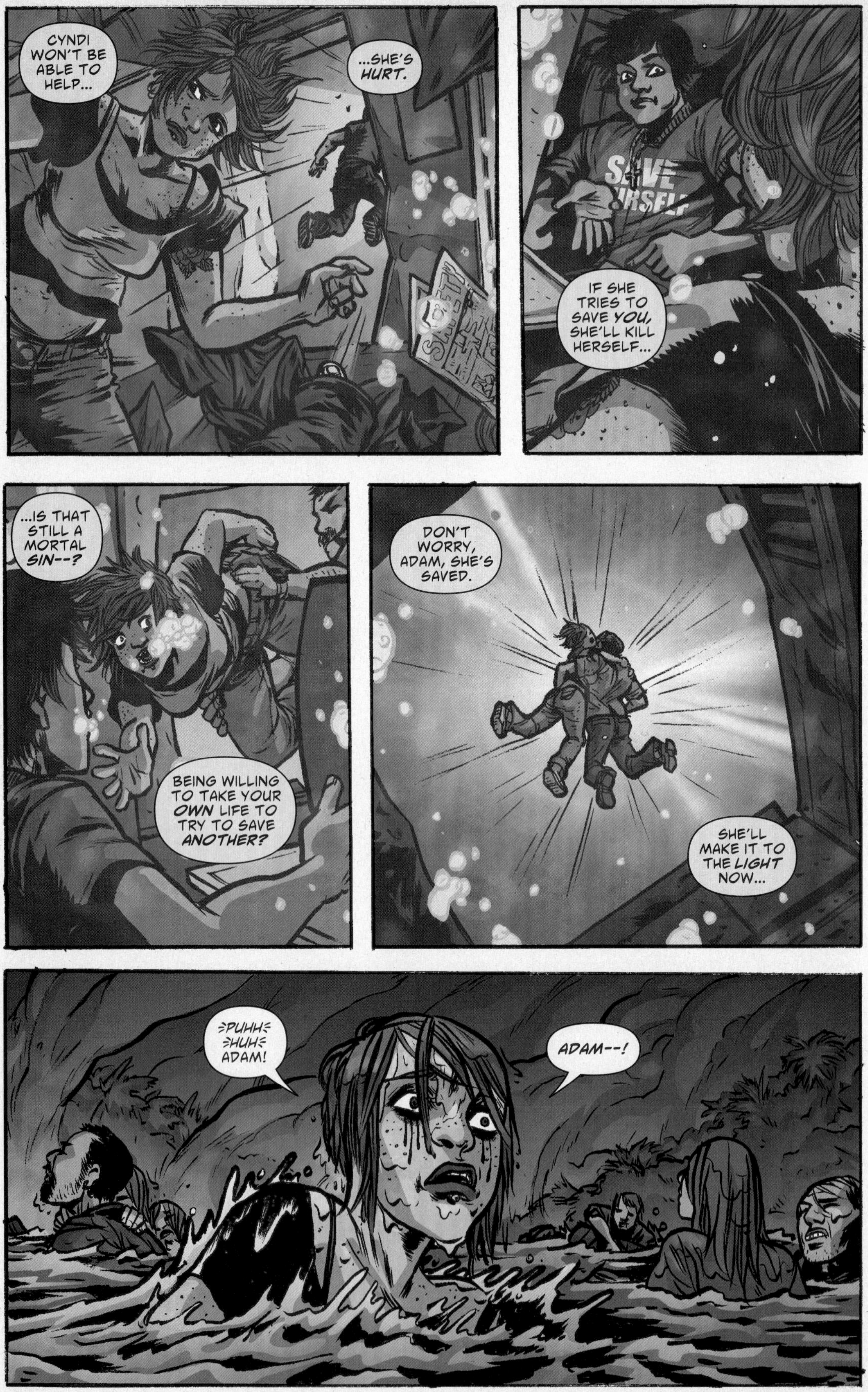
CYNDI WON'T BE ABLE TO HELP...
...SHE'S HURT.
IF SHE TRIES TO SAVE YOU, SHE'LL KILL HERSELF...
...IS THAT STILL A MORTAL SIN--?
BEING WILLING TO TAKE YOUR OWN LIFE TO TRY TO SAVE ANOTHER?
DON'T WORRY, ADAM, SHE'S SAVED.
SHE'LL MAKE IT TO THE LIGHT NOW...
PUHH HUH ADAM!
ADAM--!

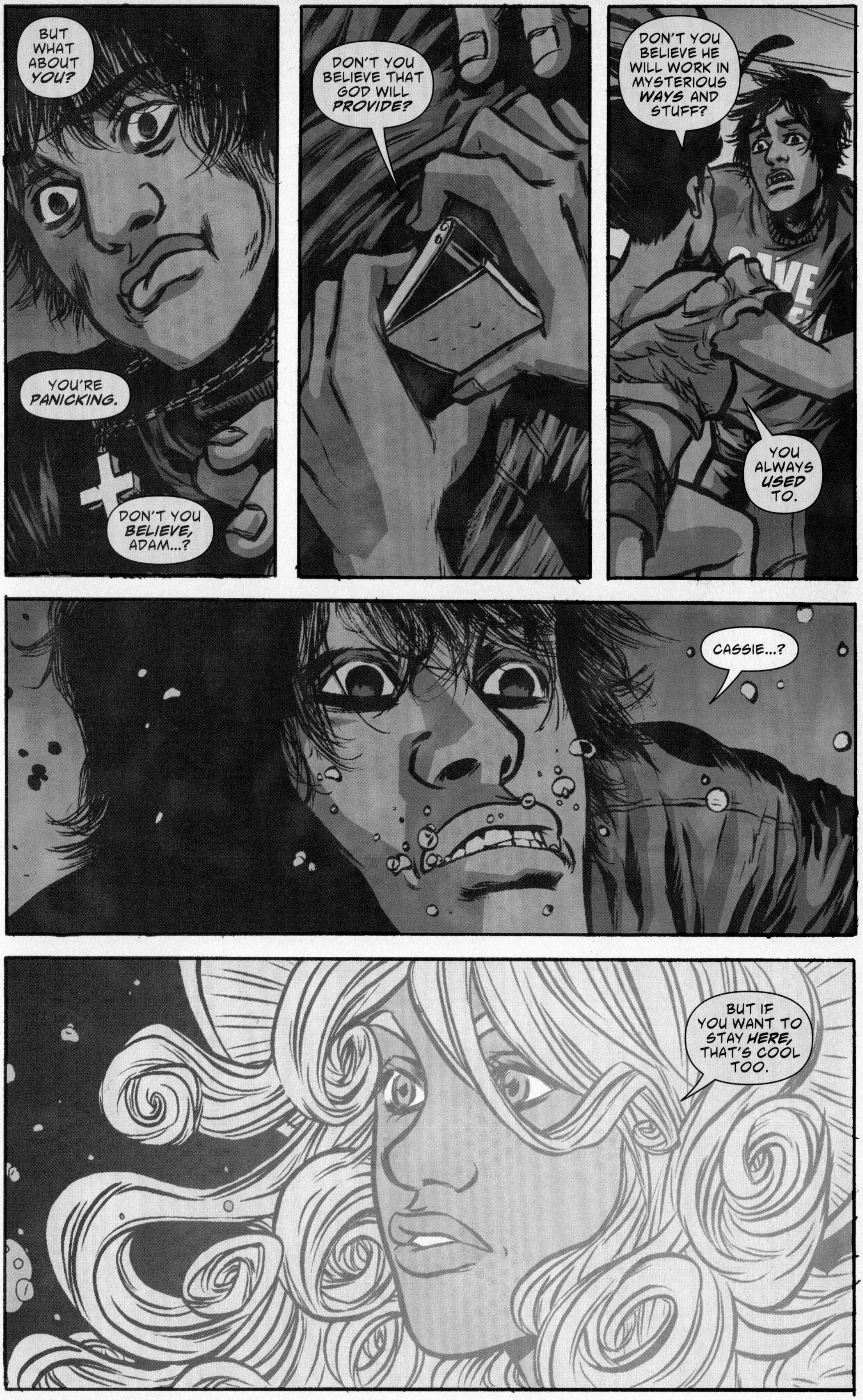

BUT WHAT ABOUT *YOU?*
YOU'RE *PANICKING.*
DON'T YOU *BELIEVE,* ADAM...?
DON'T YOU BELIEVE THAT GOD WILL *PROVIDE?*
DON'T YOU BELIEVE HE WILL WORK IN MYSTERIOUS *WAYS* AND STUFF?
YOU ALWAYS *USED* TO.
CASSIE...?
BUT IF YOU WANT TO STAY *HERE,* THAT'S COOL TOO.

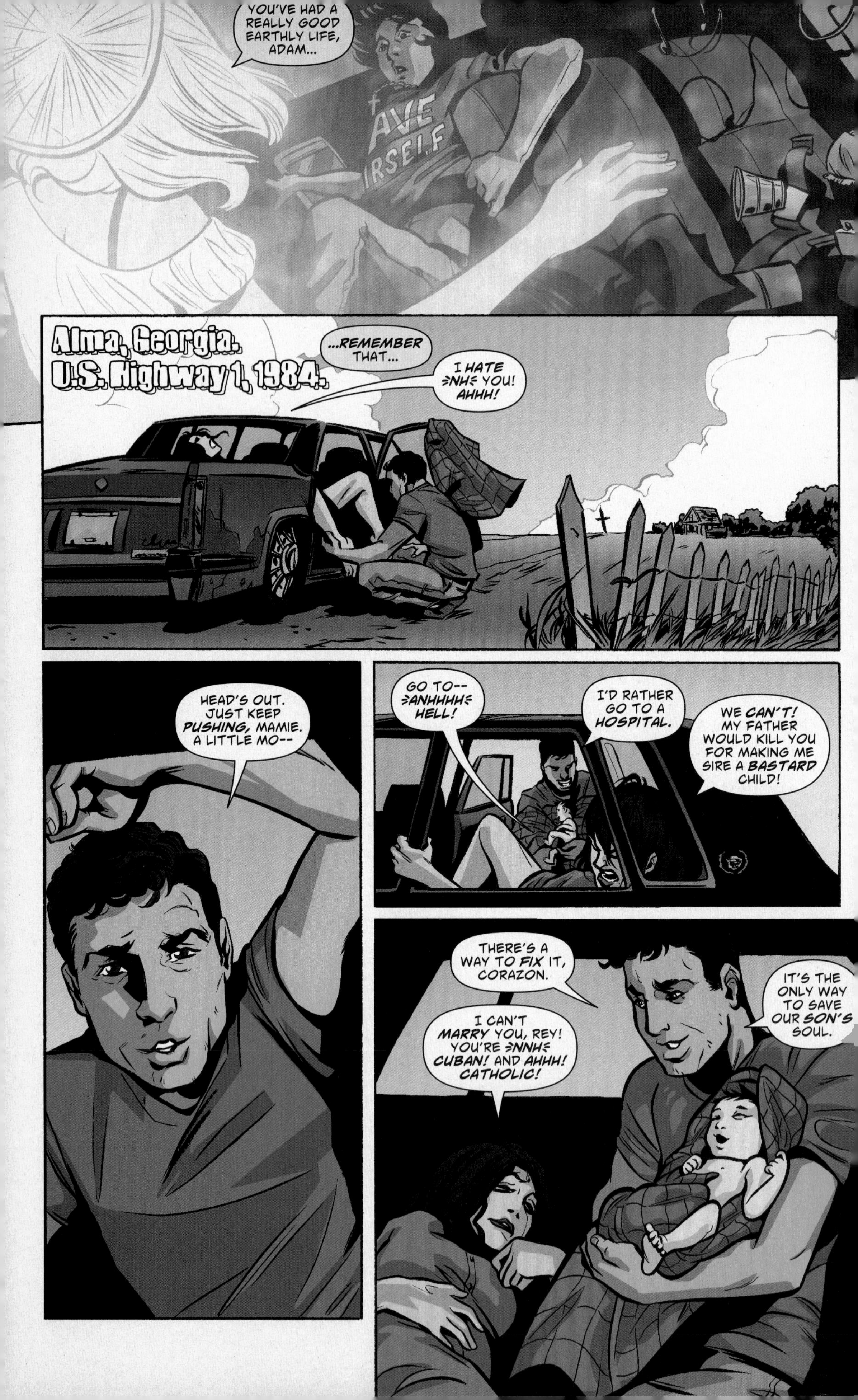
YOU'VE HAD A REALLY GOOD EARTHLY LIFE, ADAM...
Alma, Georgia. U.S. Highway 1, 1984.
...REMEMBER THAT...
I HATE NH YOU! AHHH!
HEAD'S OUT. JUST KEEP PUSHING, MAMIE. A LITTLE MO--
GO TO-- ANHHHH HELL!
I'D RATHER GO TO A HOSPITAL.
WE CAN'T! MY FATHER WOULD KILL YOU FOR MAKING ME SIRE A BASTARD CHILD!
THERE'S A WAY TO FIX IT, CORAZON.
I CAN'T MARRY YOU, REY! YOU'RE NNH CUBAN! AND AHHH! CATHOLIC!
IT'S THE ONLY WAY TO SAVE OUR SON'S SOUL.

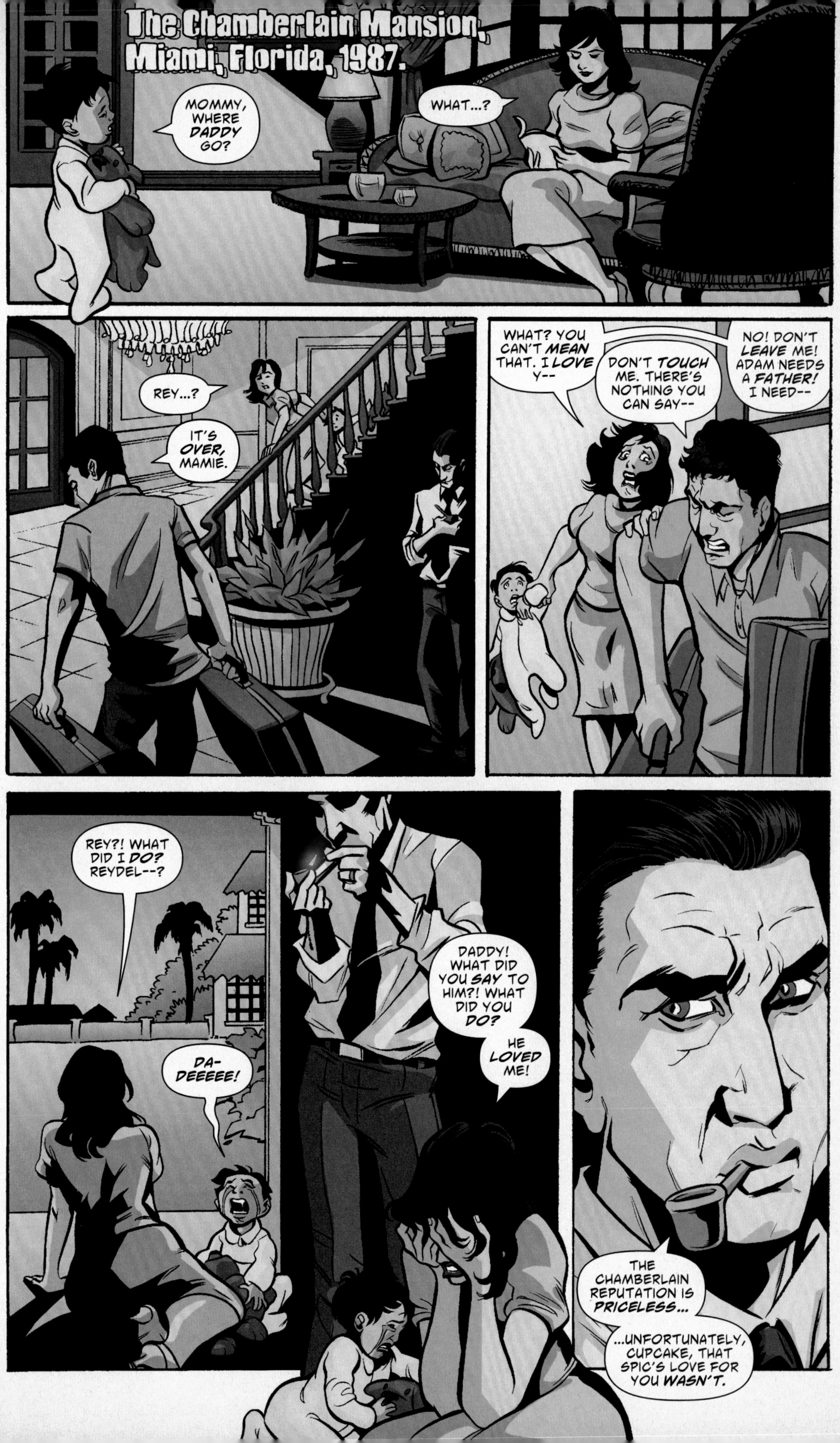

The Chamberlain Mansion, Miami, Florida, 1987.
MOMMY, WHERE DADDY GO?
WHAT...?
REY...?
IT'S OVER, MAMIE.
WHAT? YOU CAN'T MEAN THAT. I LOVE Y--
DON'T TOUCH ME. THERE'S NOTHING YOU CAN SAY--
NO! DON'T LEAVE ME! ADAM NEEDS A FATHER! I NEED--
REY?! WHAT DID I DO? REYDEL--?
DA-DEEEEEE!
DADDY! WHAT DID YOU SAY TO HIM?! WHAT DID YOU DO?
HE LOVED ME!
THE CHAMBERLAIN REPUTATION IS PRICELESS...
...UNFORTUNATELY, CUPCAKE, THAT SPIC'S LOVE FOR YOU WASN'T.

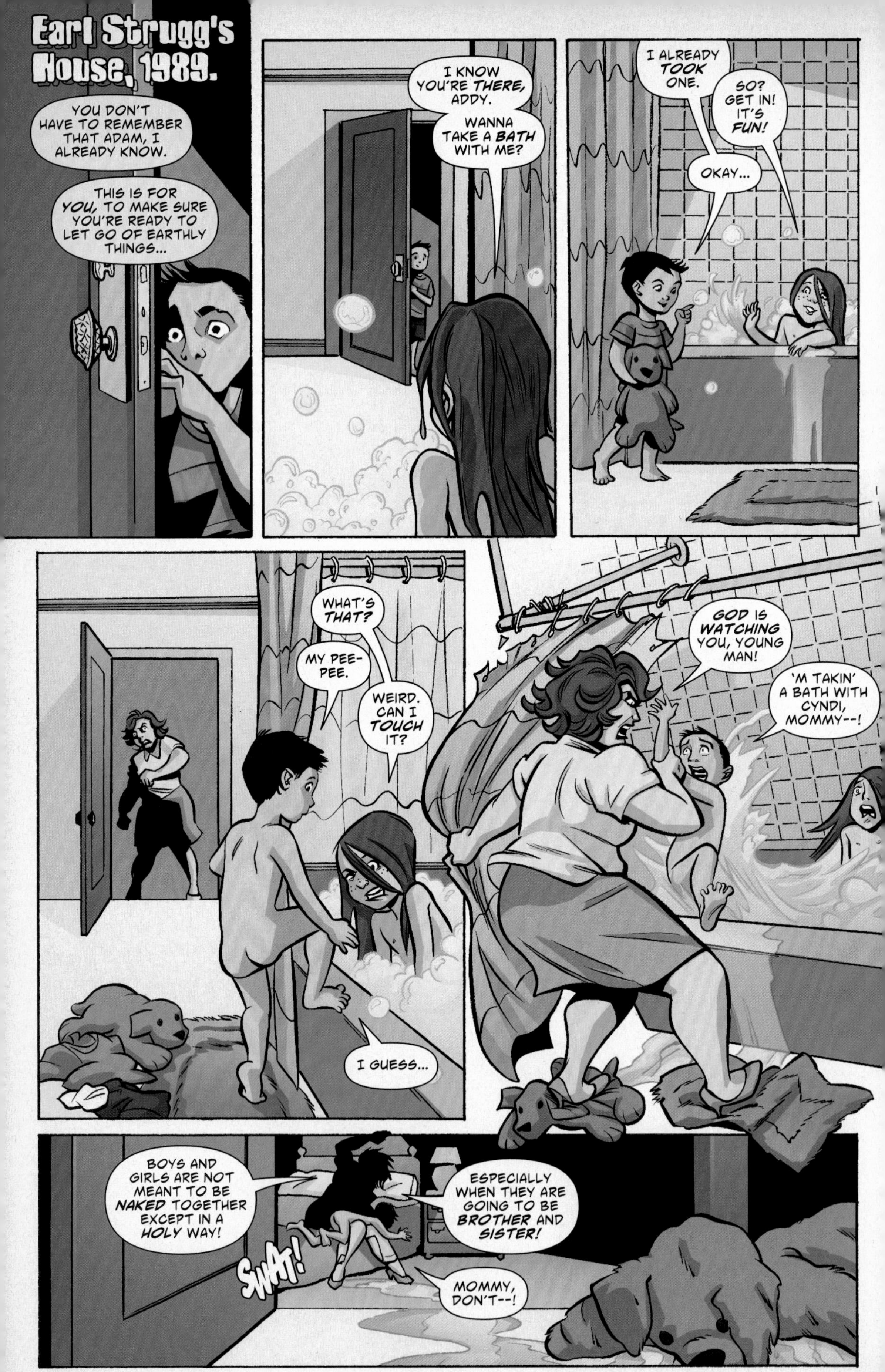

Earl Strugg's House, 1989.
YOU DON'T HAVE TO REMEMBER THAT ADAM, I ALREADY KNOW.
THIS IS FOR YOU, TO MAKE SURE YOU'RE READY TO LET GO OF EARTHLY THINGS...
I KNOW YOU'RE THERE, ADDY.
WANNA TAKE A BATH WITH ME?
I ALREADY TOOK ONE.
SO? GET IN! IT'S FUN!
OKAY...
WHAT'S THAT?
MY PEE-PEE.
WEIRD. CAN I TOUCH IT?
I GUESS...
GOD IS WATCHING YOU, YOUNG MAN!
'M TAKIN' A BATH WITH CYNDI, MOMMY--!
BOYS AND GIRLS ARE NOT MEANT TO BE NAKED TOGETHER EXCEPT IN A HOLY WAY!
SWAT!
ESPECIALLY WHEN THEY ARE GOING TO BE BROTHER AND SISTER!
MOMMY, DON'T--!

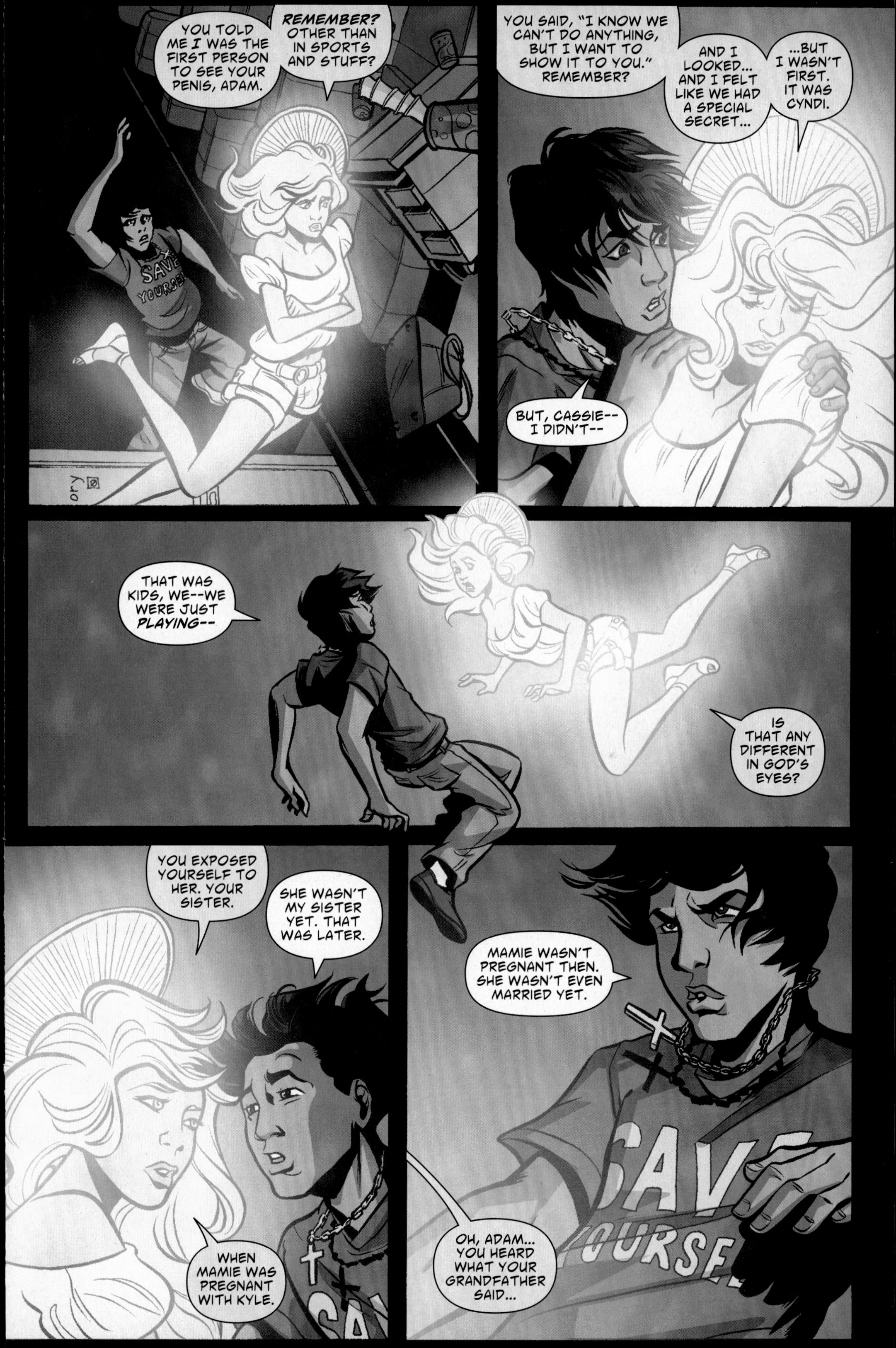
YOU TOLD ME I WAS THE FIRST PERSON TO SEE YOUR PENIS, ADAM.
REMEMBER? OTHER THAN IN SPORTS AND STUFF?
SAVE YOURSELF
YOU SAID, "I KNOW WE CAN'T DO ANYTHING, BUT I WANT TO SHOW IT TO YOU." REMEMBER?
AND I LOOKED... AND I FELT LIKE WE HAD A SPECIAL SECRET...
...BUT I WASN'T FIRST. IT WAS CYNDI.
BUT, CASSIE-- I DIDN'T--
THAT WAS KIDS, WE--WE WERE JUST PLAYING--
IS THAT ANY DIFFERENT IN GOD'S EYES?
YOU EXPOSED YOURSELF TO HER. YOUR SISTER.
SHE WASN'T MY SISTER YET. THAT WAS LATER.
WHEN MAMIE WAS PREGNANT WITH KYLE.
MAMIE WASN'T PREGNANT THEN. SHE WASN'T EVEN MARRIED YET.
OH, ADAM... YOU HEARD WHAT YOUR GRANDFATHER SAID...

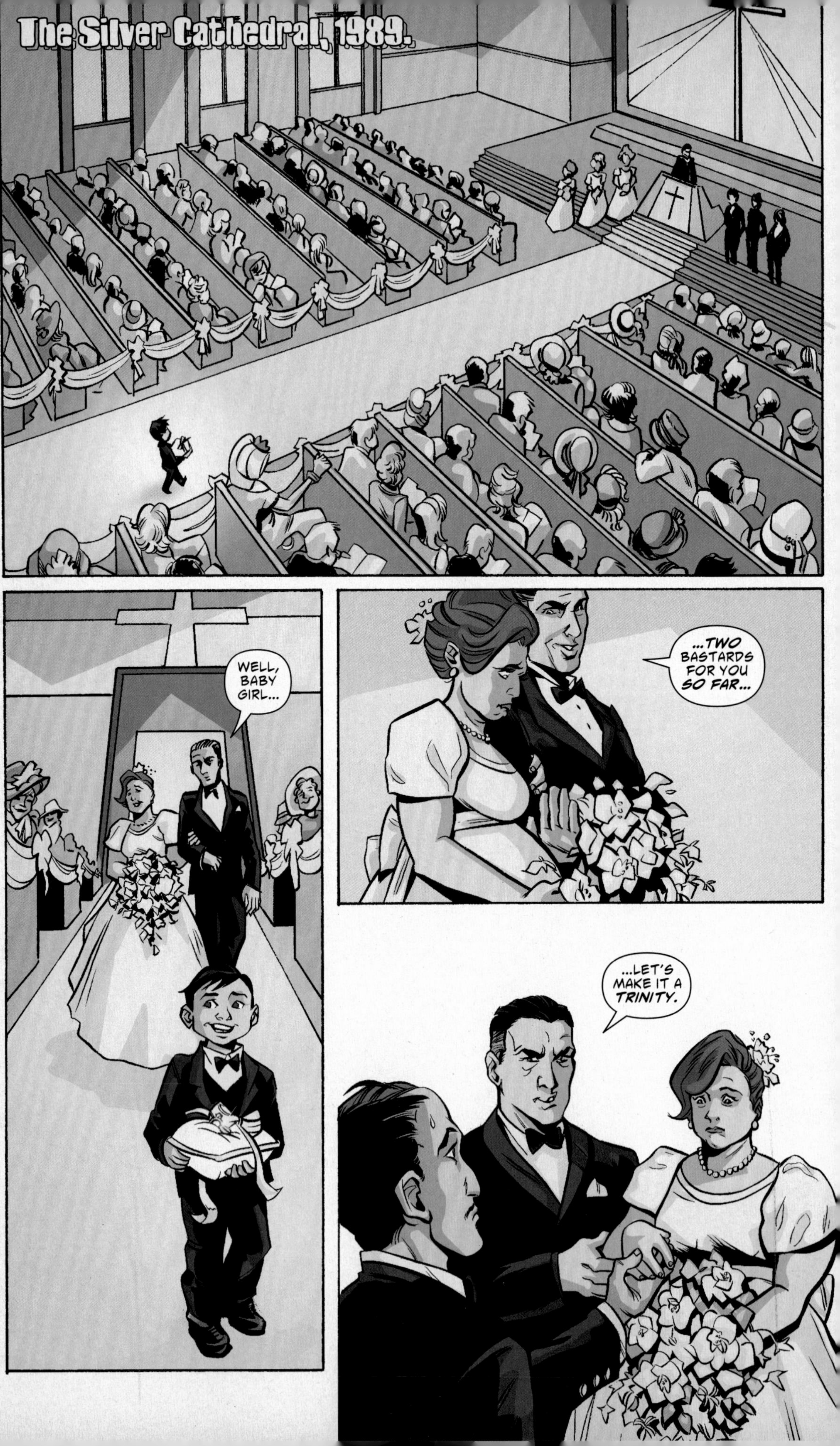
The Silver Cathedral, 1989.
WELL, BABY GIRL...
...TWO BASTARDS FOR YOU SO FAR...
...LET'S MAKE IT A TRINITY.

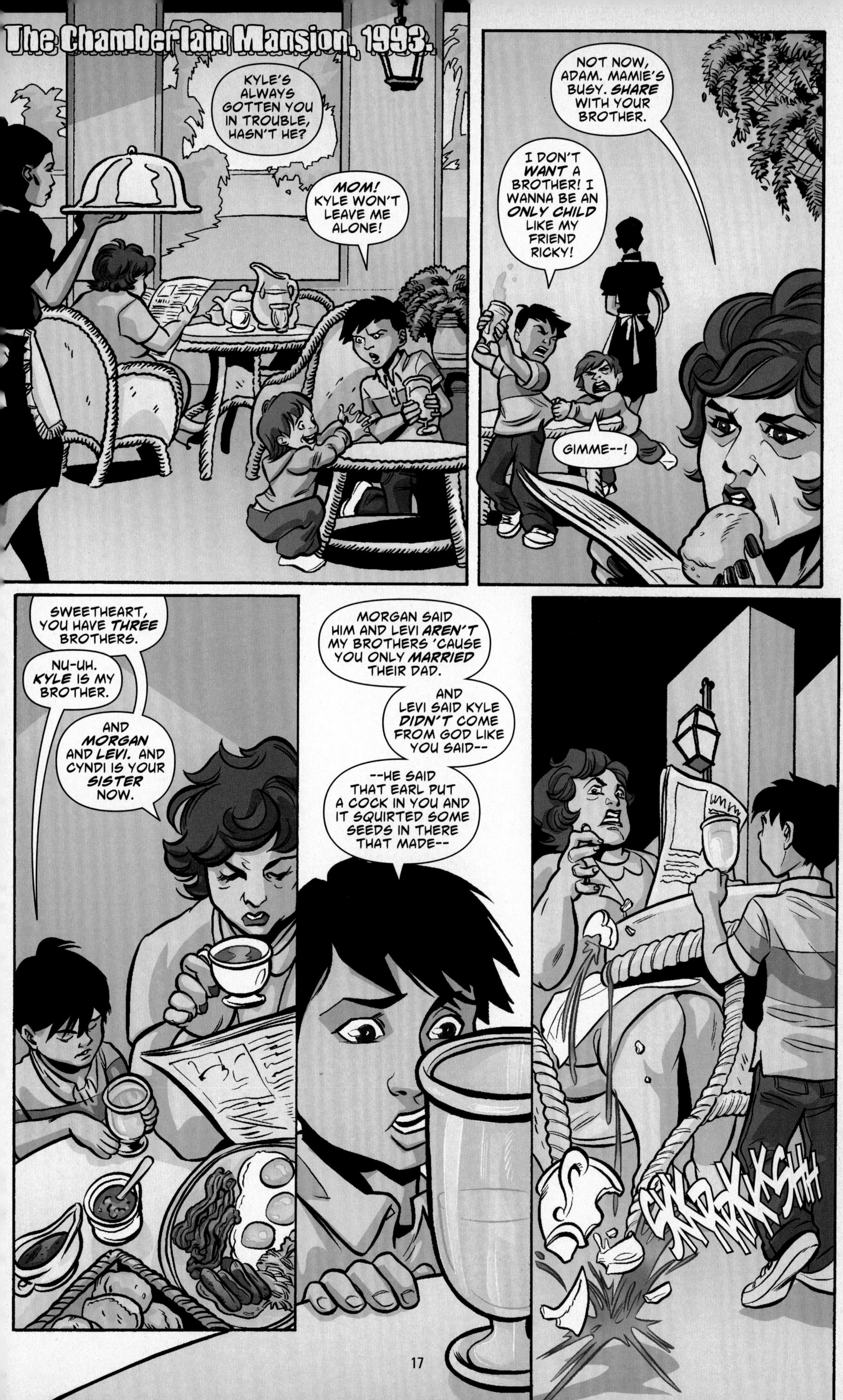
The Chamberlain Mansion, 1993.
KYLE'S ALWAYS GOTTEN YOU IN TROUBLE, HASN'T HE?
MOM! KYLE WON'T LEAVE ME ALONE!
NOT NOW, ADAM. MAMIE'S BUSY. SHARE WITH YOUR BROTHER.
I DON'T WANT A BROTHER! I WANNA BE AN ONLY CHILD LIKE MY FRIEND RICKY!
GIMME--!
SWEETHEART, YOU HAVE THREE BROTHERS.
NU-UH. KYLE IS MY BROTHER.
AND MORGAN AND LEVI. AND CYNDI IS YOUR SISTER NOW.
MORGAN SAID HIM AND LEVI AREN'T MY BROTHERS 'CAUSE YOU ONLY MARRIED THEIR DAD.
AND LEVI SAID KYLE DIDN'T COME FROM GOD LIKE YOU SAID--
--HE SAID THAT EARL PUT A COCK IN YOU AND IT SQUIRTED SOME SEEDS IN THERE THAT MADE--
CRRKKSSHH

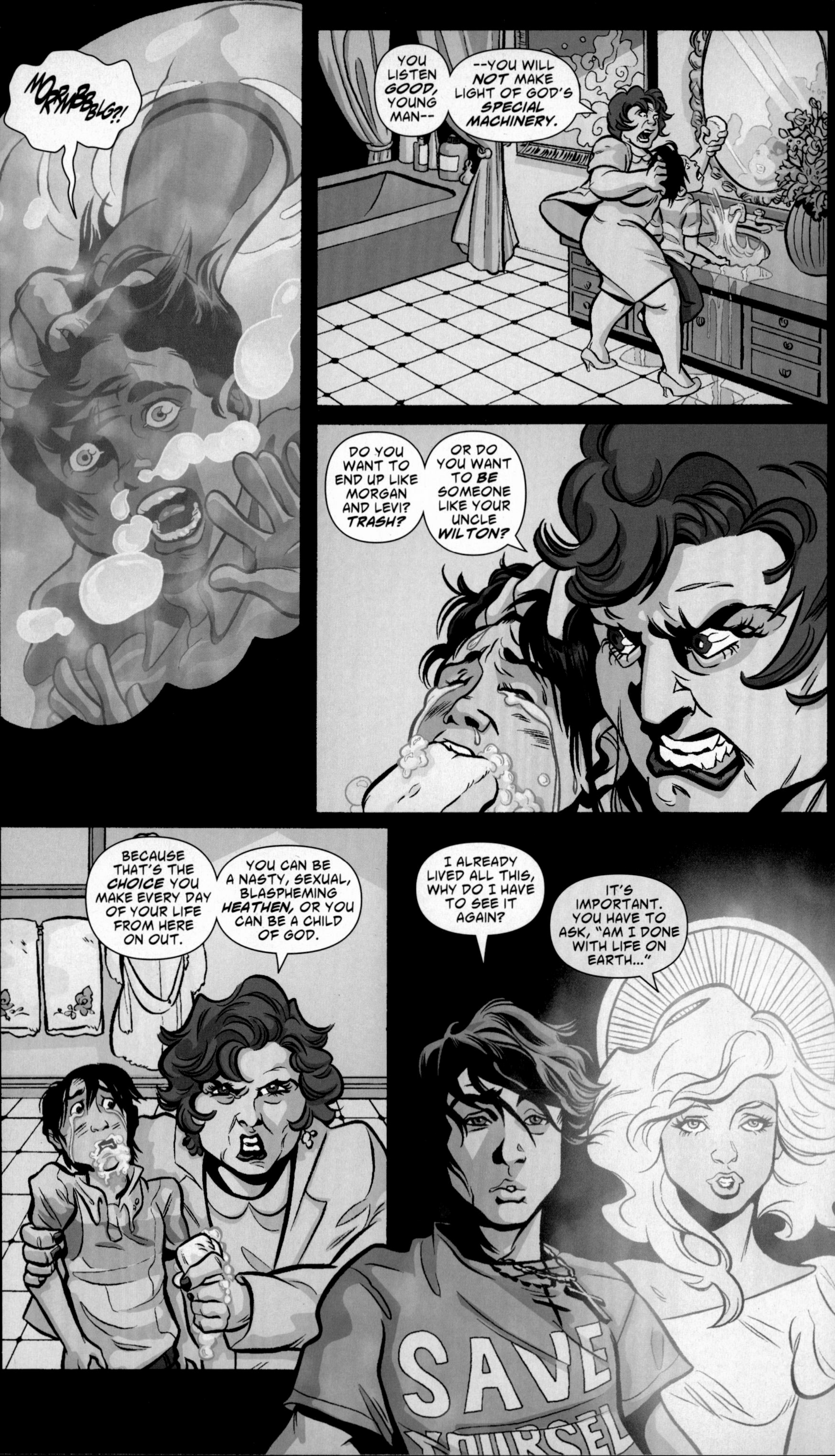
MORRMBBBLG?!
YOU LISTEN GOOD, YOUNG MAN--
--YOU WILL NOT MAKE LIGHT OF GOD'S SPECIAL MACHINERY.
DO YOU WANT TO END UP LIKE MORGAN AND LEVI? TRASH?
OR DO YOU WANT TO BE SOMEONE LIKE YOUR UNCLE WILTON?
BECAUSE THAT'S THE CHOICE YOU MAKE EVERY DAY OF YOUR LIFE FROM HERE ON OUT.
YOU CAN BE A NASTY, SEXUAL, BLASPHEMING HEATHEN, OR YOU CAN BE A CHILD OF GOD.
I ALREADY LIVED ALL THIS, WHY DO I HAVE TO SEE IT AGAIN?
IT'S IMPORTANT. YOU HAVE TO ASK, "AM I DONE WITH LIFE ON EARTH..."
SAVE

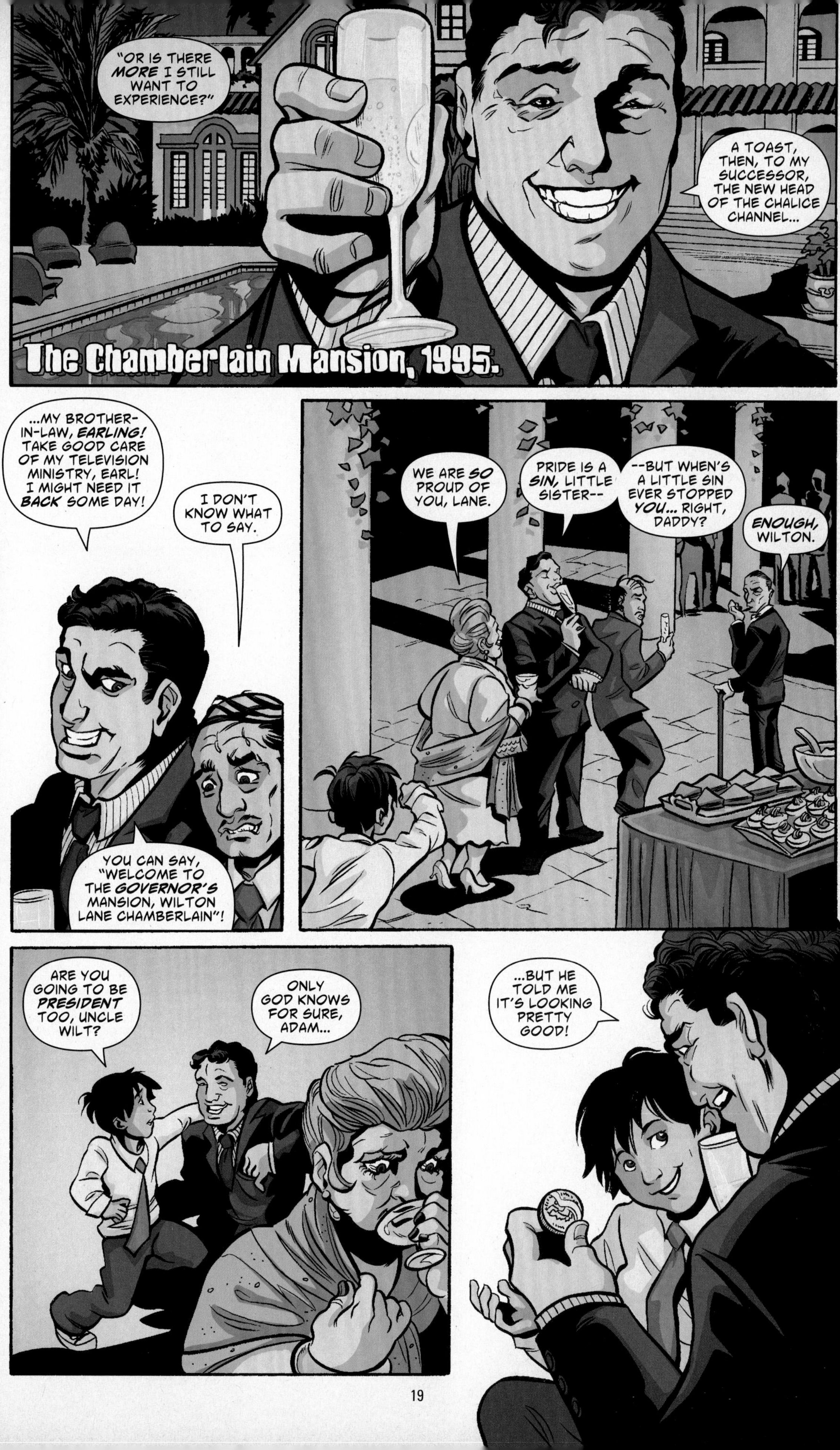
"OR IS THERE MORE I STILL WANT TO EXPERIENCE?"
A TOAST, THEN, TO MY SUCCESSOR, THE NEW HEAD OF THE CHALICE CHANNEL...
The Chamberlain Mansion, 1995.
...MY BROTHER-IN-LAW, EARLING! TAKE GOOD CARE OF MY TELEVISION MINISTRY, EARL! I MIGHT NEED IT BACK SOME DAY!
I DON'T KNOW WHAT TO SAY.
YOU CAN SAY, "WELCOME TO THE GOVERNOR'S MANSION, WILTON LANE CHAMBERLAIN"!
WE ARE SO PROUD OF YOU, LANE.
PRIDE IS A SIN, LITTLE SISTER--
--BUT WHEN'S A LITTLE SIN EVER STOPPED YOU... RIGHT, DADDY?
ENOUGH, WILTON.
ARE YOU GOING TO BE PRESIDENT TOO, UNCLE WILT?
ONLY GOD KNOWS FOR SURE, ADAM...
...BUT HE TOLD ME IT'S LOOKING PRETTY GOOD!

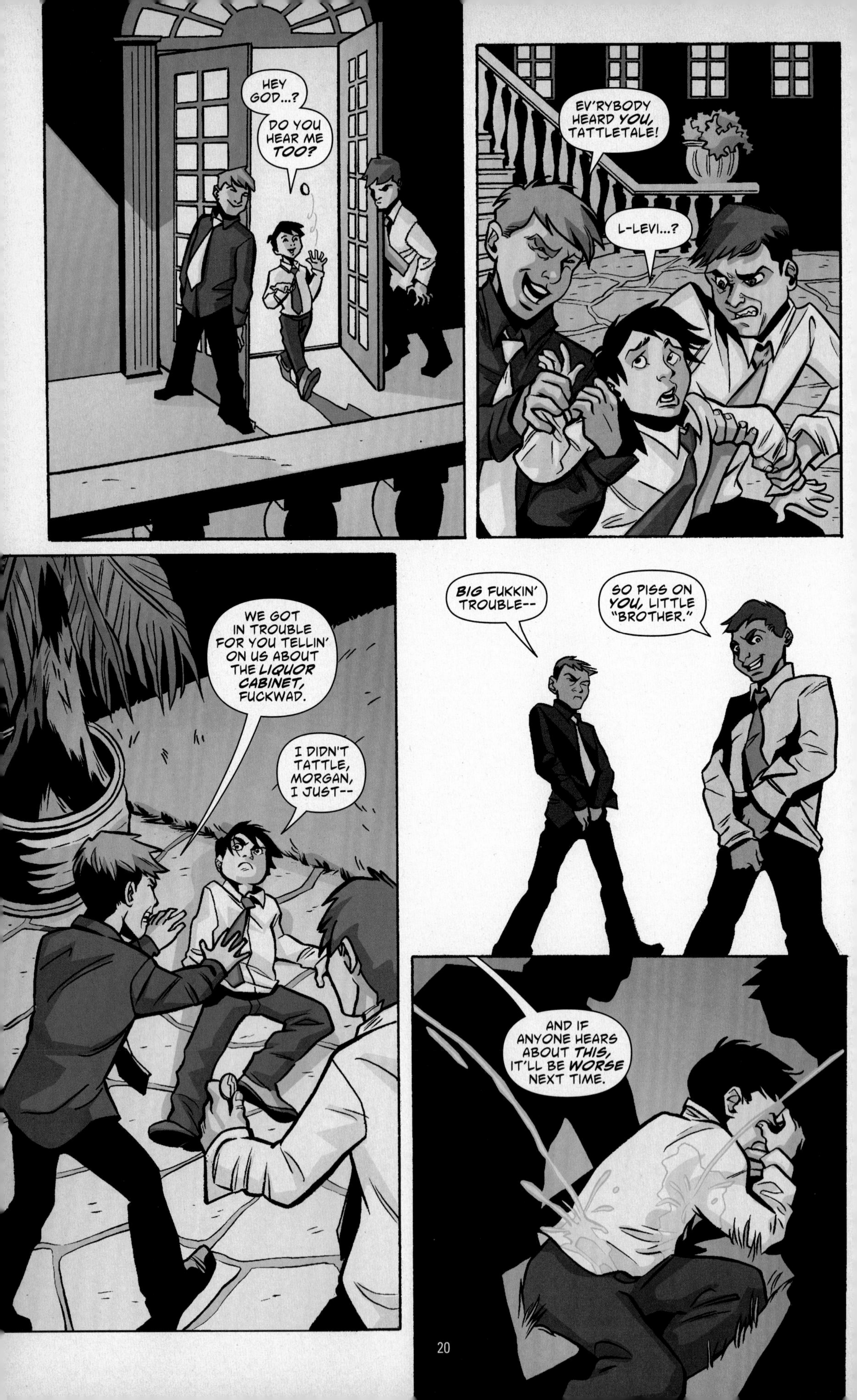
HEY GOD...?
DO YOU HEAR ME TOO?
EV'RYBODY HEARD YOU, TATTLETALE!
L-LEVI...?
WE GOT IN TROUBLE FOR YOU TELLIN' ON US ABOUT THE LIQUOR CABINET, FUCKWAD.
I DIDN'T TATTLE, MORGAN, I JUST--
BIG FUKKIN' TROUBLE--
SO PISS ON YOU, LITTLE "BROTHER."
AND IF ANYONE HEARS ABOUT THIS, IT'LL BE WORSE NEXT TIME.

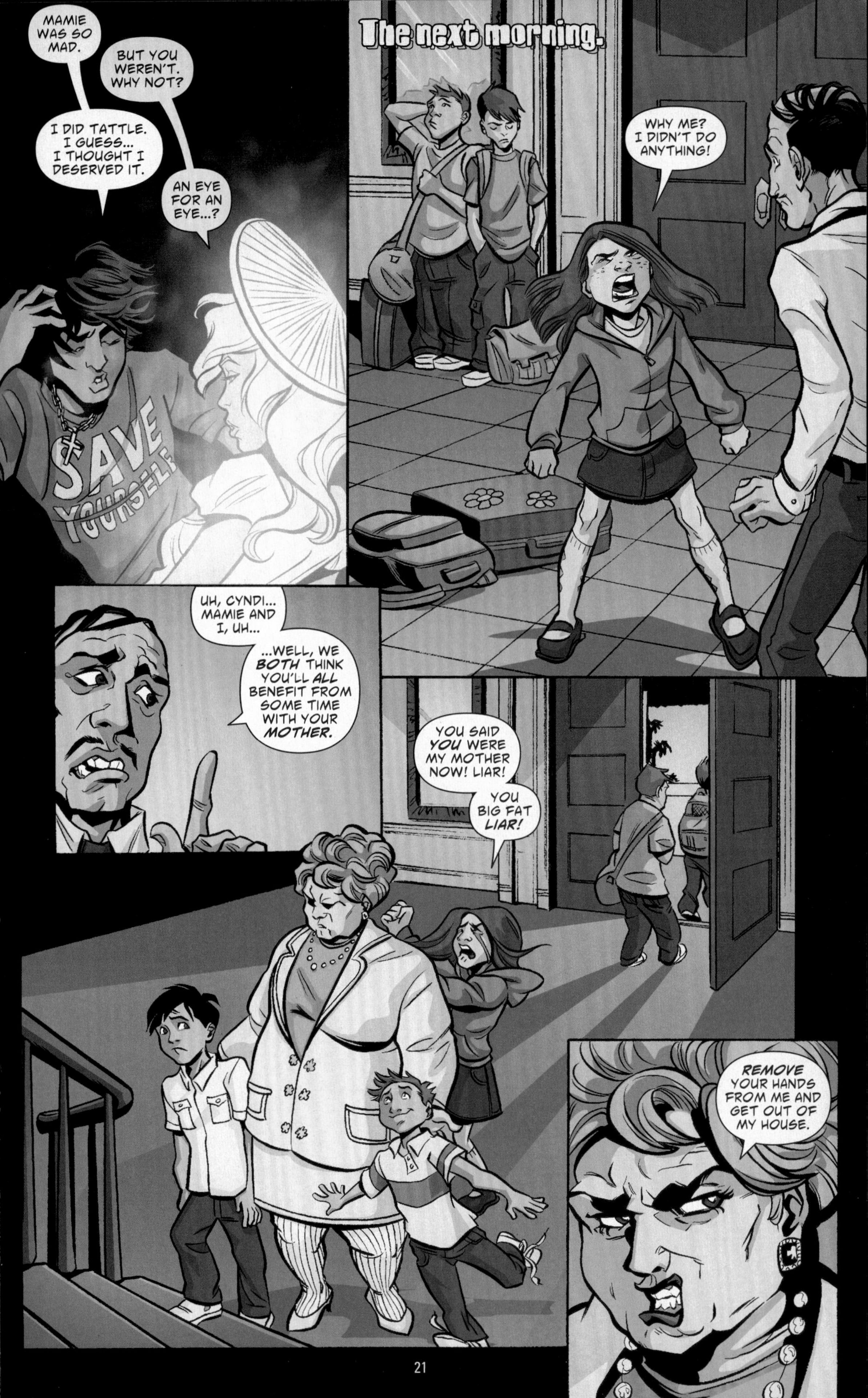

MAMIE WAS SO MAD.
BUT YOU WEREN'T. WHY NOT?
I DID TATTLE. I GUESS... I THOUGHT I DESERVED IT.
AN EYE FOR AN EYE...?
The next morning.
WHY ME? I DIDN'T DO ANYTHING!
SAVE YOURSELF
UH, CYNDI... MAMIE AND I, UH...
...WELL, WE BOTH THINK YOU'LL ALL BENEFIT FROM SOME TIME WITH YOUR MOTHER.
YOU SAID YOU WERE MY MOTHER NOW! LIAR!
YOU BIG FAT LIAR!
REMOVE YOUR HANDS FROM ME AND GET OUT OF MY HOUSE.

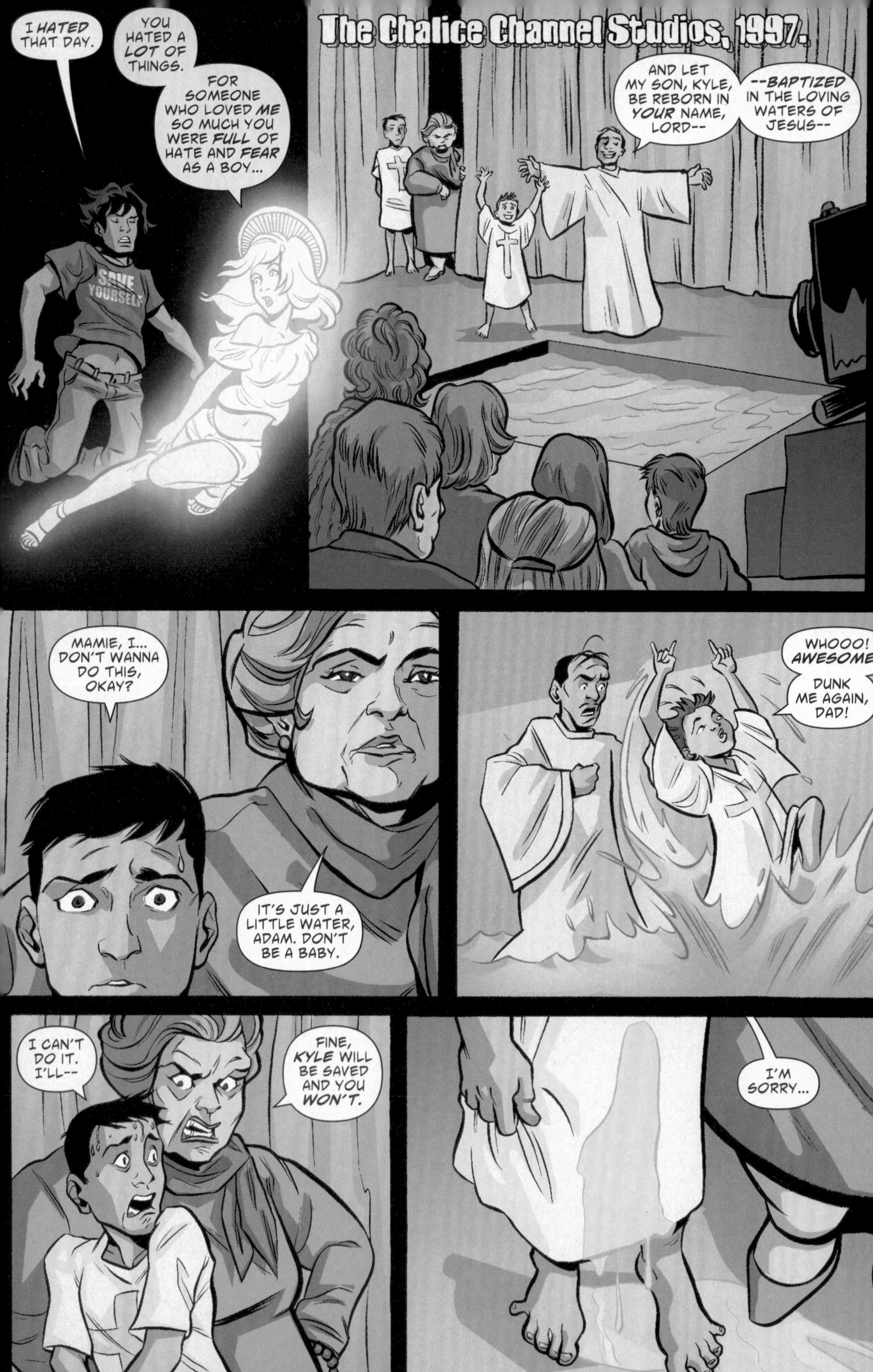

I HATED THAT DAY.
YOU HATED A LOT OF THINGS.
FOR SOMEONE WHO LOVED ME SO MUCH YOU WERE FULL OF HATE AND FEAR AS A BOY...
The Chalice Channel Studios, 1997.
AND LET MY SON, KYLE, BE REBORN IN YOUR NAME, LORD--
--BAPTIZED IN THE LOVING WATERS OF JESUS--
SAVE YOURSELF
MAMIE, I... DON'T WANNA DO THIS, OKAY?
IT'S JUST A LITTLE WATER, ADAM. DON'T BE A BABY.
WHOOO! AWESOME!
DUNK ME AGAIN, DAD!
I CAN'T DO IT. I'LL--
FINE, KYLE WILL BE SAVED AND YOU WON'T.
I'M SORRY...

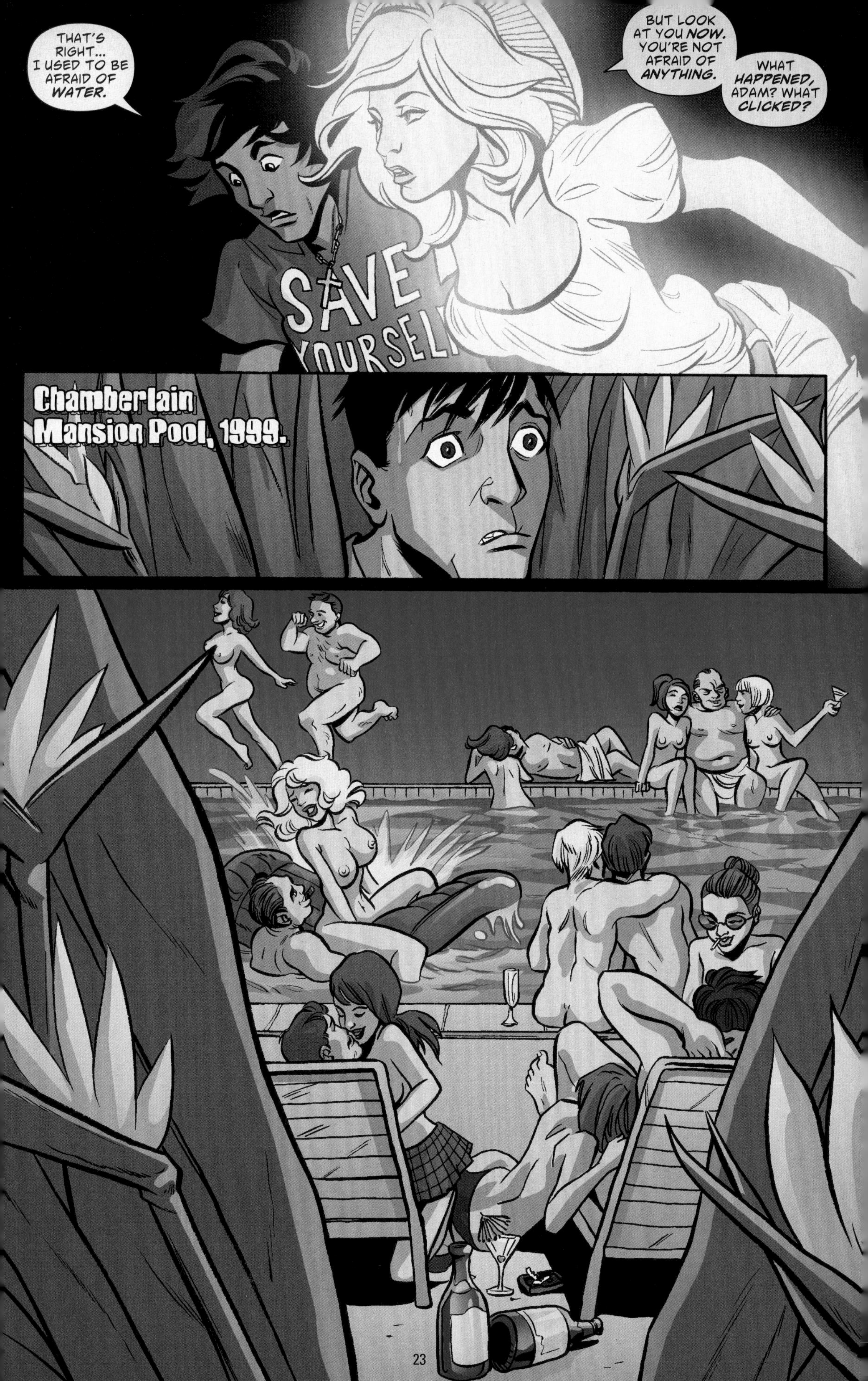
THAT'S RIGHT... I USED TO BE AFRAID OF WATER.
BUT LOOK AT YOU NOW. YOU'RE NOT AFRAID OF ANYTHING.
WHAT HAPPENED, ADAM? WHAT CLICKED?
SAVE YOURSEL
Chamberlain Mansion Pool, 1999.

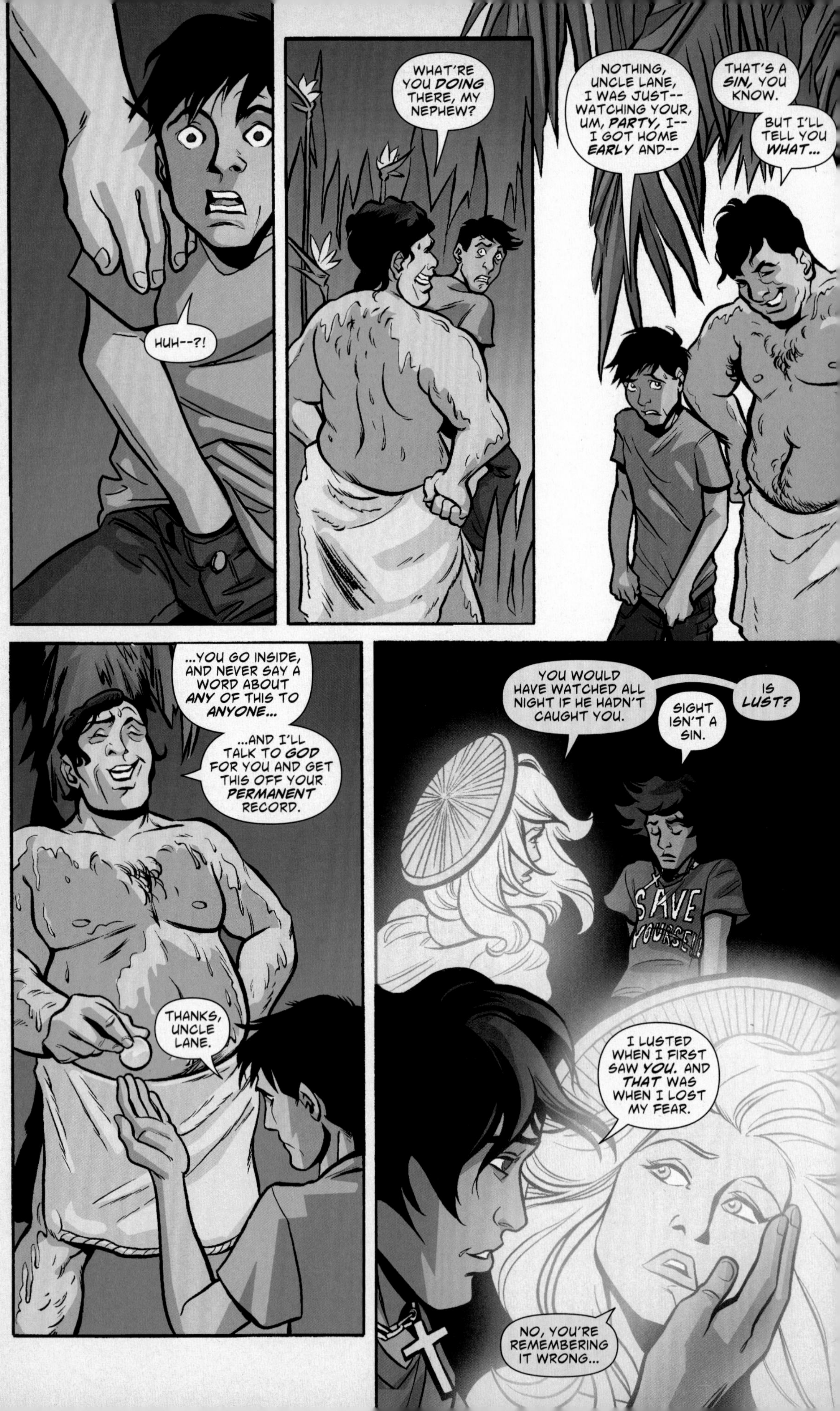
HUH--?!
WHAT'RE YOU DOING THERE, MY NEPHEW?
NOTHING, UNCLE LANE, I WAS JUST-- WATCHING YOUR, UM, PARTY, I-- I GOT HOME EARLY AND--
THAT'S A SIN, YOU KNOW.
BUT I'LL TELL YOU WHAT...
...YOU GO INSIDE, AND NEVER SAY A WORD ABOUT ANY OF THIS TO ANYONE...
...AND I'LL TALK TO GOD FOR YOU AND GET THIS OFF YOUR PERMANENT RECORD.
THANKS, UNCLE LANE.
YOU WOULD HAVE WATCHED ALL NIGHT IF HE HADN'T CAUGHT YOU.
SIGHT ISN'T A SIN.
IS LUST?
SAVE YOURSELF
I LUSTED WHEN I FIRST SAW YOU. AND THAT WAS WHEN I LOST MY FEAR.
NO, YOU'RE REMEMBERING IT WRONG...

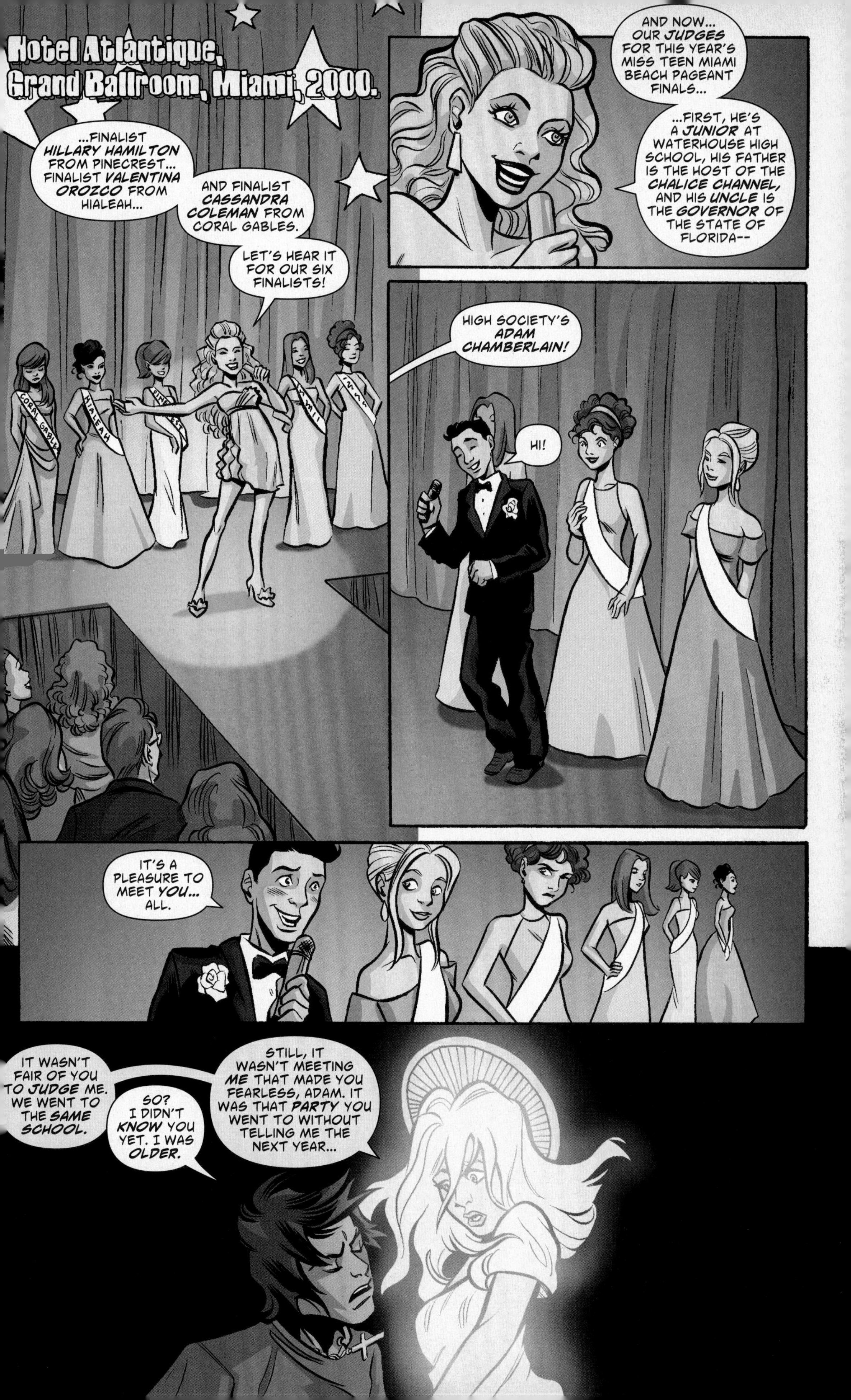
Hotel Atlantique, Grand Ballroom, Miami, 2000.
...FINALIST HILLARY HAMILTON FROM PINECREST... FINALIST VALENTINA OROZCO FROM HIALEAH...
AND FINALIST CASSANDRA COLEMAN FROM CORAL GABLES.
LET'S HEAR IT FOR OUR SIX FINALISTS!
CORAL GABLES
HIALEAH
AND NOW... OUR JUDGES FOR THIS YEAR'S MISS TEEN MIAMI BEACH PAGEANT FINALS...
...FIRST, HE'S A JUNIOR AT WATERHOUSE HIGH SCHOOL, HIS FATHER IS THE HOST OF THE CHALICE CHANNEL, AND HIS UNCLE IS THE GOVERNOR OF THE STATE OF FLORIDA--
HIGH SOCIETY'S ADAM CHAMBERLAIN!
HI!
IT'S A PLEASURE TO MEET YOU... ALL.
IT WASN'T FAIR OF YOU TO JUDGE ME. WE WENT TO THE SAME SCHOOL.
SO? I DIDN'T KNOW YOU YET. I WAS OLDER.
STILL, IT WASN'T MEETING ME THAT MADE YOU FEARLESS, ADAM. IT WAS THAT PARTY YOU WENT TO WITHOUT TELLING ME THE NEXT YEAR...

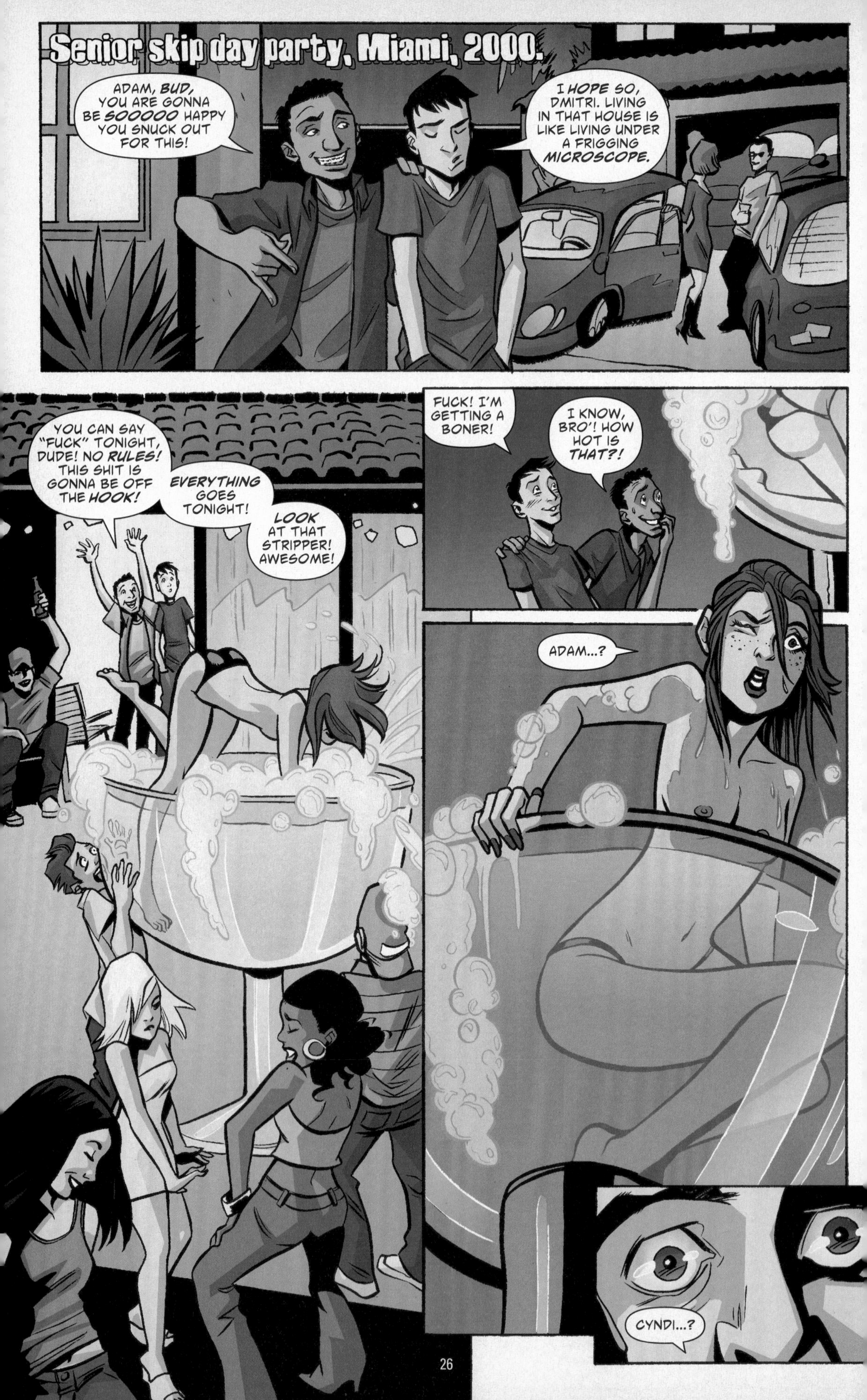
Senior skip day party, Miami, 2000.
ADAM, BUD, YOU ARE GONNA BE SOOOOOO HAPPY YOU SNUCK OUT FOR THIS!
I HOPE SO, DMITRI. LIVING IN THAT HOUSE IS LIKE LIVING UNDER A FRIGGING MICROSCOPE.
YOU CAN SAY "FUCK" TONIGHT, DUDE! NO RULES! THIS SHIT IS GONNA BE OFF THE HOOK!
EVERYTHING GOES TONIGHT!
LOOK AT THAT STRIPPER! AWESOME!
FUCK! I'M GETTING A BONER!
I KNOW, BRO'! HOW HOT IS THAT?!
ADAM...?
CYNDI...?

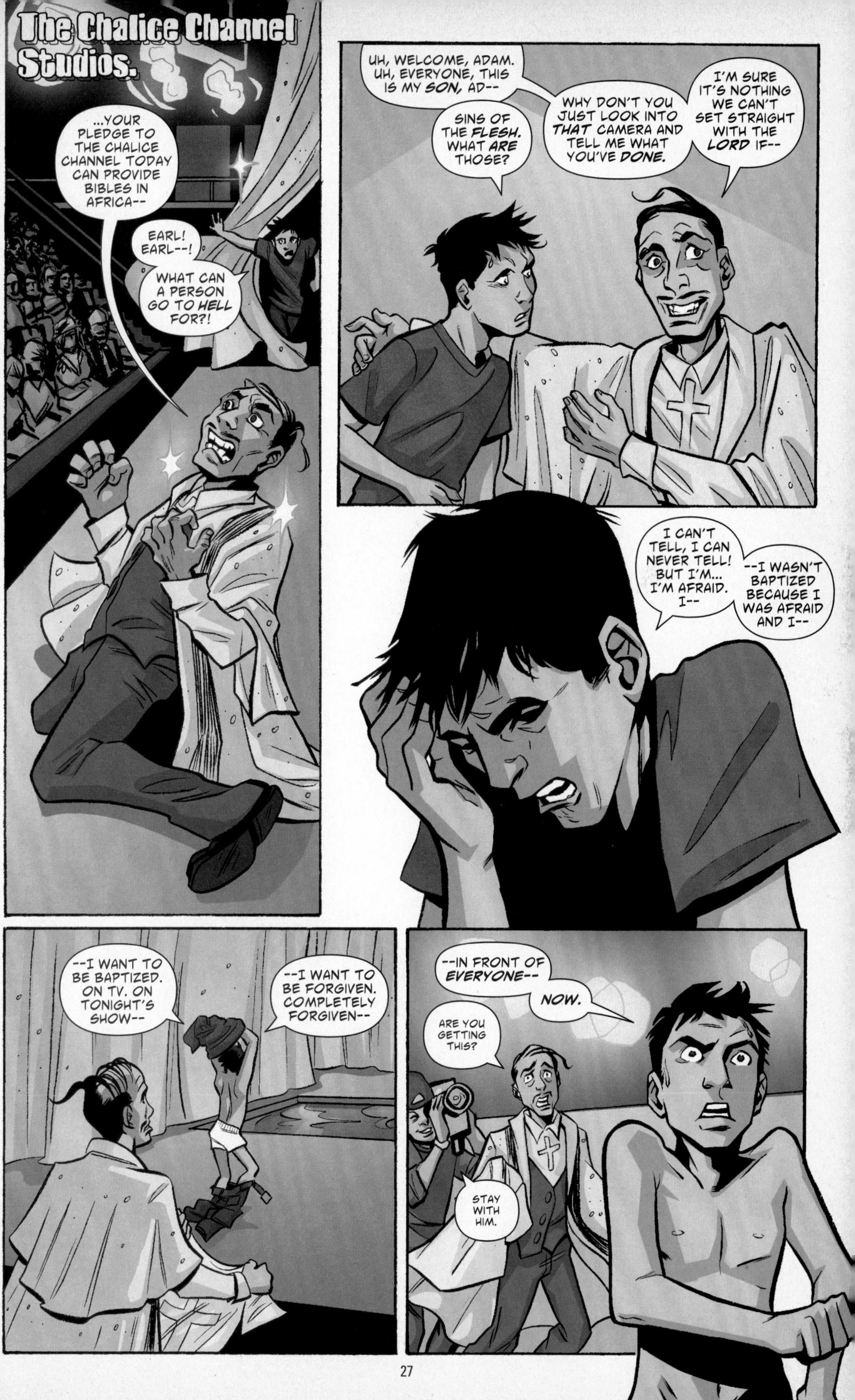
The Chalice Channel Studios.
...YOUR PLEDGE TO THE CHALICE CHANNEL TODAY CAN PROVIDE BIBLES IN AFRICA--
EARL! EARL--!
WHAT CAN A PERSON GO TO HELL FOR?!
UH, WELCOME, ADAM. UH, EVERYONE, THIS IS MY SON, AD--
SINS OF THE FLESH. WHAT ARE THOSE?
WHY DON'T YOU JUST LOOK INTO THAT CAMERA AND TELL ME WHAT YOU'VE DONE.
I'M SURE IT'S NOTHING WE CAN'T SET STRAIGHT WITH THE LORD IF--
I CAN'T TELL, I CAN NEVER TELL! BUT I'M... I'M AFRAID. I--
--I WASN'T BAPTIZED BECAUSE I WAS AFRAID AND I--
--I WANT TO BE BAPTIZED. ON TV. ON TONIGHT'S SHOW--
--I WANT TO BE FORGIVEN. COMPLETELY FORGIVEN--
--IN FRONT OF EVERYONE--
NOW.
ARE YOU GETTING THIS?
STAY WITH HIM.

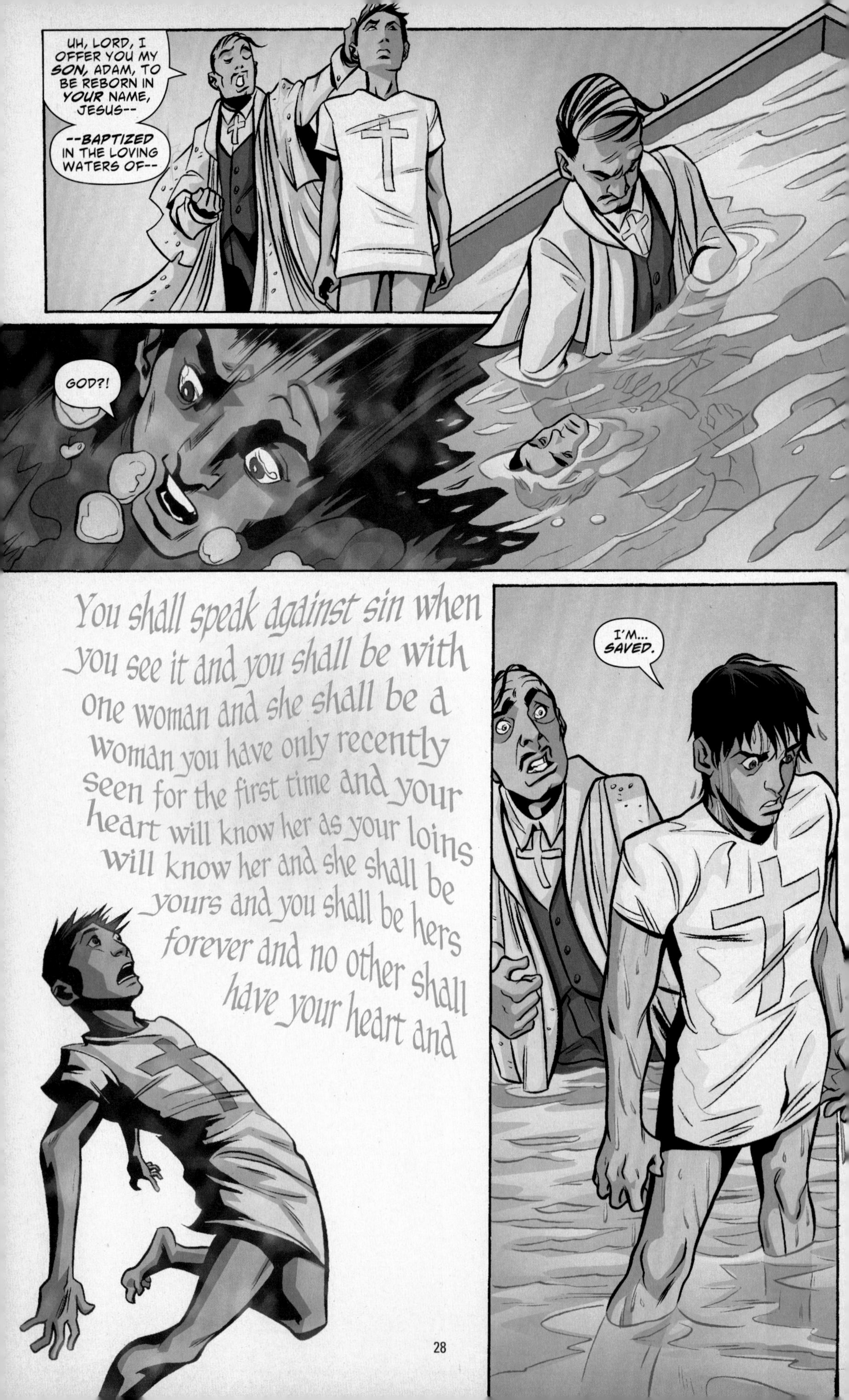
UH, LORD, I OFFER YOU MY SON, ADAM, TO BE REBORN IN YOUR NAME, JESUS--
--BAPTIZED IN THE LOVING WATERS OF--
GOD?!
You shall speak against sin when you see it and you shall be with one woman and she shall be a woman you have only recently seen for the first time and your heart will know her as your loins will know her and she shall be yours and you shall be hers forever and no other shall have your heart and
I'M... SAVED.

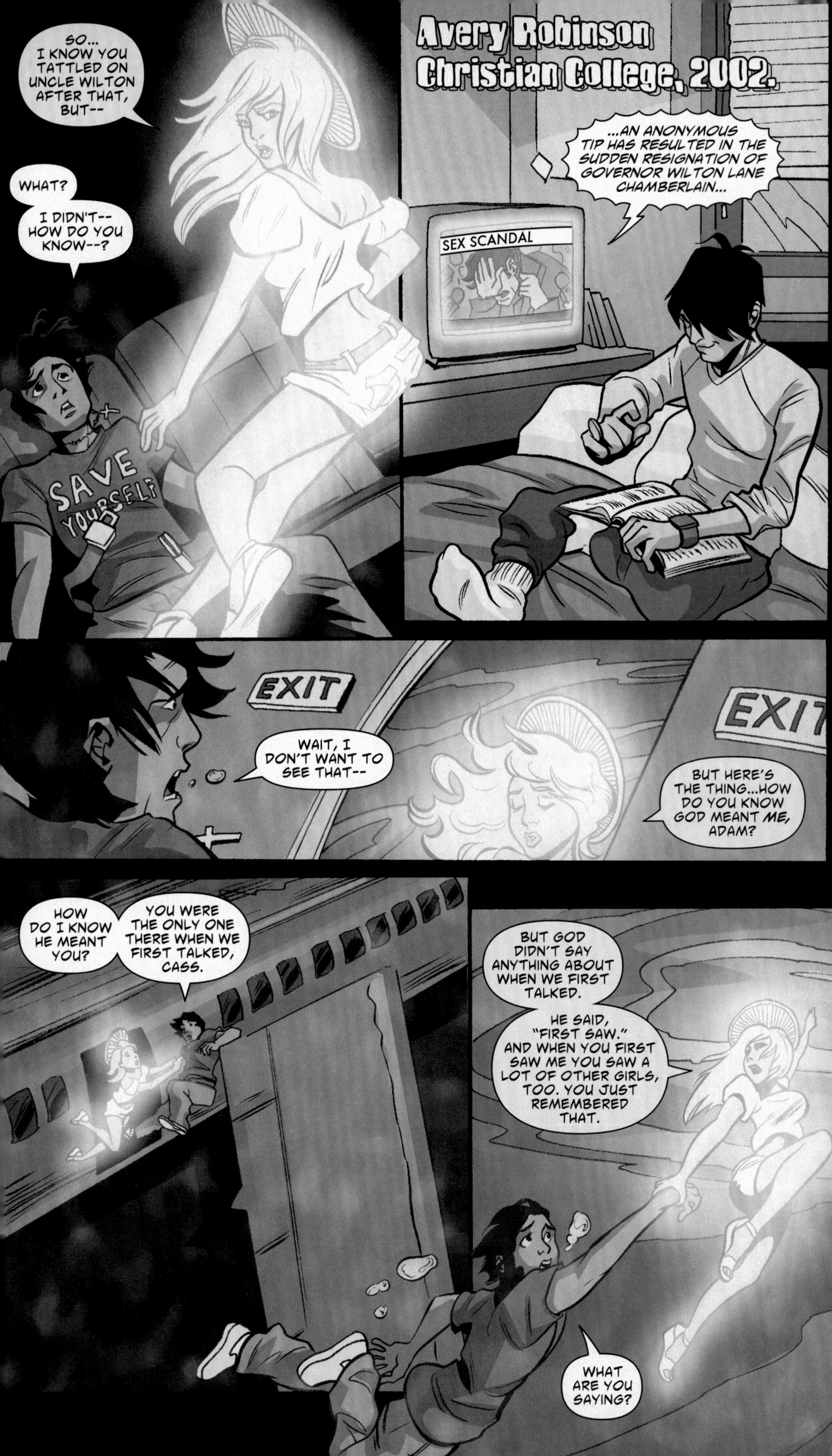
SO... I KNOW YOU TATTLED ON UNCLE WILTON AFTER THAT, BUT--
WHAT?
I DIDN'T-- HOW DO YOU KNOW--?
SAVE YOURSELF
Avery Robinson Christian College, 2002.
...AN ANONYMOUS TIP HAS RESULTED IN THE SUDDEN RESIGNATION OF GOVERNOR WILTON LANE CHAMBERLAIN...
SEX SCANDAL
EXIT
WAIT, I DON'T WANT TO SEE THAT--
EXIT
BUT HERE'S THE THING...HOW DO YOU KNOW GOD MEANT *ME*, ADAM?
HOW DO I KNOW HE MEANT YOU?
YOU WERE THE ONLY ONE THERE WHEN WE FIRST TALKED, CASS.
BUT GOD DIDN'T SAY ANYTHING ABOUT WHEN WE FIRST TALKED.
HE SAID, "FIRST SAW." AND WHEN YOU FIRST SAW ME YOU SAW A LOT OF OTHER GIRLS, TOO. YOU JUST REMEMBERED THAT.
WHAT ARE YOU SAYING?

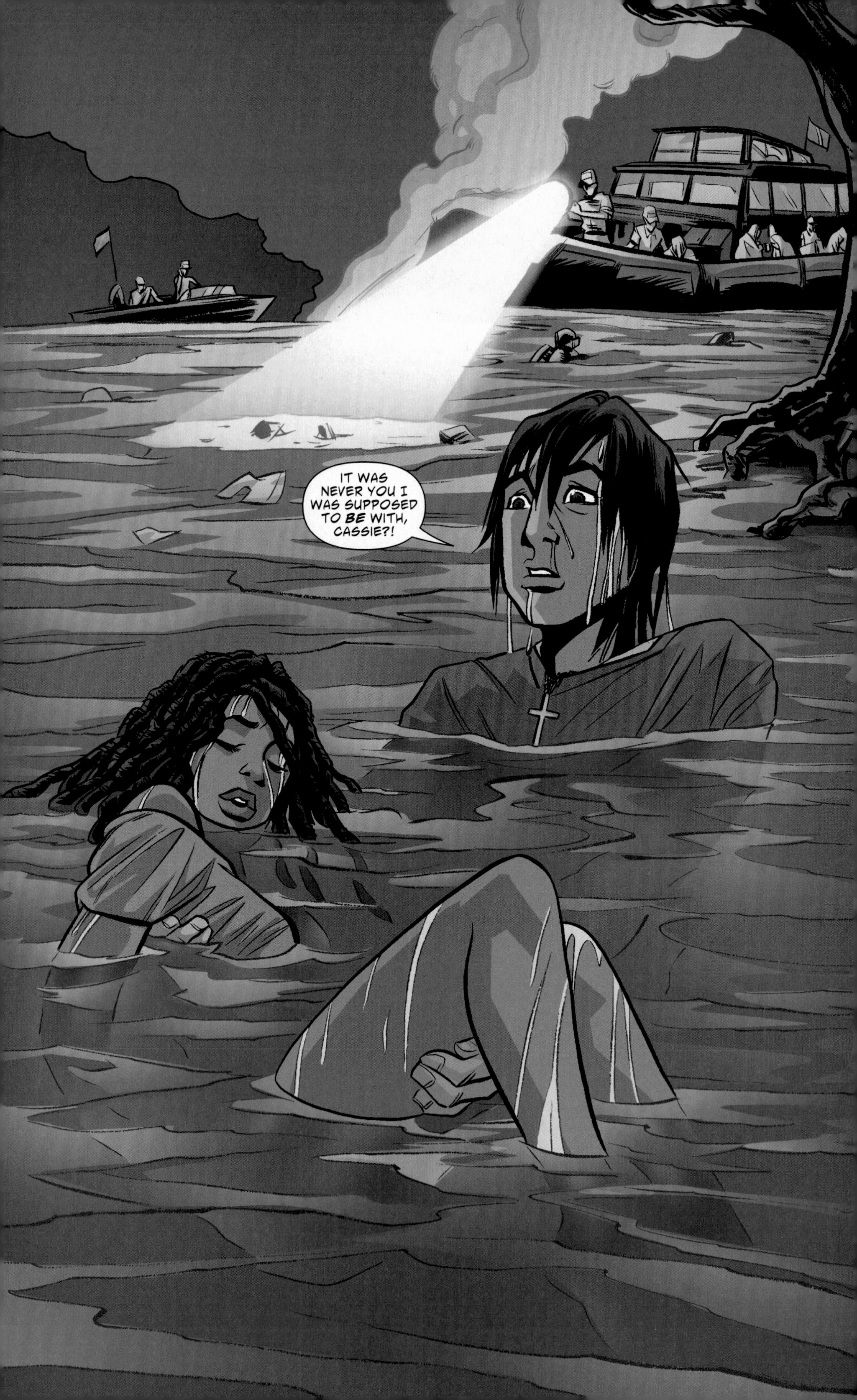
IT WAS NEVER YOU I WAS SUPPOSED TO *BE* WITH, CASSIE?!

CHAPTER TWO

Chapter art by Becky Cloonan

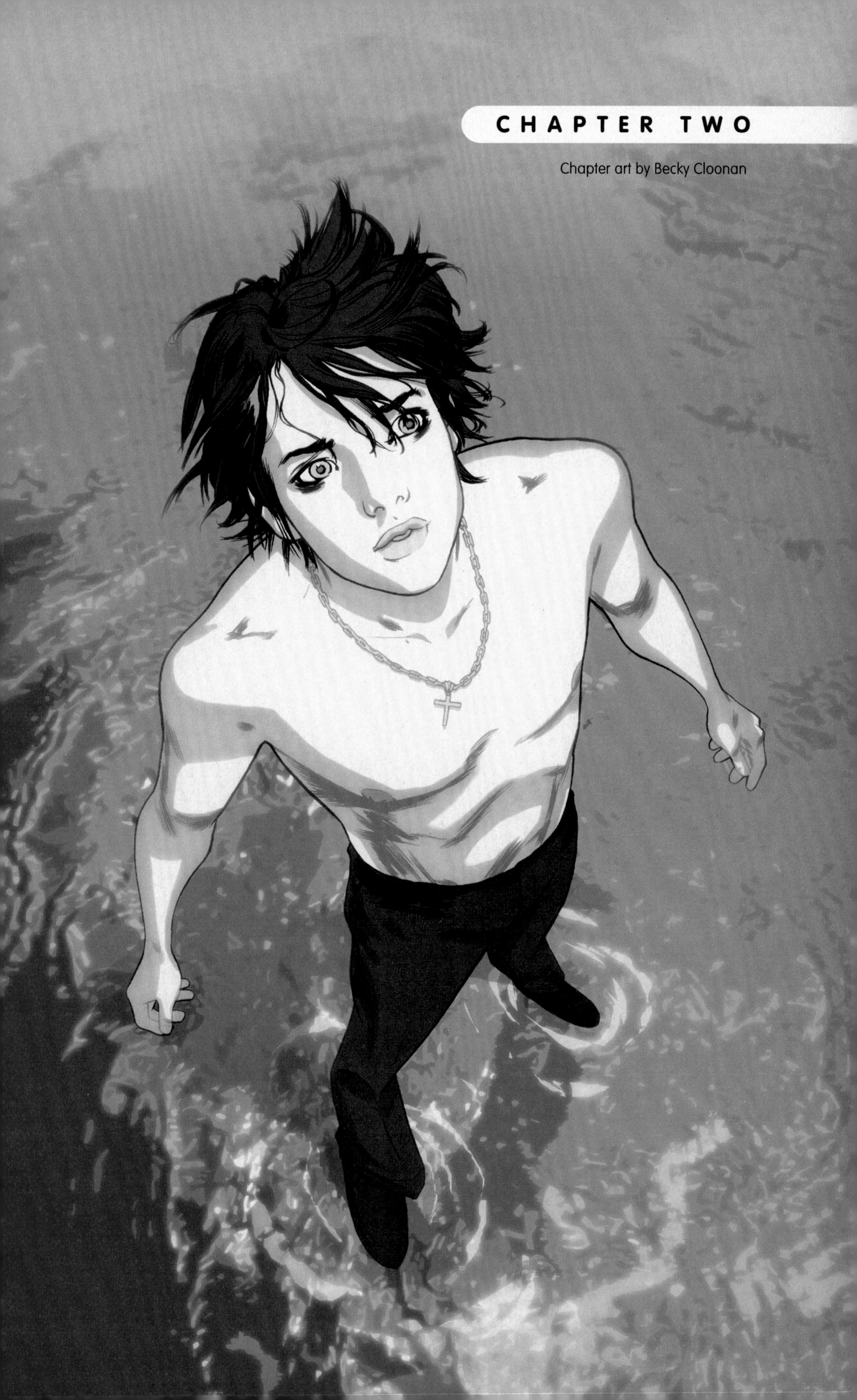

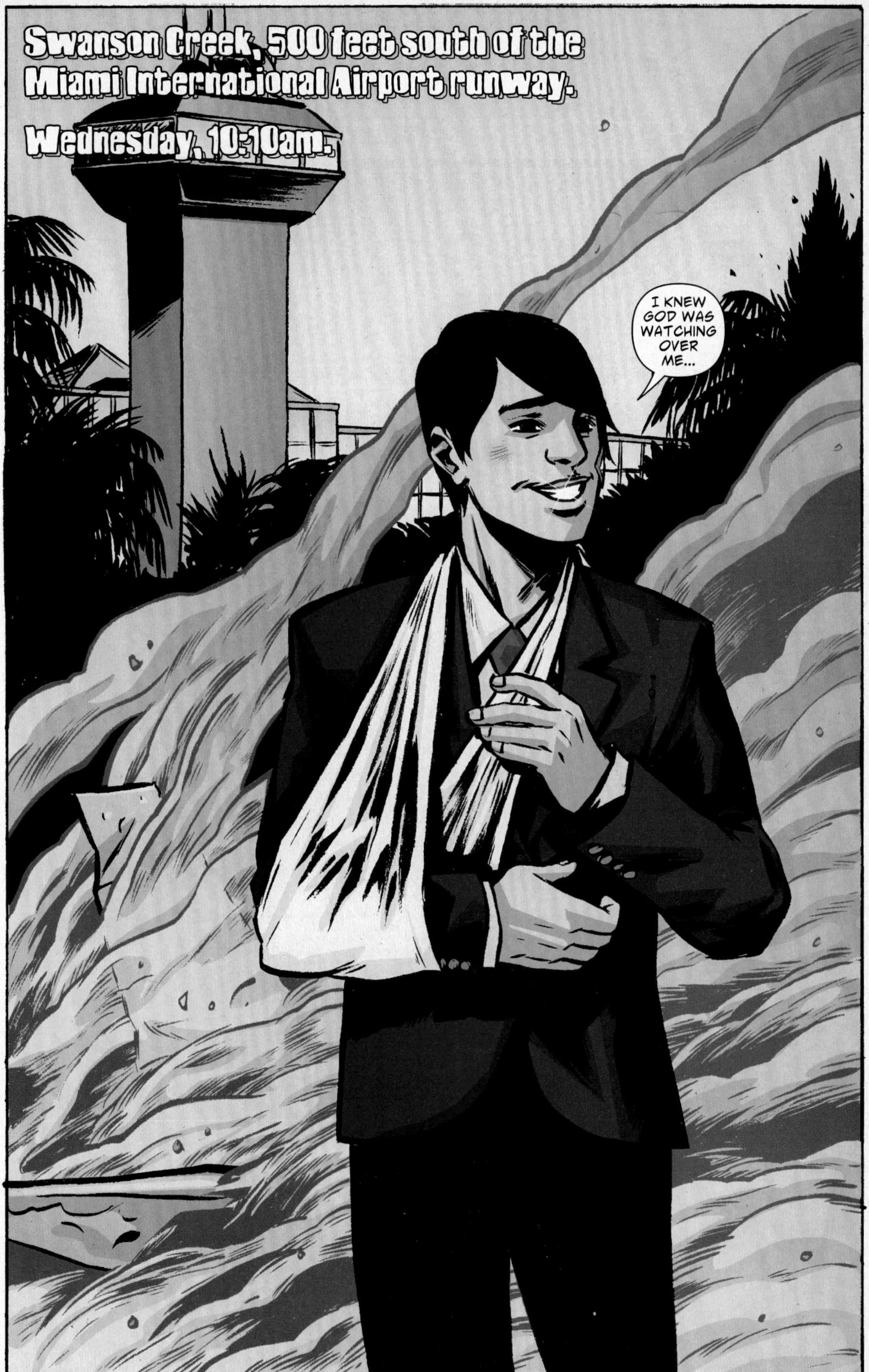
Swanson Creek, 500 feet south of the Miami International Airport runway.
Wednesday, 10:10am.
I KNEW GOD WAS WATCHING OVER ME...

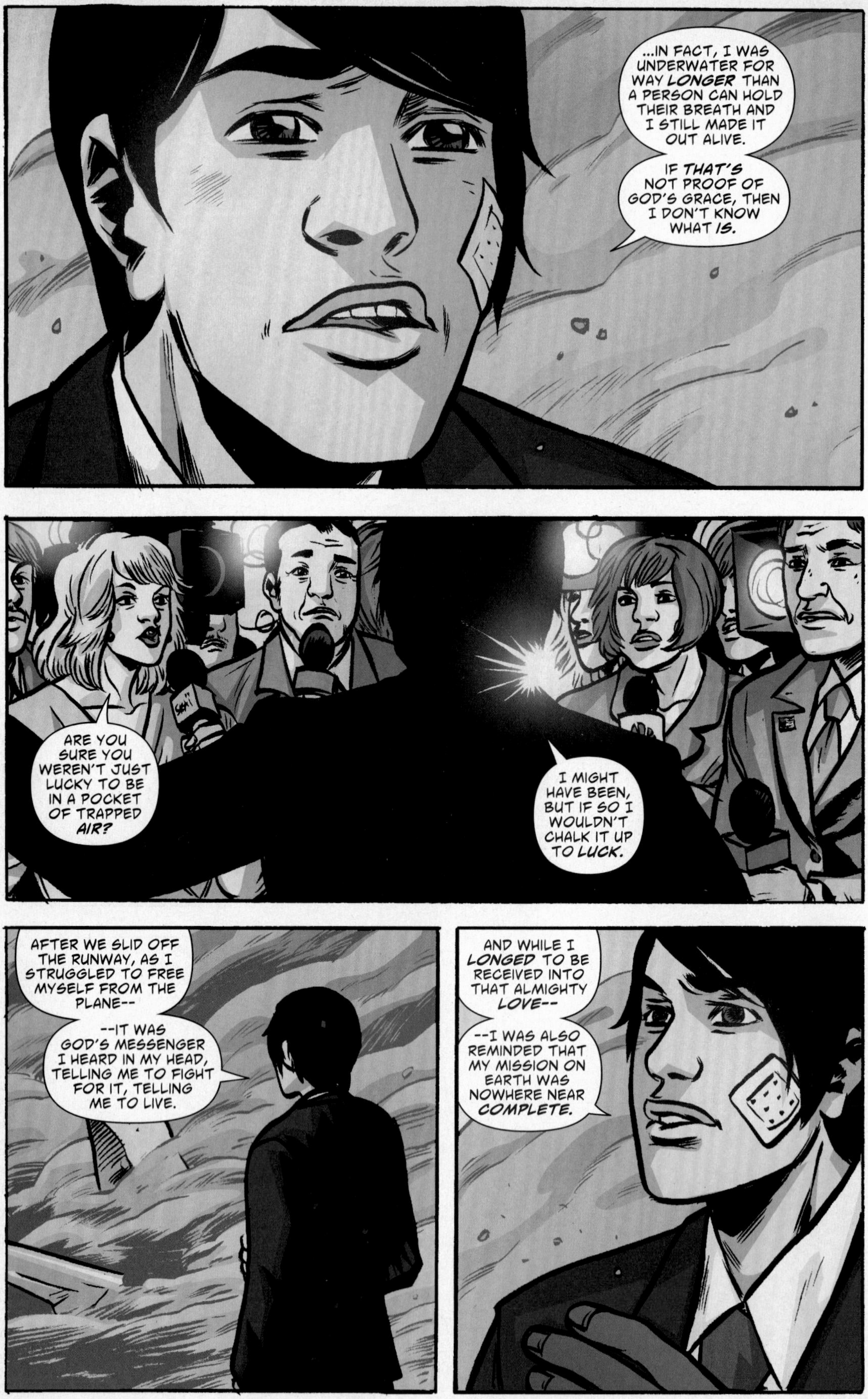
...IN FACT, I WAS UNDERWATER FOR WAY LONGER THAN A PERSON CAN HOLD THEIR BREATH AND I STILL MADE IT OUT ALIVE.
IF THAT'S NOT PROOF OF GOD'S GRACE, THEN I DON'T KNOW WHAT IS.
ARE YOU SURE YOU WEREN'T JUST LUCKY TO BE IN A POCKET OF TRAPPED AIR?
I MIGHT HAVE BEEN, BUT IF SO I WOULDN'T CHALK IT UP TO LUCK.
AFTER WE SLID OFF THE RUNWAY, AS I STRUGGLED TO FREE MYSELF FROM THE PLANE--
--IT WAS GOD'S MESSENGER I HEARD IN MY HEAD, TELLING ME TO FIGHT FOR IT, TELLING ME TO LIVE.
AND WHILE I LONGED TO BE RECEIVED INTO THAT ALMIGHTY LOVE--
--I WAS ALSO REMINDED THAT MY MISSION ON EARTH WAS NOWHERE NEAR COMPLETE.

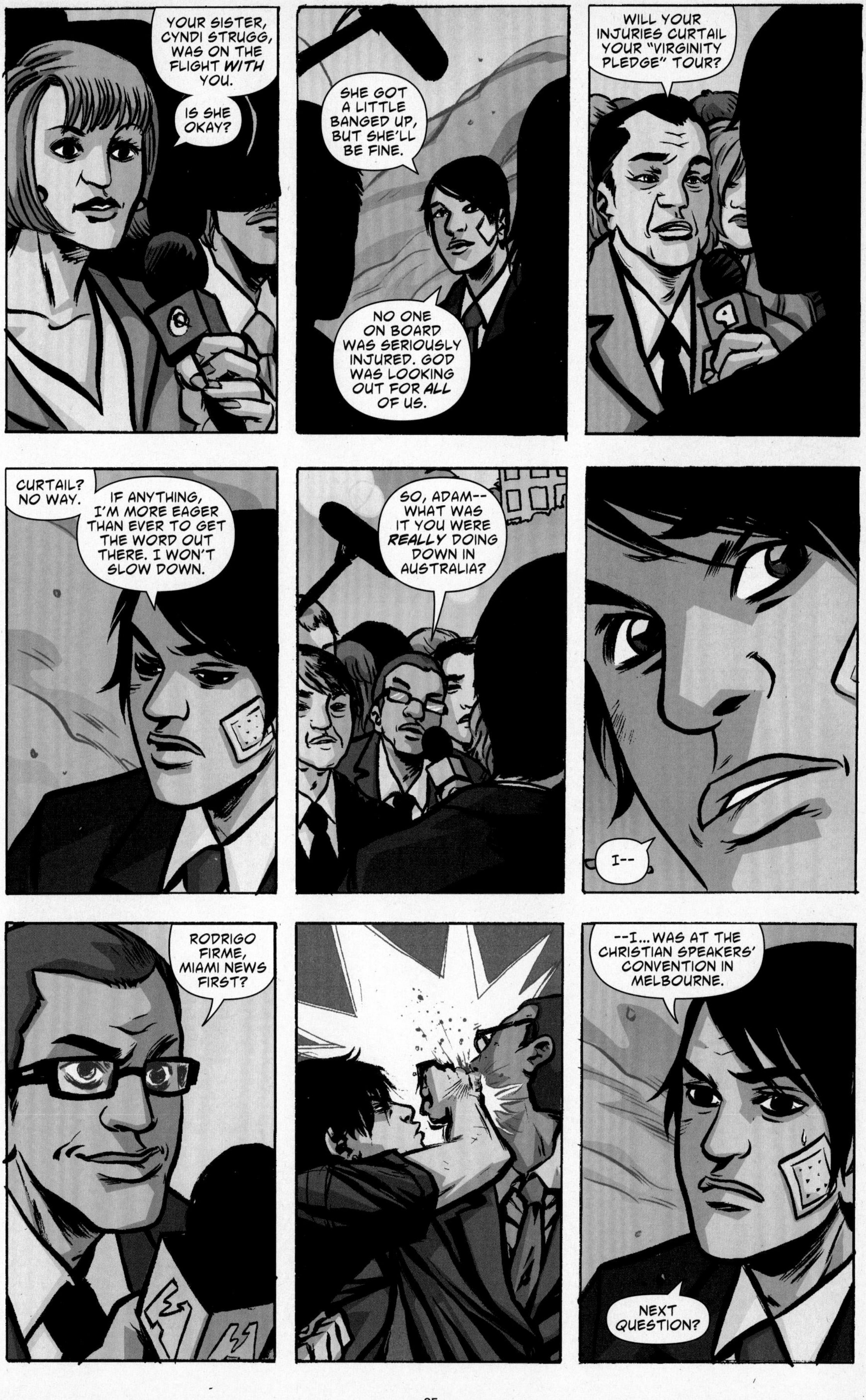
YOUR SISTER, CYNDI STRUGG, WAS ON THE FLIGHT WITH YOU.
IS SHE OKAY?
SHE GOT A LITTLE BANGED UP, BUT SHE'LL BE FINE.
NO ONE ON BOARD WAS SERIOUSLY INJURED. GOD WAS LOOKING OUT FOR ALL OF US.
WILL YOUR INJURIES CURTAIL YOUR "VIRGINITY PLEDGE" TOUR?
CURTAIL? NO WAY.
IF ANYTHING, I'M MORE EAGER THAN EVER TO GET THE WORD OUT THERE. I WON'T SLOW DOWN.
SO, ADAM-- WHAT WAS IT YOU WERE REALLY DOING DOWN IN AUSTRALIA?
I--
RODRIGO FIRME, MIAMI NEWS FIRST?
--I...WAS AT THE CHRISTIAN SPEAKERS' CONVENTION IN MELBOURNE.
NEXT QUESTION?

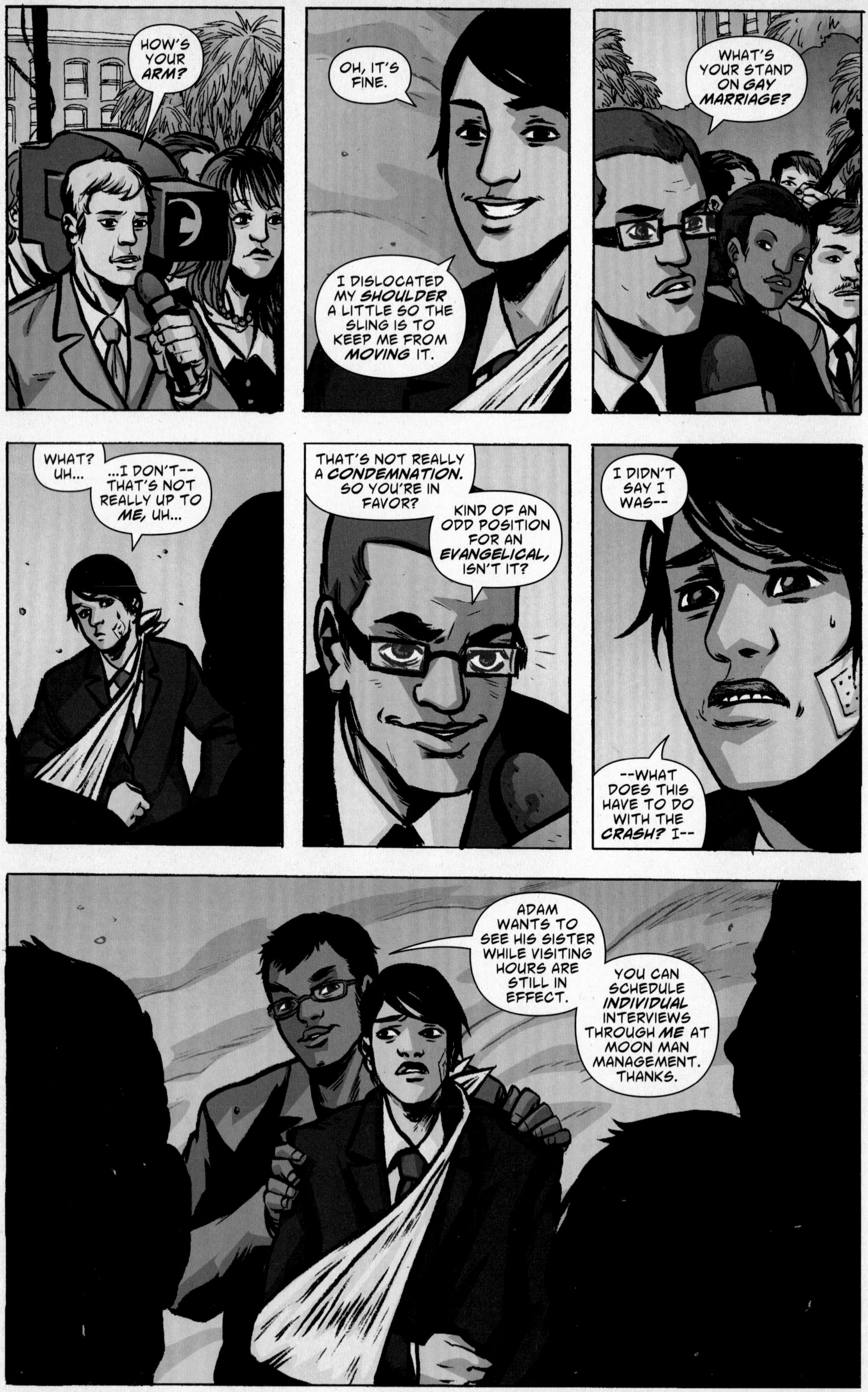
HOW'S YOUR ARM?
OH, IT'S FINE.
I DISLOCATED MY SHOULDER A LITTLE SO THE SLING IS TO KEEP ME FROM MOVING IT.
WHAT'S YOUR STAND ON GAY MARRIAGE?
WHAT? UH...
...I DON'T-- THAT'S NOT REALLY UP TO ME, UH...
THAT'S NOT REALLY A CONDEMNATION. SO YOU'RE IN FAVOR?
KIND OF AN ODD POSITION FOR AN EVANGELICAL, ISN'T IT?
I DIDN'T SAY I WAS--
--WHAT DOES THIS HAVE TO DO WITH THE CRASH? I--
ADAM WANTS TO SEE HIS SISTER WHILE VISITING HOURS ARE STILL IN EFFECT.
YOU CAN SCHEDULE INDIVIDUAL INTERVIEWS THROUGH ME AT MOON MAN MANAGEMENT. THANKS.

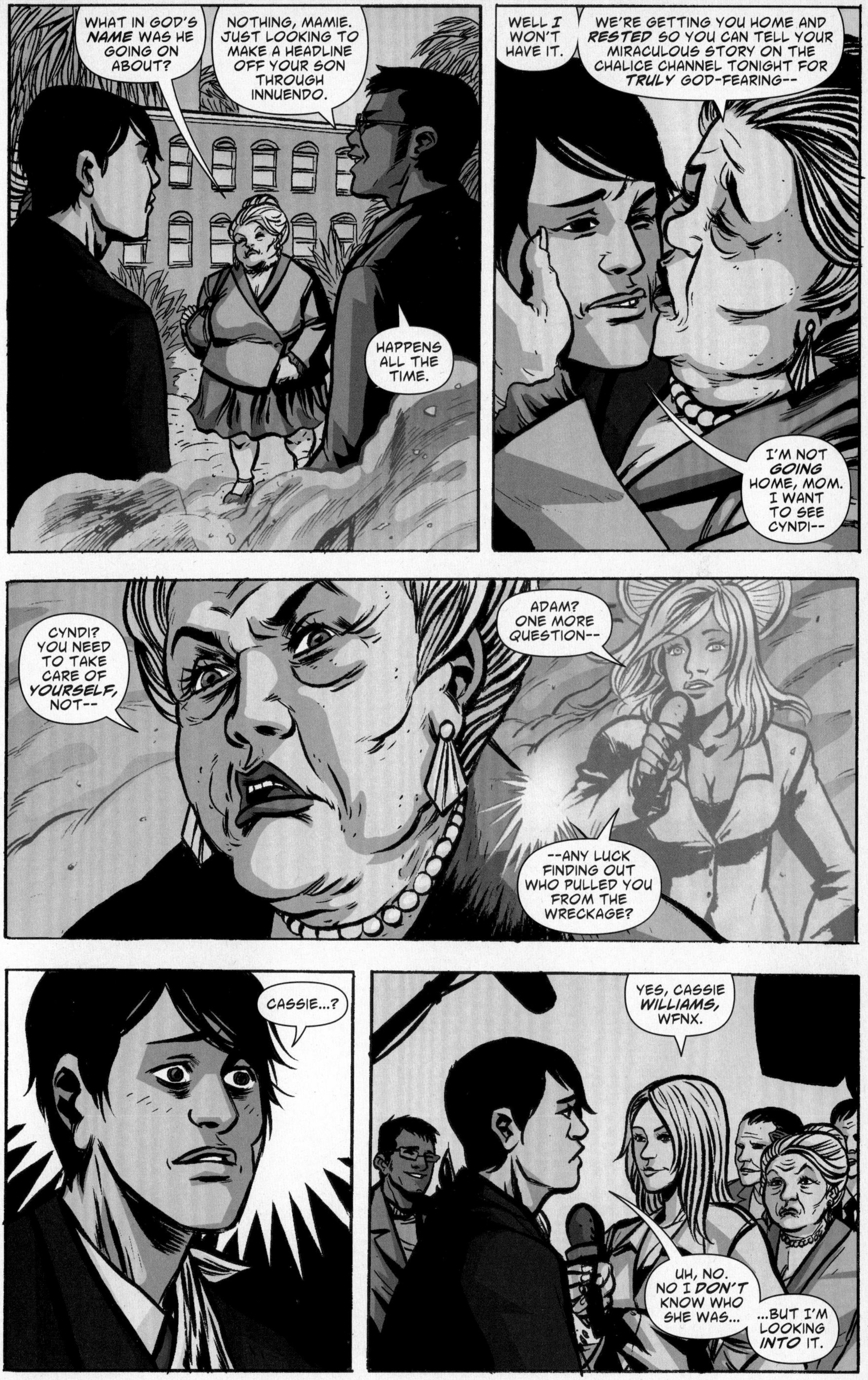
WHAT IN GOD'S NAME WAS HE GOING ON ABOUT?
NOTHING, MAMIE. JUST LOOKING TO MAKE A HEADLINE OFF YOUR SON THROUGH INNUENDO.
HAPPENS ALL THE TIME.
WELL I WON'T HAVE IT.
WE'RE GETTING YOU HOME AND RESTED SO YOU CAN TELL YOUR MIRACULOUS STORY ON THE CHALICE CHANNEL TONIGHT FOR TRULY GOD-FEARING--
I'M NOT GOING HOME, MOM. I WANT TO SEE CYNDI--
CYNDI? YOU NEED TO TAKE CARE OF YOURSELF, NOT--
ADAM? ONE MORE QUESTION--
--ANY LUCK FINDING OUT WHO PULLED YOU FROM THE WRECKAGE?
CASSIE...?
YES, CASSIE WILLIAMS, WFNX.
UH, NO. NO I DON'T KNOW WHO SHE WAS...
...BUT I'M LOOKING INTO IT.

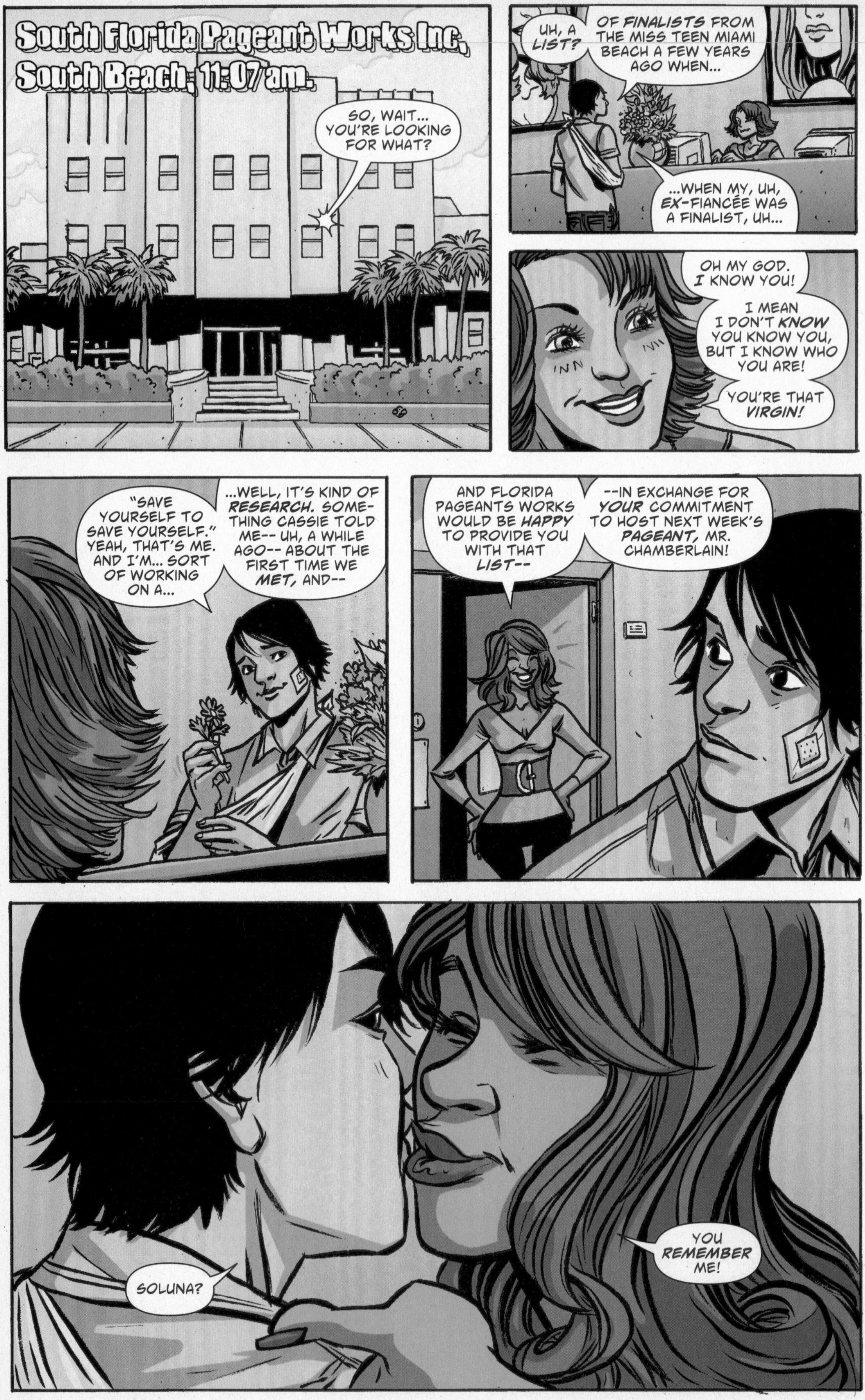

South Florida Pageant Works Inc, South Beach; 11:07 am.
SO, WAIT... YOU'RE LOOKING FOR WHAT?
UH, A LIST?
OF FINALISTS FROM THE MISS TEEN MIAMI BEACH A FEW YEARS AGO WHEN...
...WHEN MY, UH, EX-FIANCÉE WAS A FINALIST, UH...
OH MY GOD. I KNOW YOU!
I MEAN I DON'T KNOW YOU KNOW YOU, BUT I KNOW WHO YOU ARE!
YOU'RE THAT VIRGIN!
"SAVE YOURSELF TO SAVE YOURSELF." YEAH, THAT'S ME. AND I'M... SORT OF WORKING ON A...
...WELL, IT'S KIND OF RESEARCH. SOMETHING CASSIE TOLD ME-- UH, A WHILE AGO-- ABOUT THE FIRST TIME WE MET, AND--
AND FLORIDA PAGEANTS WORKS WOULD BE HAPPY TO PROVIDE YOU WITH THAT LIST--
--IN EXCHANGE FOR YOUR COMMITMENT TO HOST NEXT WEEK'S PAGEANT, MR. CHAMBERLAIN!
SOLUNA?
YOU REMEMBER ME!

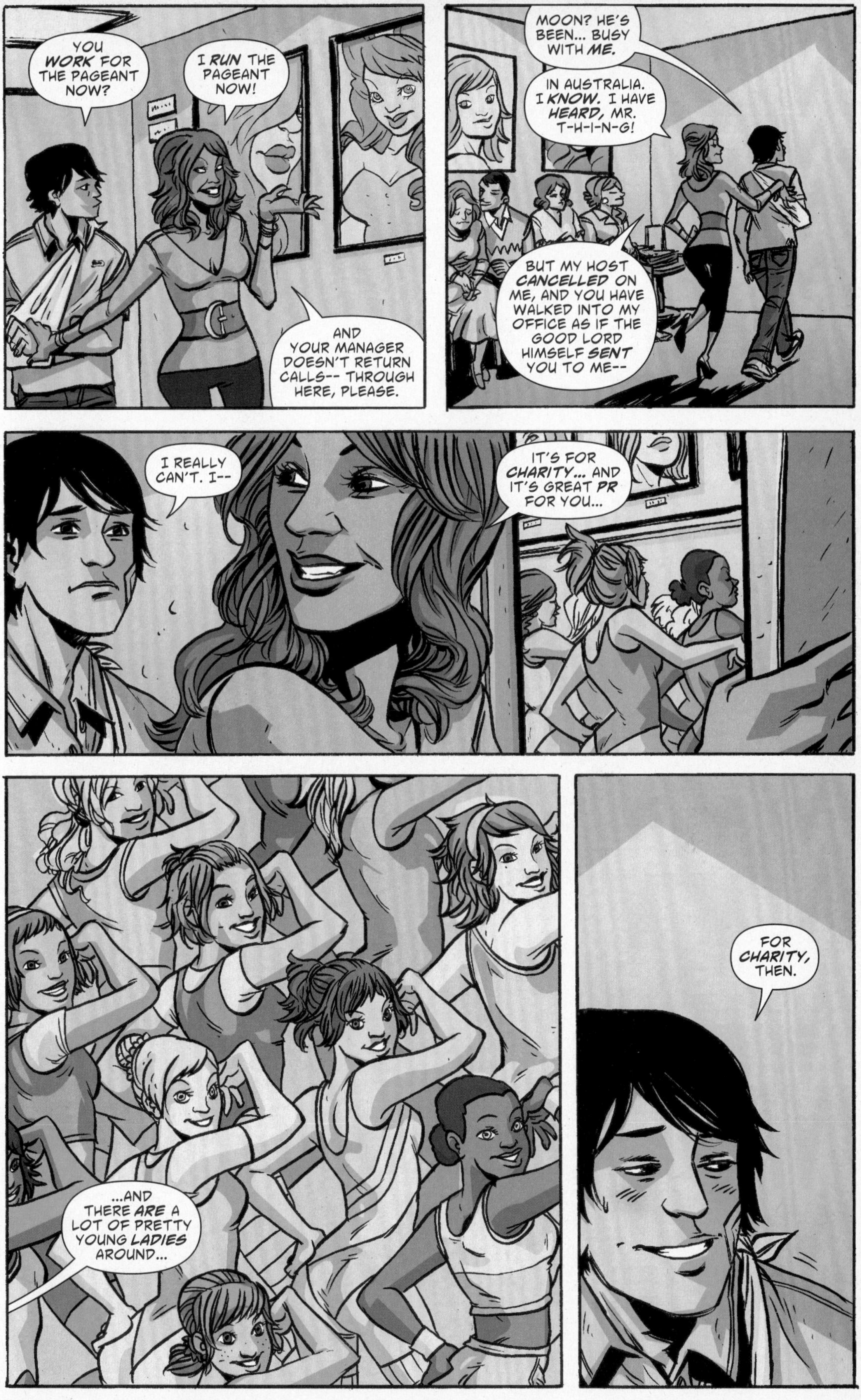
YOU WORK FOR THE PAGEANT NOW?
I RUN THE PAGEANT NOW!
AND YOUR MANAGER DOESN'T RETURN CALLS-- THROUGH HERE, PLEASE.
MOON? HE'S BEEN... BUSY WITH ME.
IN AUSTRALIA. I KNOW. I HAVE HEARD, MR. T-H-I-N-G!
BUT MY HOST CANCELLED ON ME, AND YOU HAVE WALKED INTO MY OFFICE AS IF THE GOOD LORD HIMSELF SENT YOU TO ME--
I REALLY CAN'T. I--
IT'S FOR CHARITY... AND IT'S GREAT PR FOR YOU...
...AND THERE ARE A LOT OF PRETTY YOUNG LADIES AROUND...
FOR CHARITY, THEN.

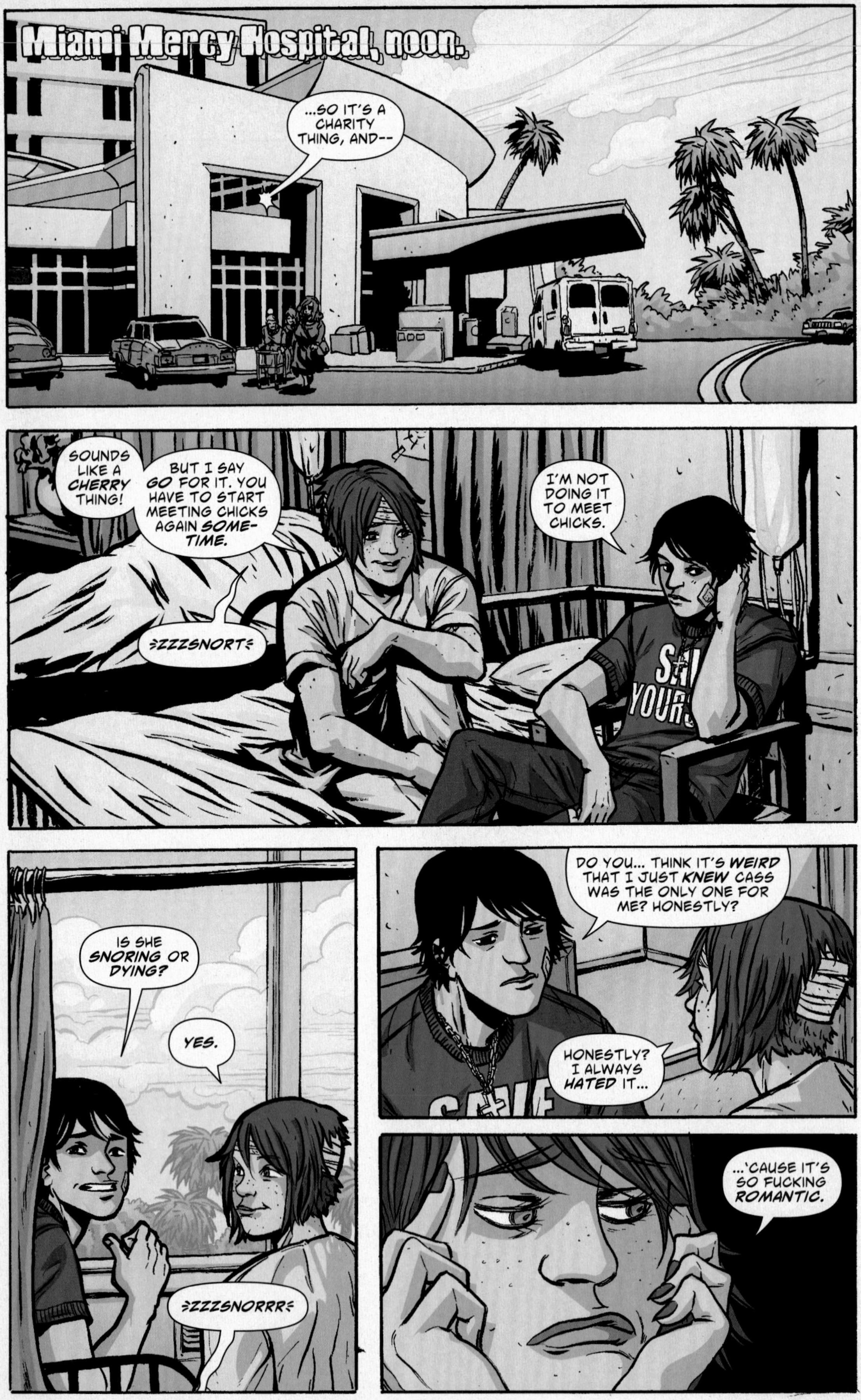
Miami Mercy Hospital, noon.
...SO IT'S A CHARITY THING, AND--
SOUNDS LIKE A CHERRY THING!
BUT I SAY GO FOR IT. YOU HAVE TO START MEETING CHICKS AGAIN SOME-TIME.
≷ZZZSNORT≶
I'M NOT DOING IT TO MEET CHICKS.
IS SHE SNORING OR DYING?
YES.
≷ZZZSNORRR≶
DO YOU... THINK IT'S WEIRD THAT I JUST KNEW CASS WAS THE ONLY ONE FOR ME? HONESTLY?
HONESTLY? I ALWAYS HATED IT...
...'CAUSE IT'S SO FUCKING ROMANTIC.

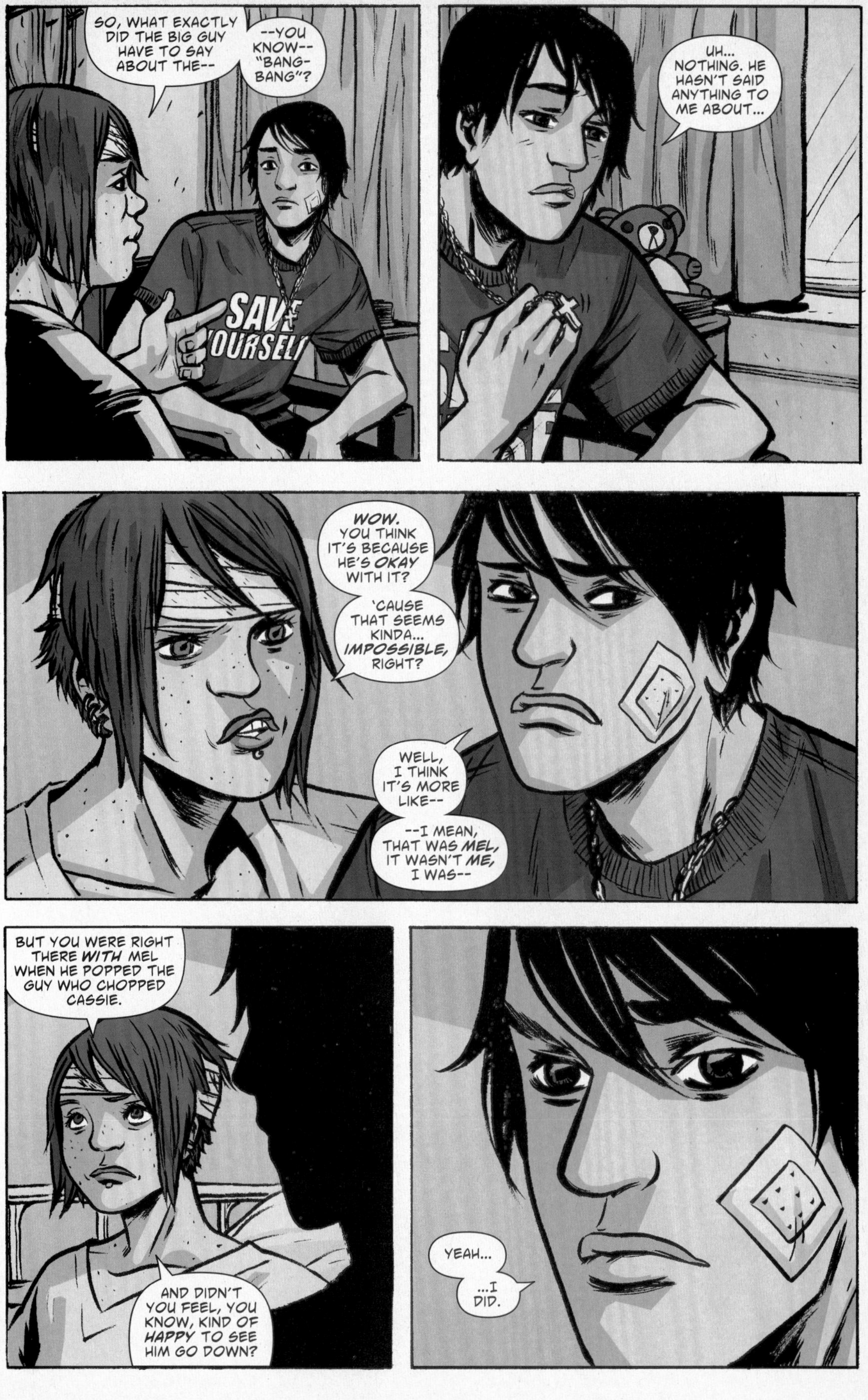
SO, WHAT EXACTLY DID THE BIG GUY HAVE TO SAY ABOUT THE--
--YOU KNOW-- "BANG-BANG"?
SAVE YOURSELF
UH... NOTHING. HE HASN'T SAID ANYTHING TO ME ABOUT...
WOW. YOU THINK IT'S BECAUSE HE'S OKAY WITH IT?
'CAUSE THAT SEEMS KINDA... IMPOSSIBLE, RIGHT?
WELL, I THINK IT'S MORE LIKE--
--I MEAN, THAT WAS MEL, IT WASN'T ME, I WAS--
BUT YOU WERE RIGHT THERE WITH MEL WHEN HE POPPED THE GUY WHO CHOPPED CASSIE.
AND DIDN'T YOU FEEL, YOU KNOW, KIND OF HAPPY TO SEE HIM GO DOWN?
YEAH...
...I DID.

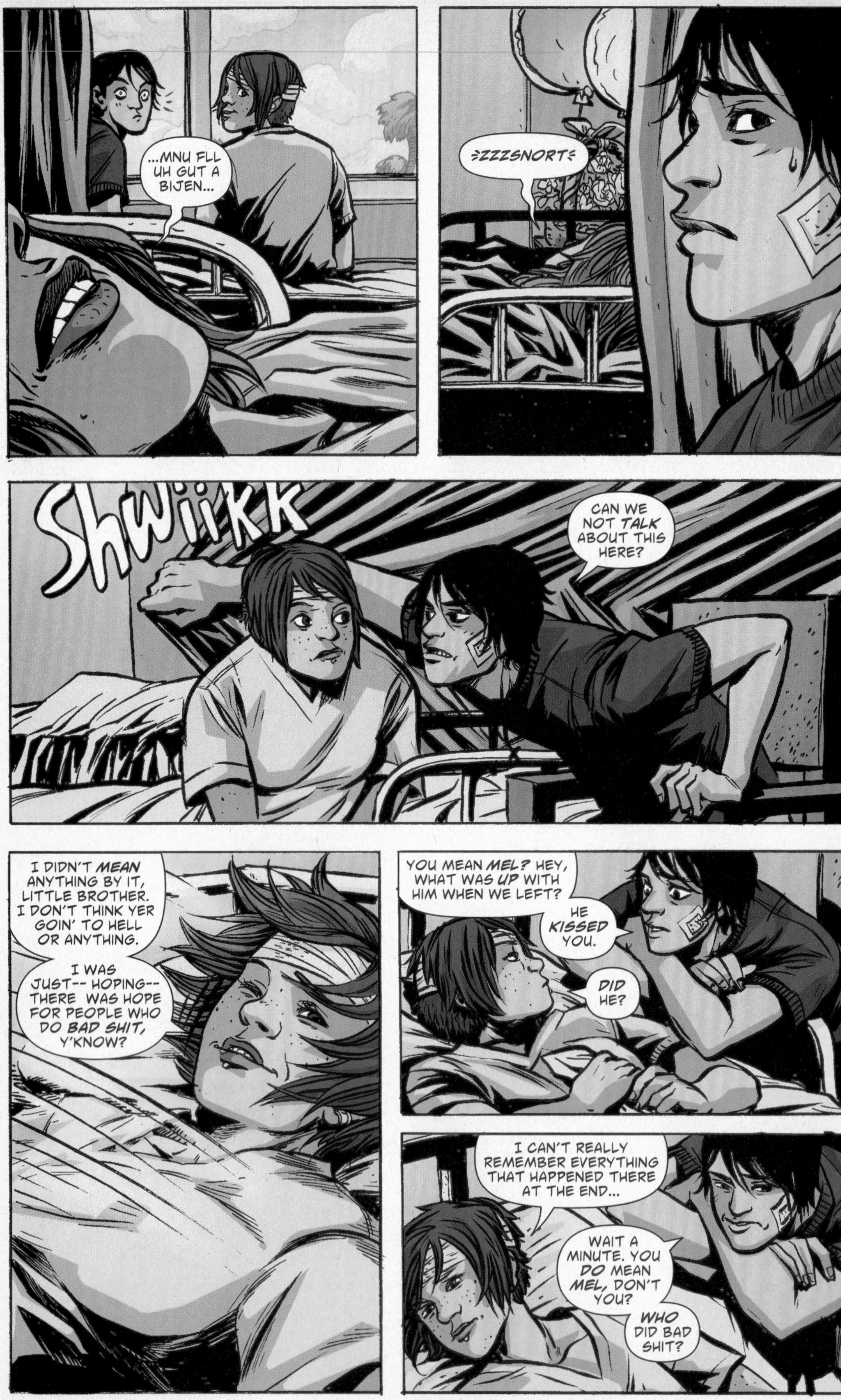
...MNU FLL UH GUT A BIJEN...
ZZZSNORT
SHWIIKK
CAN WE NOT TALK ABOUT THIS HERE?
I DIDN'T MEAN ANYTHING BY IT, LITTLE BROTHER. I DON'T THINK YER GOIN' TO HELL OR ANYTHING.
I WAS JUST-- HOPING-- THERE WAS HOPE FOR PEOPLE WHO DO BAD SHIT, Y'KNOW?
YOU MEAN MEL? HEY, WHAT WAS UP WITH HIM WHEN WE LEFT?
HE KISSED YOU.
DID HE?
I CAN'T REALLY REMEMBER EVERYTHING THAT HAPPENED THERE AT THE END...
WAIT A MINUTE. YOU DO MEAN MEL, DON'T YOU?
WHO DID BAD SHIT?

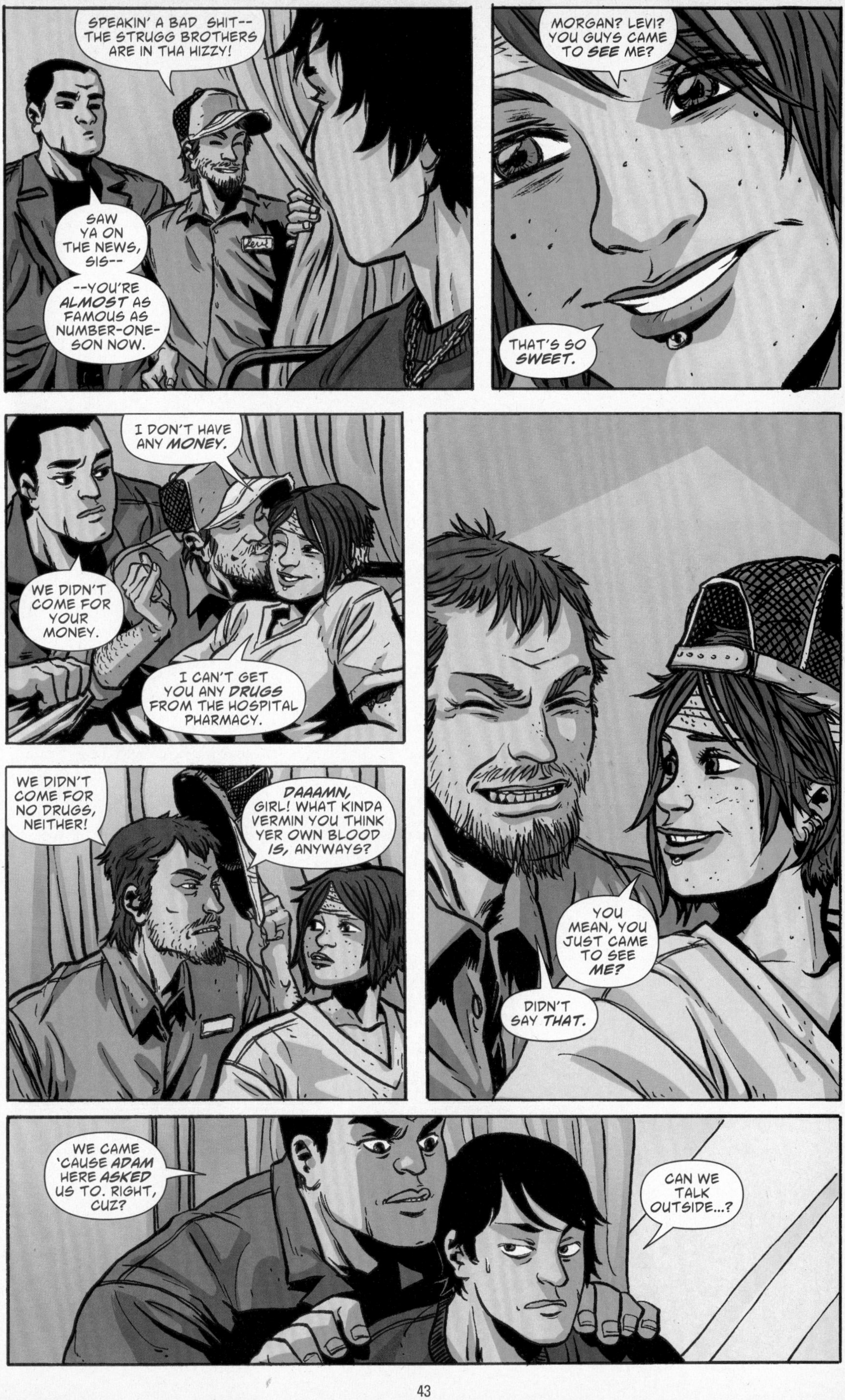
SPEAKIN' A BAD SHIT-- THE STRUGG BROTHERS ARE IN THA HIZZY!
SAW YA ON THE NEWS, SIS--
--YOU'RE ALMOST AS FAMOUS AS NUMBER-ONE-SON NOW.
MORGAN? LEVI? YOU GUYS CAME TO SEE ME?
THAT'S SO SWEET.
I DON'T HAVE ANY MONEY.
WE DIDN'T COME FOR YOUR MONEY.
I CAN'T GET YOU ANY DRUGS FROM THE HOSPITAL PHARMACY.
WE DIDN'T COME FOR NO DRUGS, NEITHER!
DAAAMN, GIRL! WHAT KINDA VERMIN YOU THINK YER OWN BLOOD IS, ANYWAYS?
YOU MEAN, YOU JUST CAME TO SEE ME?
DIDN'T SAY THAT.
WE CAME 'CAUSE ADAM HERE ASKED US TO. RIGHT, CUZ?
CAN WE TALK OUTSIDE...?

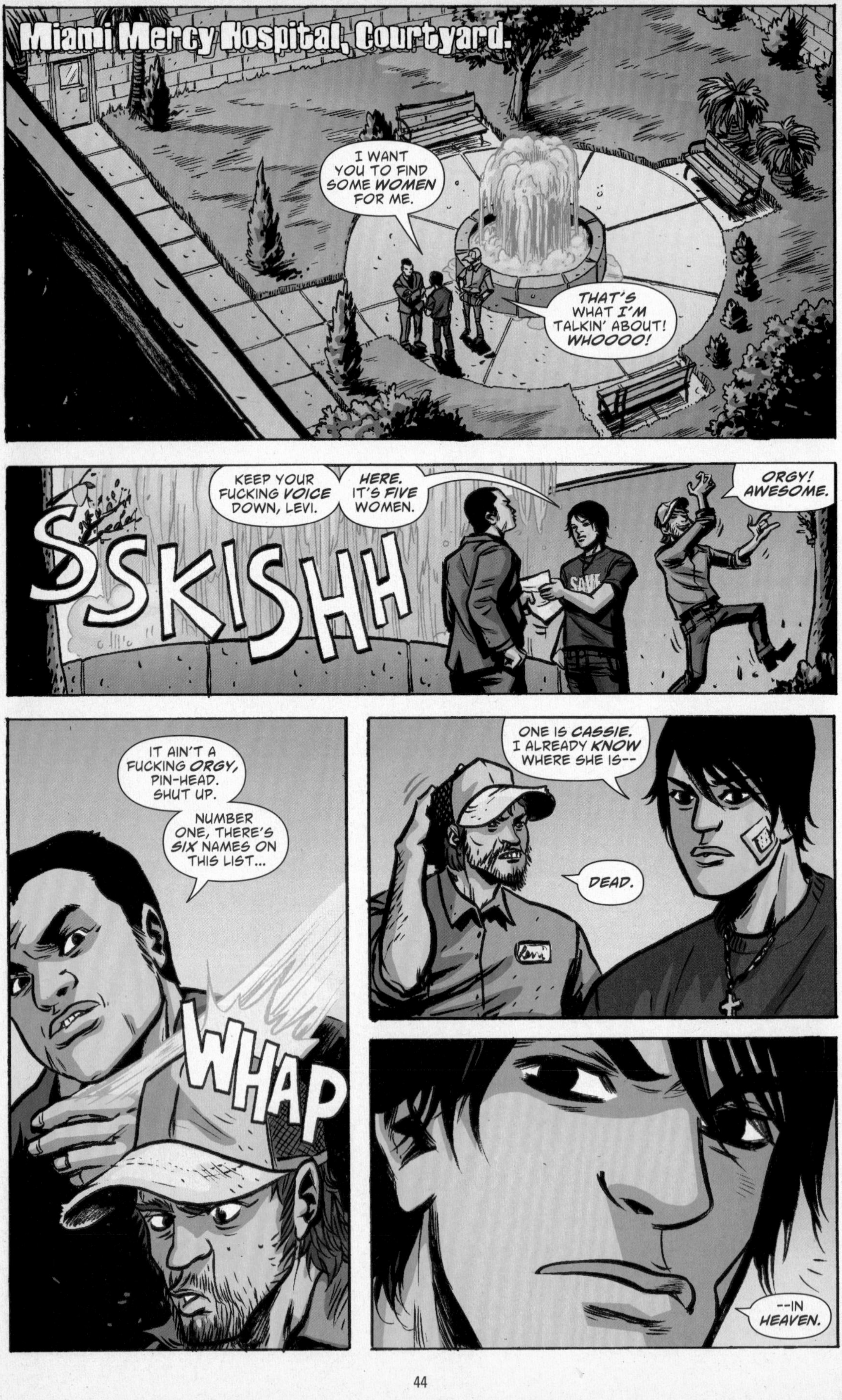
Miami Mercy Hospital, Courtyard.
I WANT YOU TO FIND SOME WOMEN FOR ME.
THAT'S WHAT I'M TALKIN' ABOUT! WHOOOO!
SSKISHH
KEEP YOUR FUCKING VOICE DOWN, LEVI.
HERE. IT'S FIVE WOMEN.
ORGY! AWESOME.
IT AIN'T A FUCKING ORGY, PIN-HEAD. SHUT UP.
NUMBER ONE, THERE'S SIX NAMES ON THIS LIST...
WHAP
ONE IS CASSIE. I ALREADY KNOW WHERE SHE IS--
DEAD.
--IN HEAVEN.

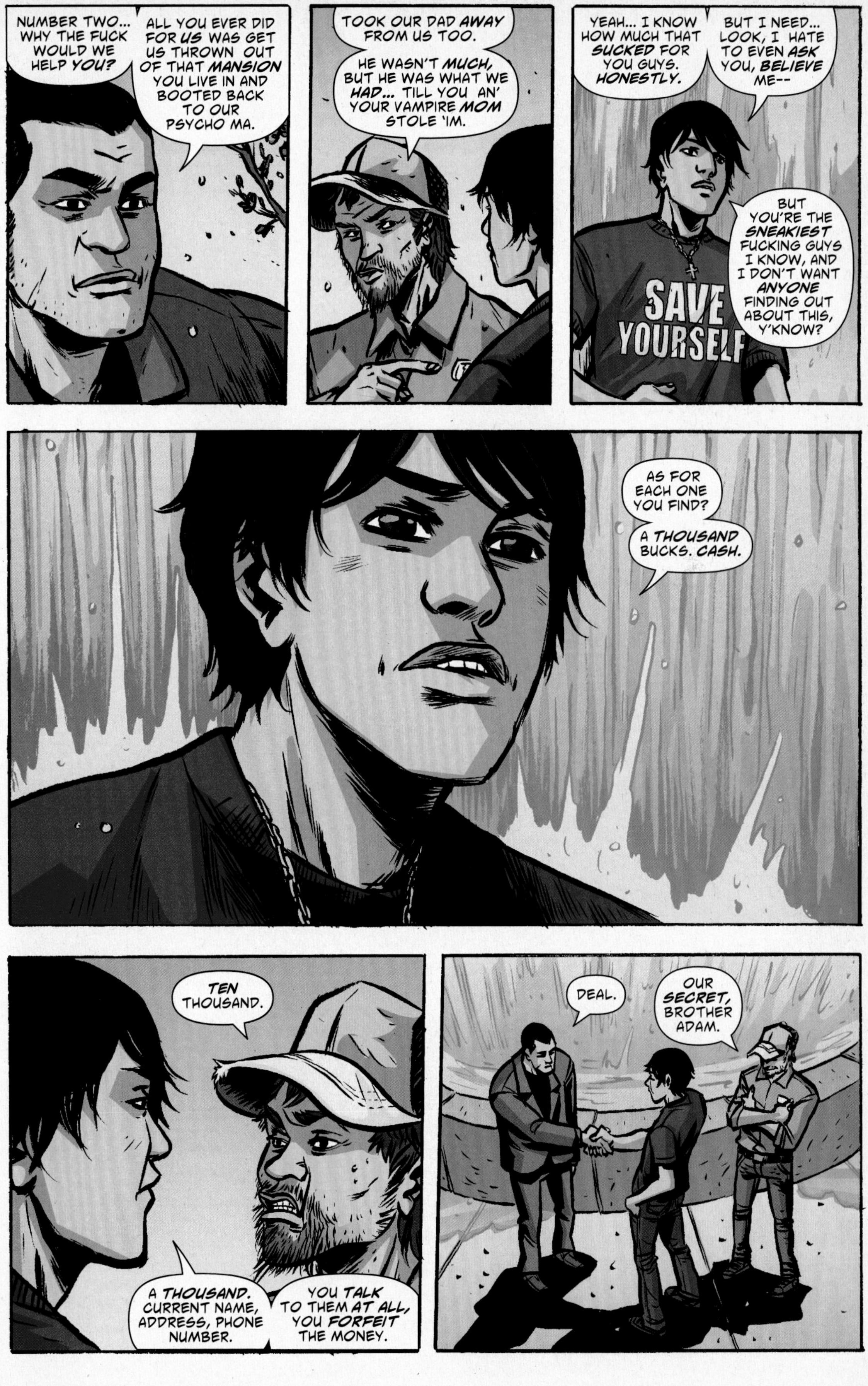

NUMBER TWO... WHY THE FUCK WOULD WE HELP *YOU?*
ALL YOU EVER DID FOR *US* WAS GET US THROWN OUT OF THAT *MANSION* YOU LIVE IN AND BOOTED BACK TO OUR PSYCHO MA.
TOOK OUR DAD *AWAY* FROM US TOO.
HE WASN'T *MUCH,* BUT HE WAS WHAT WE *HAD...* TILL YOU AN' YOUR VAMPIRE *MOM* STOLE 'IM.
YEAH... I KNOW HOW MUCH THAT *SUCKED* FOR YOU GUYS. *HONESTLY.*
BUT I NEED... LOOK, I HATE TO EVEN *ASK* YOU, *BELIEVE* ME--
SAVE YOURSELF
BUT YOU'RE THE *SNEAKIEST* FUCKING GUYS I KNOW, AND I DON'T WANT *ANYONE* FINDING OUT ABOUT THIS, Y'KNOW?
AS FOR EACH ONE YOU FIND?
A *THOUSAND* BUCKS. *CASH.*
TEN THOUSAND.
A *THOUSAND.* CURRENT NAME, ADDRESS, PHONE NUMBER.
YOU *TALK* TO THEM *AT ALL,* YOU *FORFEIT* THE MONEY.
DEAL.
OUR *SECRET,* BROTHER ADAM.

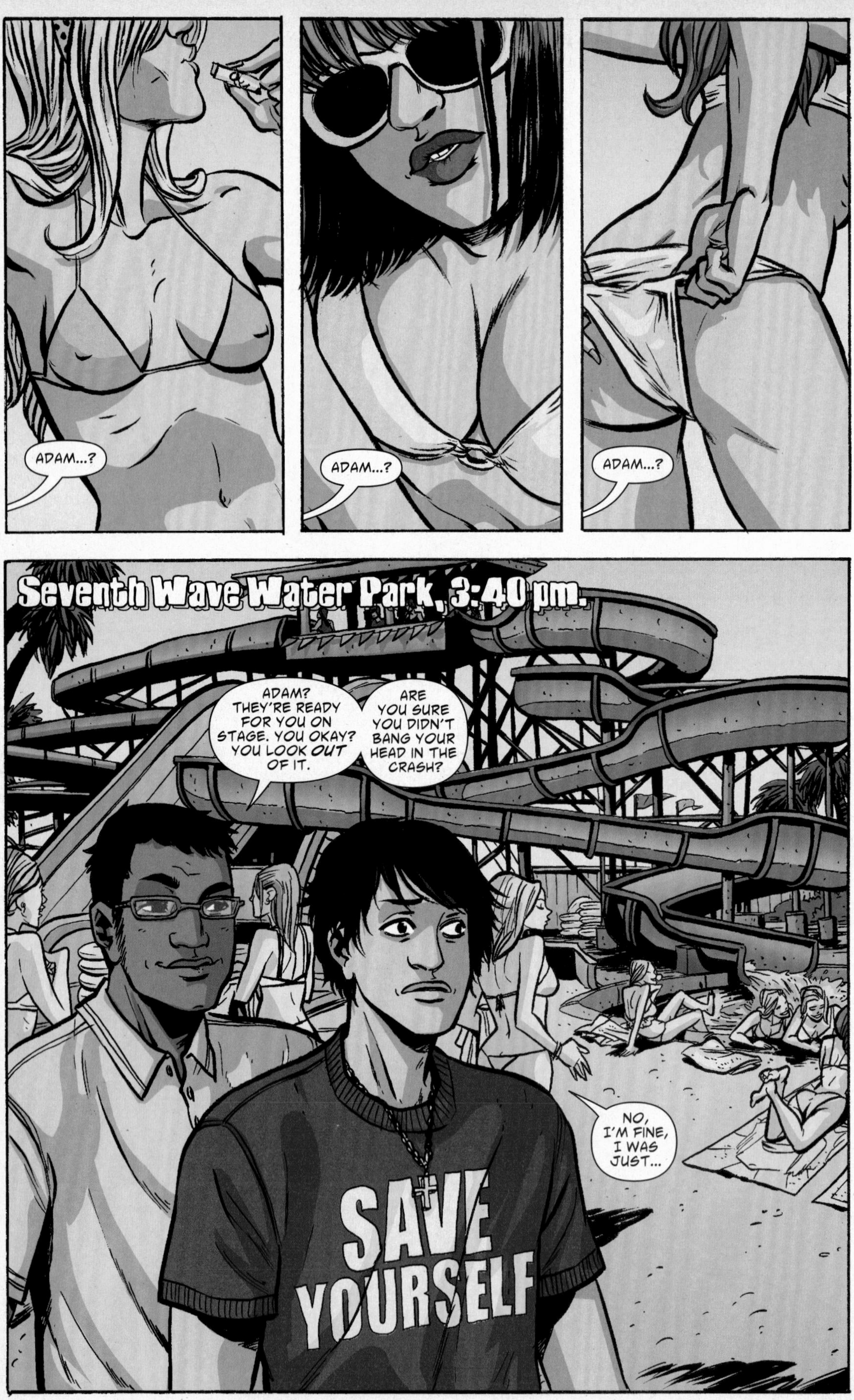
ADAM...?
ADAM...?
ADAM...?
Seventh Wave Water Park, 3:40 pm.
ADAM? THEY'RE READY FOR YOU ON STAGE. YOU OKAY? YOU LOOK OUT OF IT.
ARE YOU SURE YOU DIDN'T BANG YOUR HEAD IN THE CRASH?
NO, I'M FINE, I WAS JUST...
SAVE YOURSELF

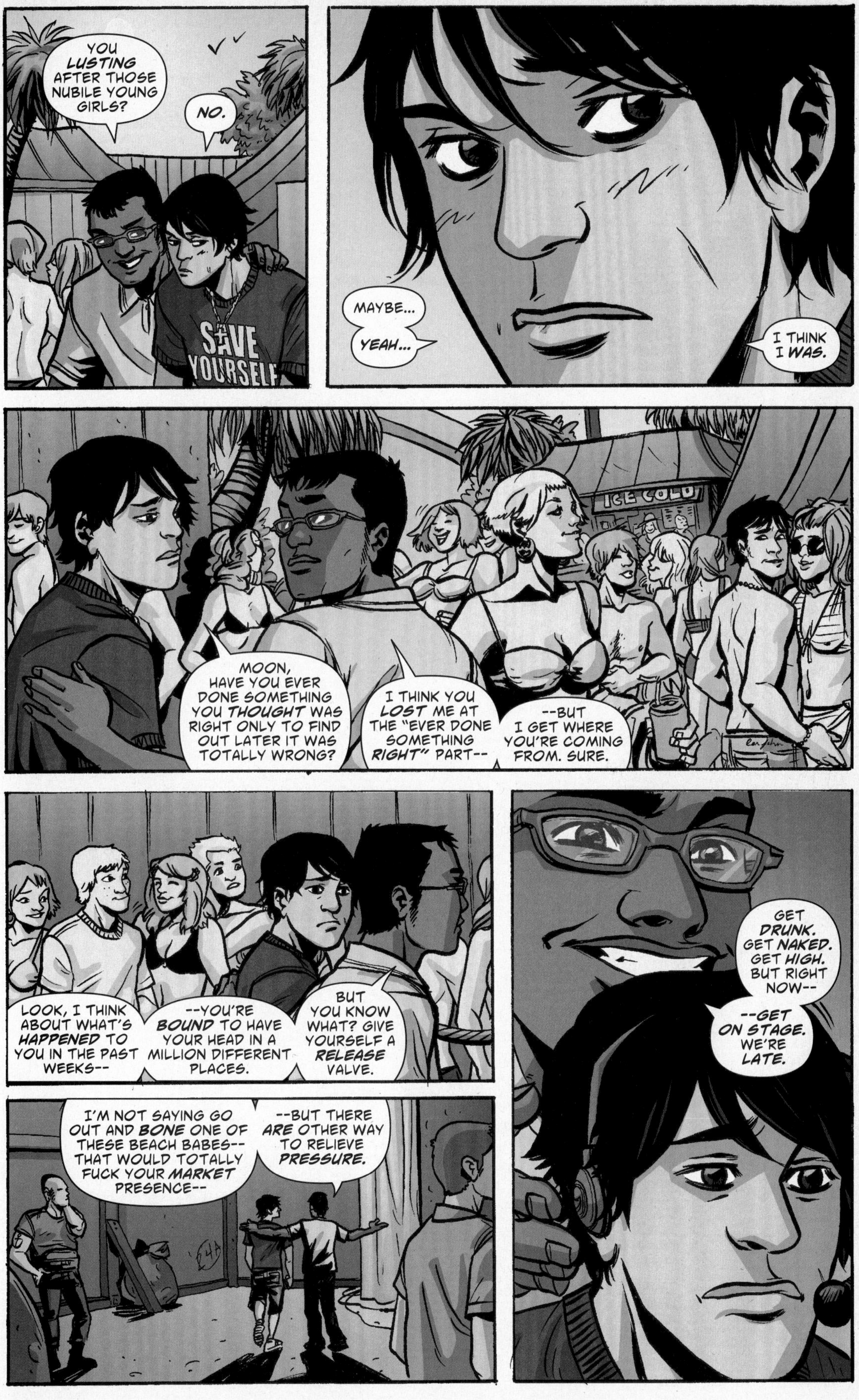
YOU LUSTING AFTER THOSE NUBILE YOUNG GIRLS?
NO.
SAVE YOURSELF
MAYBE...
YEAH...
I THINK I WAS.
ICE COLD
MOON, HAVE YOU EVER DONE SOMETHING YOU THOUGHT WAS RIGHT ONLY TO FIND OUT LATER IT WAS TOTALLY WRONG?
I THINK YOU LOST ME AT THE "EVER DONE SOMETHING RIGHT" PART--
--BUT I GET WHERE YOU'RE COMING FROM. SURE.
LOOK, I THINK ABOUT WHAT'S HAPPENED TO YOU IN THE PAST WEEKS--
--YOU'RE BOUND TO HAVE YOUR HEAD IN A MILLION DIFFERENT PLACES.
BUT YOU KNOW WHAT? GIVE YOURSELF A RELEASE VALVE.
I'M NOT SAYING GO OUT AND BONE ONE OF THESE BEACH BABES--THAT WOULD TOTALLY FUCK YOUR MARKET PRESENCE--
--BUT THERE ARE OTHER WAY TO RELIEVE PRESSURE.
GET DRUNK. GET NAKED. GET HIGH. BUT RIGHT NOW--
--GET ON STAGE. WE'RE LATE.

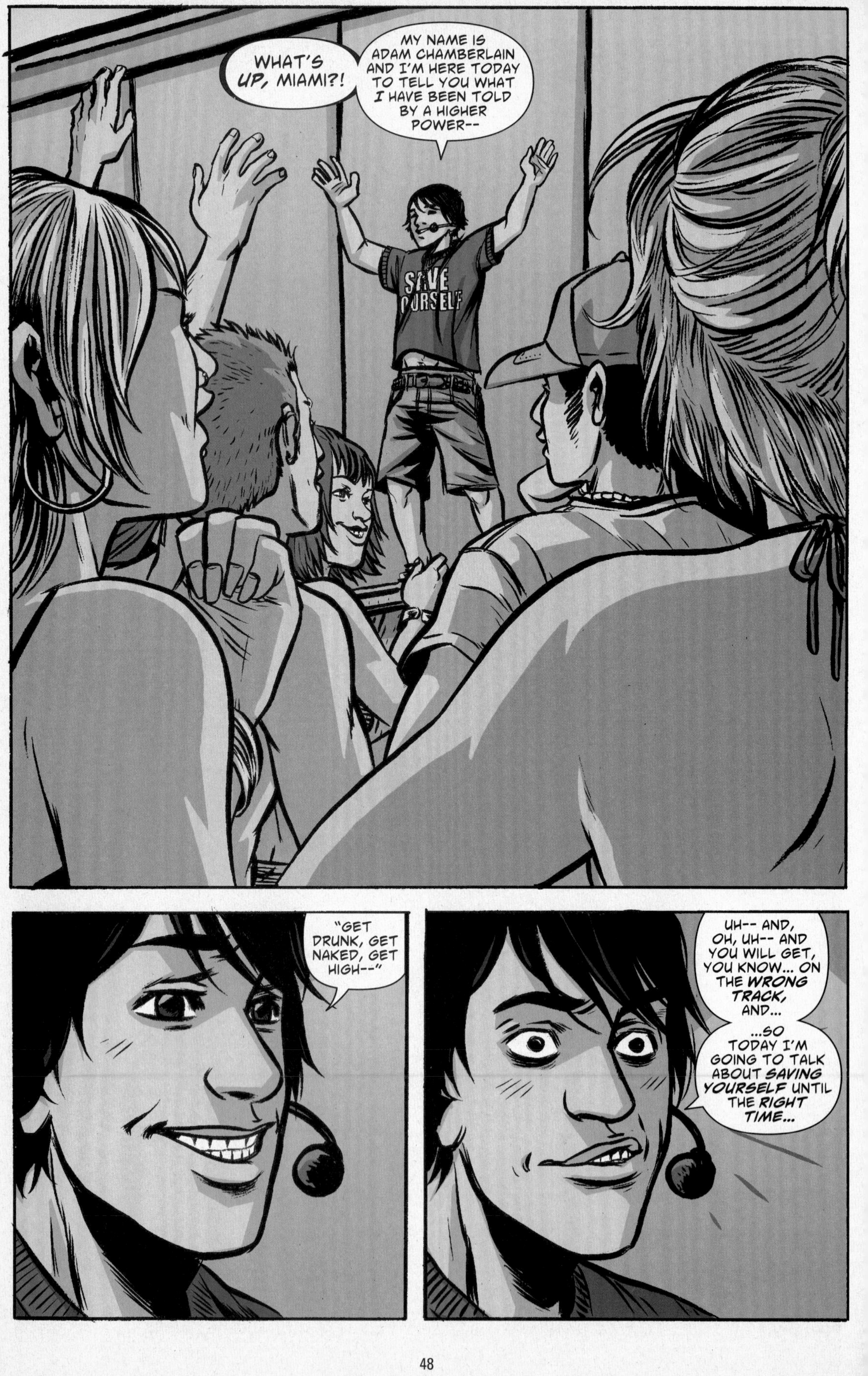
WHAT'S UP, MIAMI?!
MY NAME IS ADAM CHAMBERLAIN AND I'M HERE TODAY TO TELL YOU WHAT I HAVE BEEN TOLD BY A HIGHER POWER--
"GET DRUNK, GET NAKED, GET HIGH--"
UH-- AND, OH, UH-- AND YOU WILL GET, YOU KNOW... ON THE WRONG TRACK, AND...
...SO TODAY I'M GOING TO TALK ABOUT SAVING YOURSELF UNTIL THE RIGHT TIME...

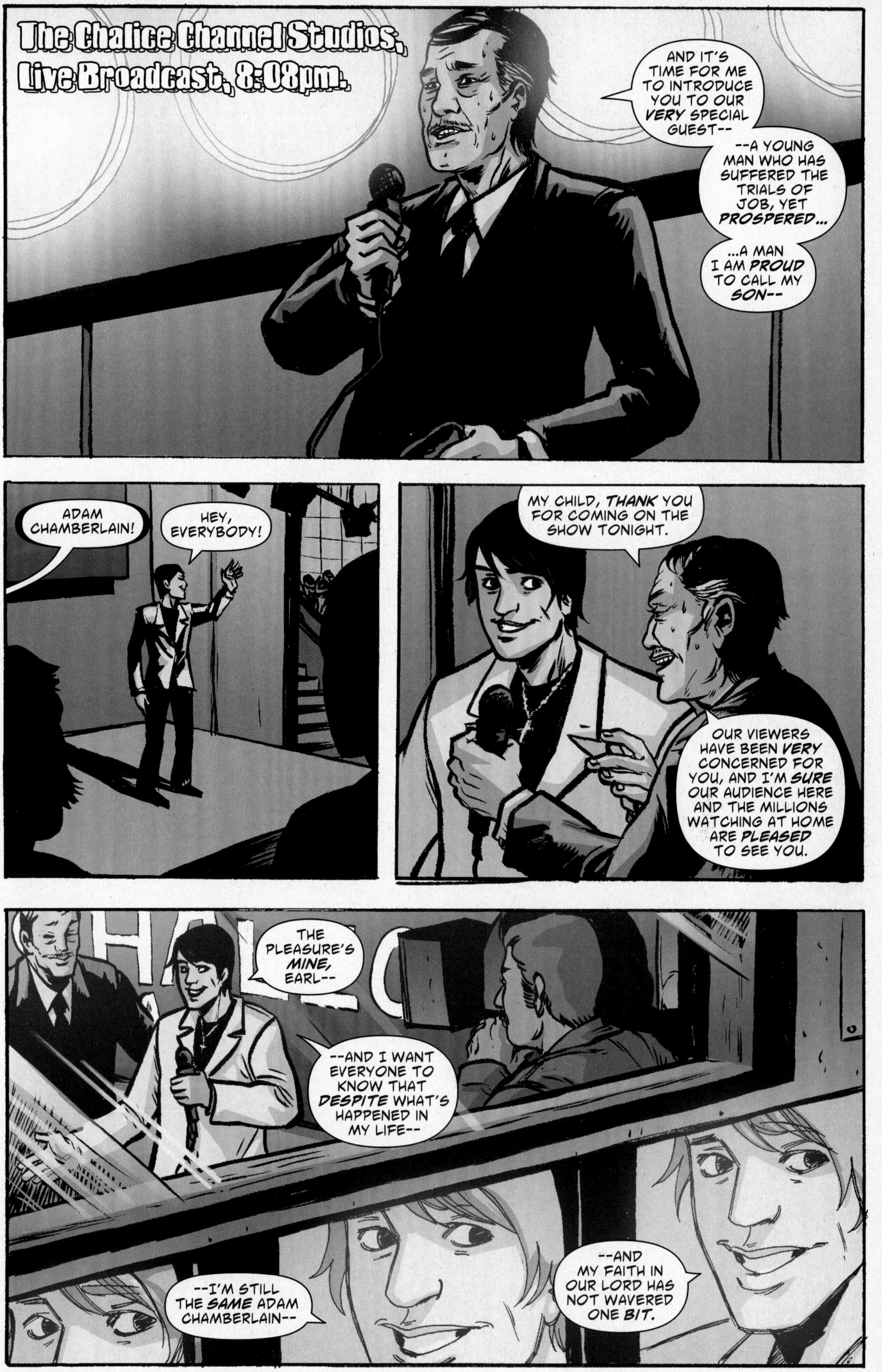
The Chalice Channel Studios, Live Broadcast, 8:08pm.
AND IT'S TIME FOR ME TO INTRODUCE YOU TO OUR VERY SPECIAL GUEST--
--A YOUNG MAN WHO HAS SUFFERED THE TRIALS OF JOB, YET PROSPERED...
...A MAN I AM PROUD TO CALL MY SON--
ADAM CHAMBERLAIN!
HEY, EVERYBODY!
MY CHILD, THANK YOU FOR COMING ON THE SHOW TONIGHT.
OUR VIEWERS HAVE BEEN VERY CONCERNED FOR YOU, AND I'M SURE OUR AUDIENCE HERE AND THE MILLIONS WATCHING AT HOME ARE PLEASED TO SEE YOU.
THE PLEASURE'S MINE, EARL--
--AND I WANT EVERYONE TO KNOW THAT DESPITE WHAT'S HAPPENED IN MY LIFE--
--I'M STILL THE SAME ADAM CHAMBERLAIN--
--AND MY FAITH IN OUR LORD HAS NOT WAVERED ONE BIT.

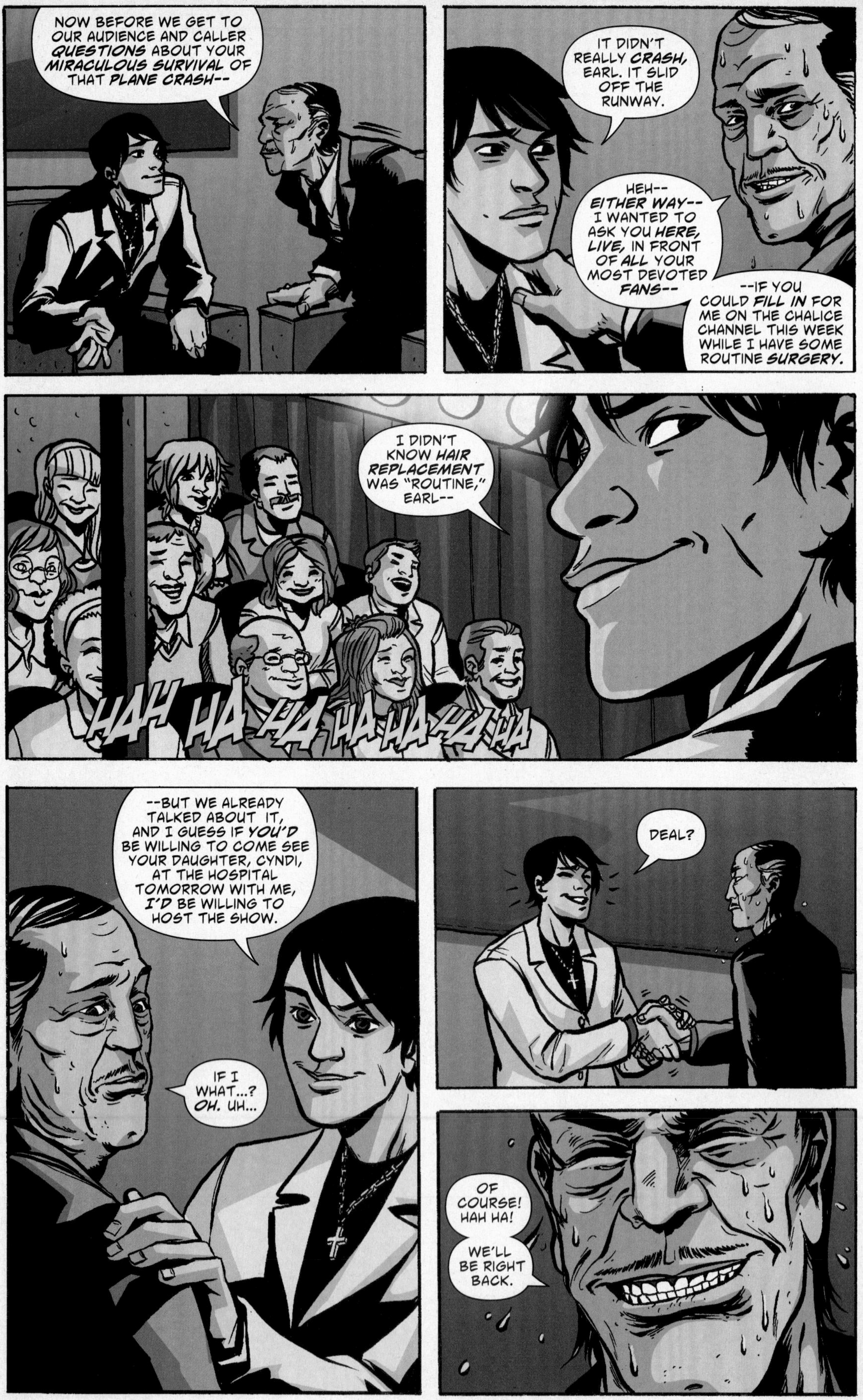
NOW BEFORE WE GET TO OUR AUDIENCE AND CALLER QUESTIONS ABOUT YOUR MIRACULOUS SURVIVAL OF THAT PLANE CRASH--
IT DIDN'T REALLY CRASH, EARL. IT SLID OFF THE RUNWAY.
HEH-- EITHER WAY-- I WANTED TO ASK YOU HERE, LIVE, IN FRONT OF ALL YOUR MOST DEVOTED FANS--
--IF YOU COULD FILL IN FOR ME ON THE CHALICE CHANNEL THIS WEEK WHILE I HAVE SOME ROUTINE SURGERY.
I DIDN'T KNOW HAIR REPLACEMENT WAS "ROUTINE," EARL--
HAH HA HA HA HA HA HA
--BUT WE ALREADY TALKED ABOUT IT, AND I GUESS IF YOU'D BE WILLING TO COME SEE YOUR DAUGHTER, CYNDI, AT THE HOSPITAL TOMORROW WITH ME, I'D BE WILLING TO HOST THE SHOW.
IF I WHAT...? OH. UH...
DEAL?
OF COURSE! HAH HA!
WE'LL BE RIGHT BACK.

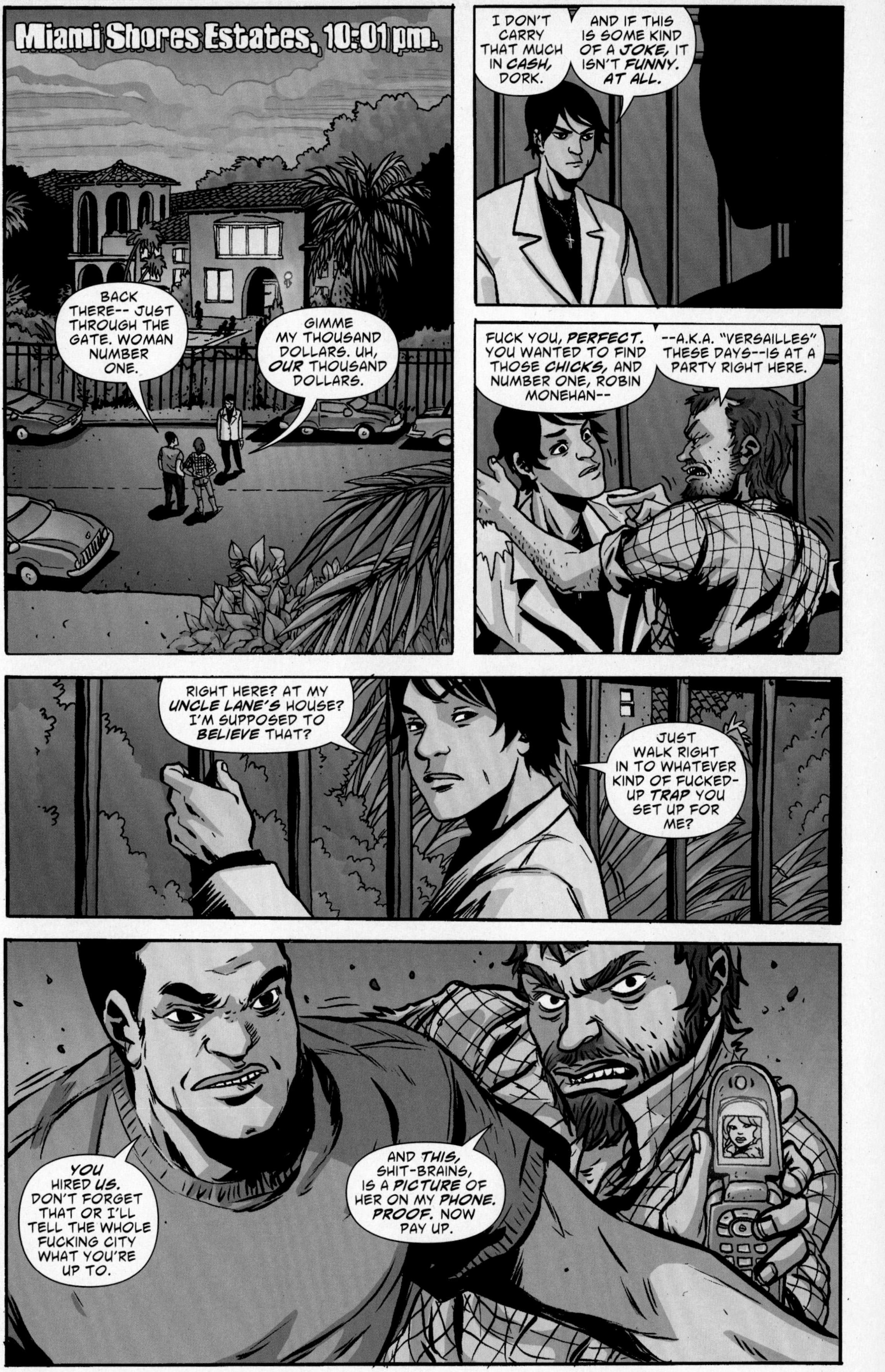

Miami Shores Estates, 10:01 pm.
BACK THERE-- JUST THROUGH THE GATE. WOMAN NUMBER ONE.
GIMME MY THOUSAND DOLLARS. UH, OUR THOUSAND DOLLARS.
I DON'T CARRY THAT MUCH IN CASH, DORK.
AND IF THIS IS SOME KIND OF A JOKE, IT ISN'T FUNNY. AT ALL.
FUCK YOU, PERFECT. YOU WANTED TO FIND THOSE CHICKS, AND NUMBER ONE, ROBIN MONEHAN--
--A.K.A. "VERSAILLES" THESE DAYS--IS AT A PARTY RIGHT HERE.
RIGHT HERE? AT MY UNCLE LANE'S HOUSE? I'M SUPPOSED TO BELIEVE THAT?
JUST WALK RIGHT IN TO WHATEVER KIND OF FUCKED-UP TRAP YOU SET UP FOR ME?
YOU HIRED US. DON'T FORGET THAT OR I'LL TELL THE WHOLE FUCKING CITY WHAT YOU'RE UP TO.
AND THIS, SHIT-BRAINS, IS A PICTURE OF HER ON MY PHONE. PROOF. NOW PAY UP.

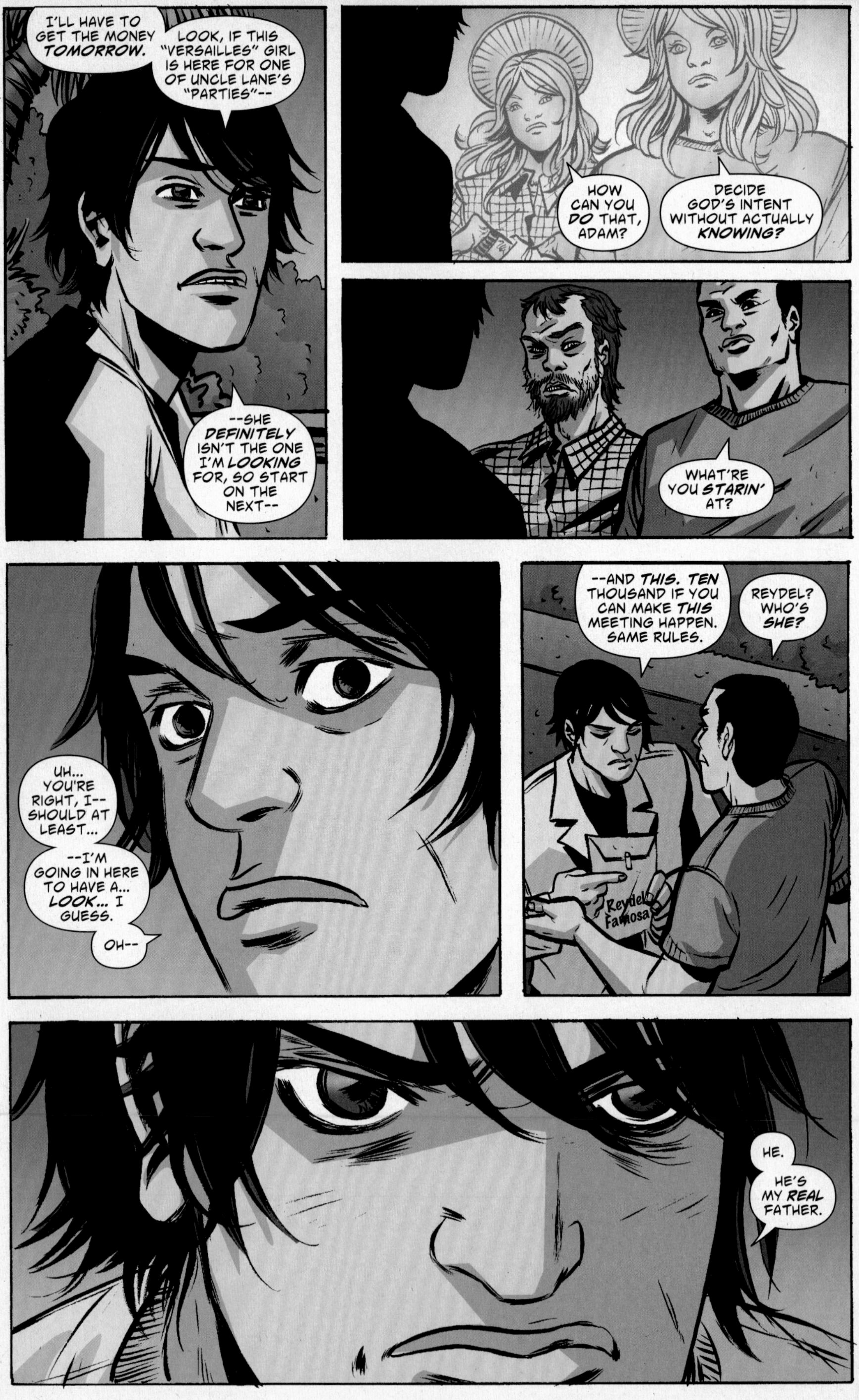
I'LL HAVE TO GET THE MONEY TOMORROW.
LOOK, IF THIS "VERSAILLES" GIRL IS HERE FOR ONE OF UNCLE LANE'S "PARTIES"--
--SHE DEFINITELY ISN'T THE ONE I'M LOOKING FOR, SO START ON THE NEXT--
HOW CAN YOU DO THAT, ADAM?
DECIDE GOD'S INTENT WITHOUT ACTUALLY KNOWING?
WHAT'RE YOU STARIN' AT?
UH... YOU'RE RIGHT, I--SHOULD AT LEAST...
--I'M GOING IN HERE TO HAVE A... LOOK... I GUESS.
OH--
--AND THIS. TEN THOUSAND IF YOU CAN MAKE THIS MEETING HAPPEN. SAME RULES.
REYDEL? WHO'S SHE?
Reydel Famosa
HE.
HE'S MY REAL FATHER.

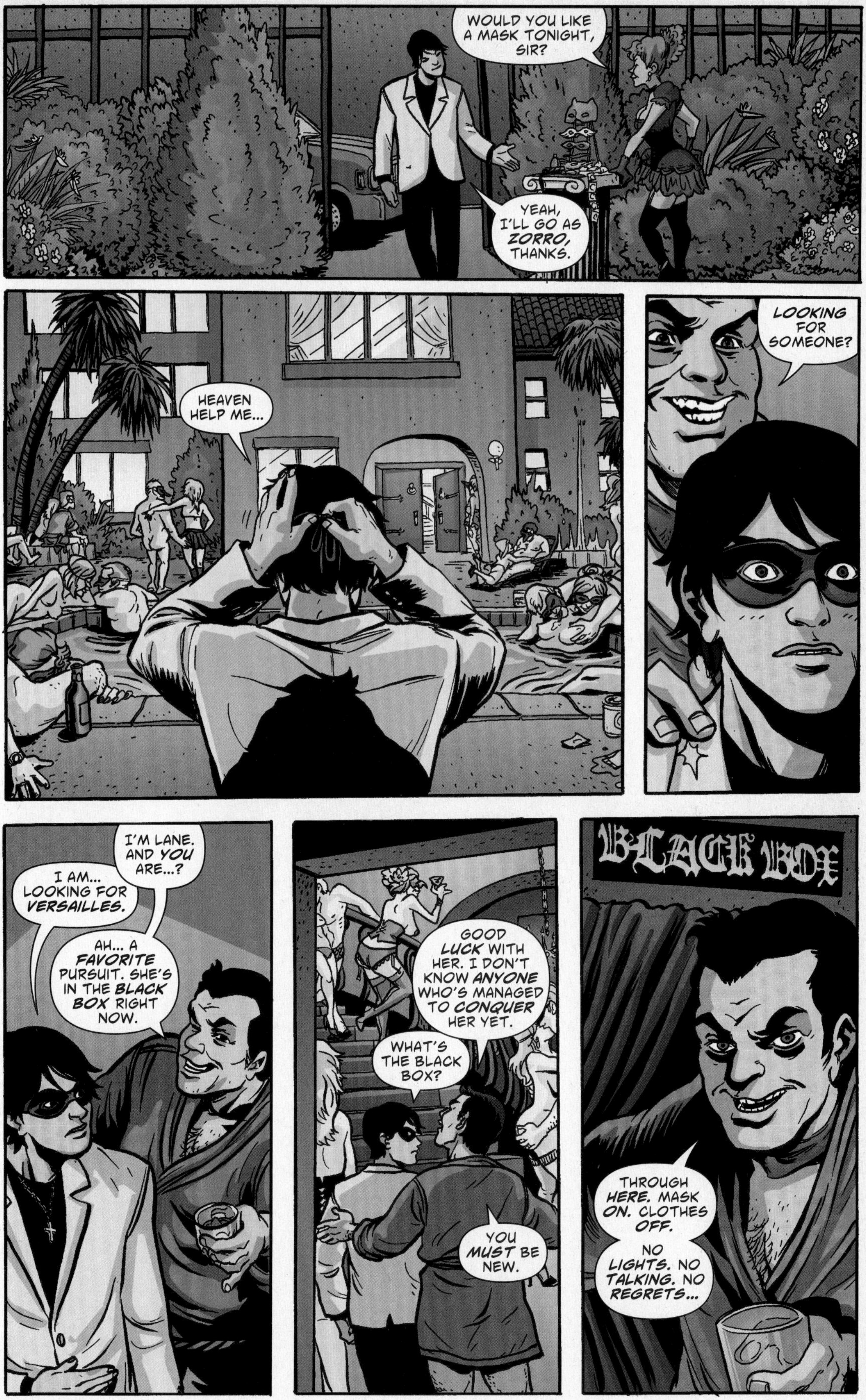
WOULD YOU LIKE A MASK TONIGHT, SIR?
YEAH, I'LL GO AS ZORRO, THANKS.
HEAVEN HELP ME...
LOOKING FOR SOMEONE?
I AM... LOOKING FOR VERSAILLES.
I'M LANE. AND YOU ARE...?
AH... A FAVORITE PURSUIT. SHE'S IN THE BLACK BOX RIGHT NOW.
GOOD LUCK WITH HER. I DON'T KNOW ANYONE WHO'S MANAGED TO CONQUER HER YET.
WHAT'S THE BLACK BOX?
YOU MUST BE NEW.
BLACK BOX
THROUGH HERE. MASK ON. CLOTHES OFF.
NO LIGHTS. NO TALKING. NO REGRETS...

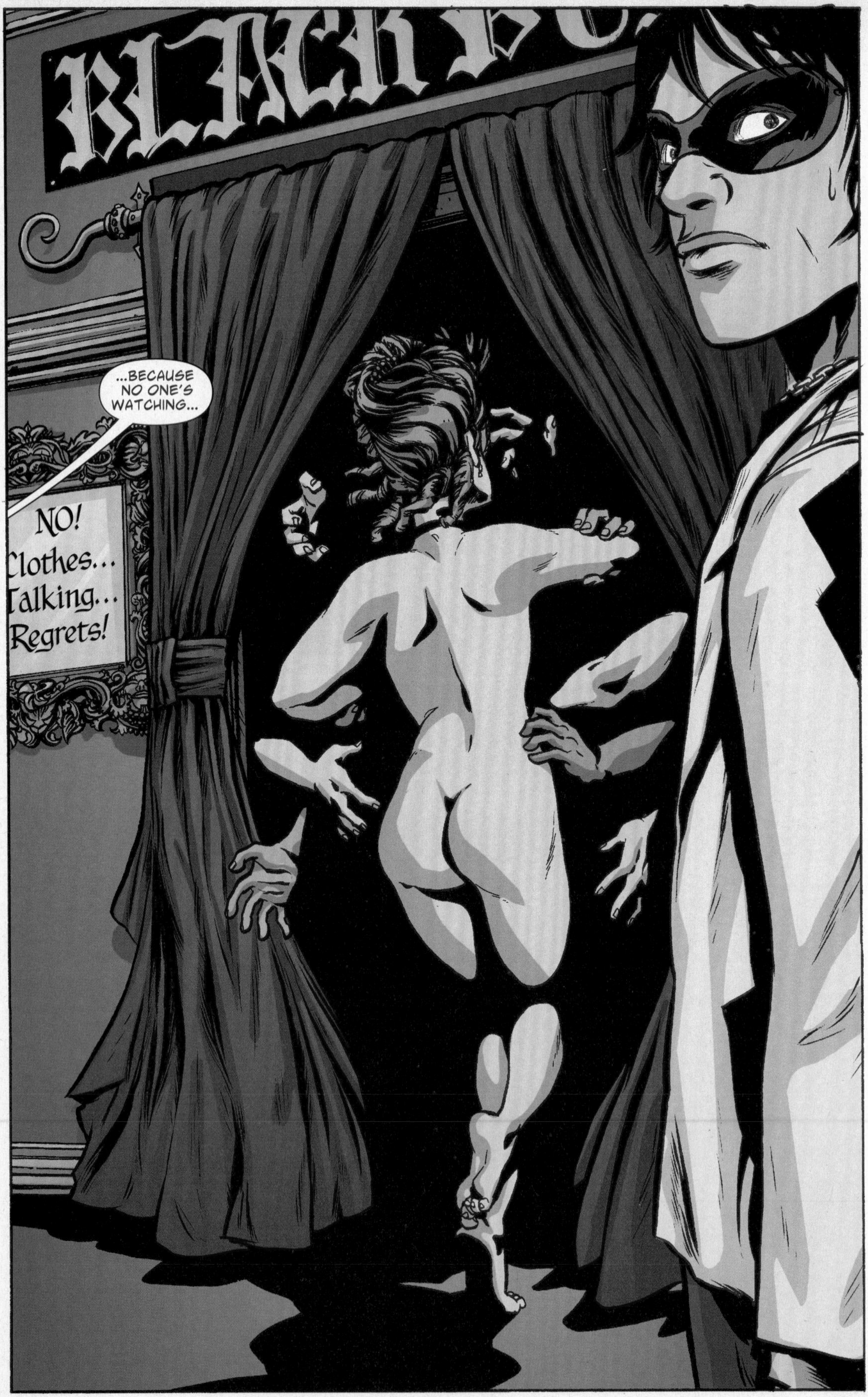
...BECAUSE NO ONE'S WATCHING...
NO!
Clothes...
Talking...
Regrets!

CHAPTER THREE

Chapter pencils by Becky Cloonan, inks by Jim Rugg

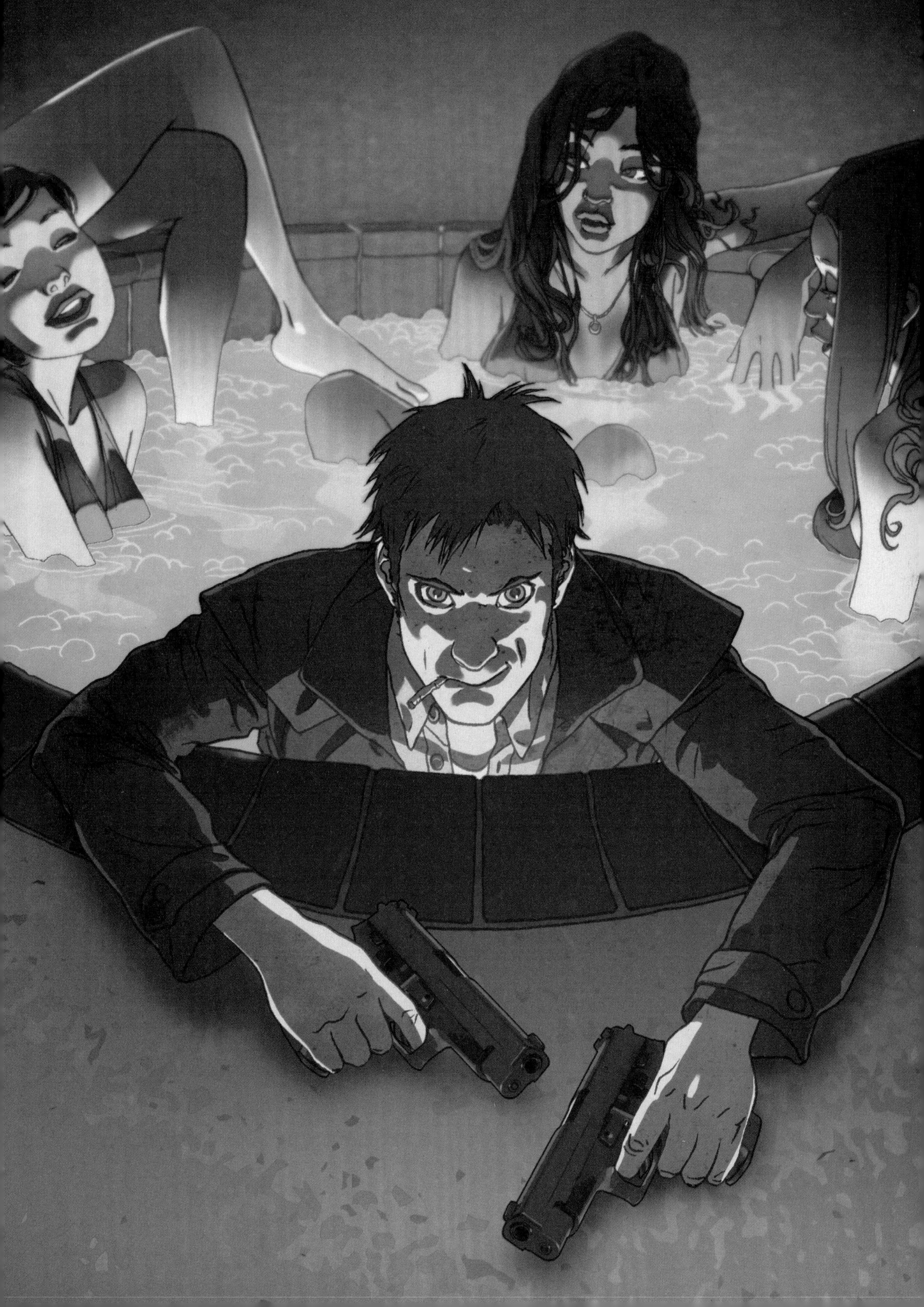

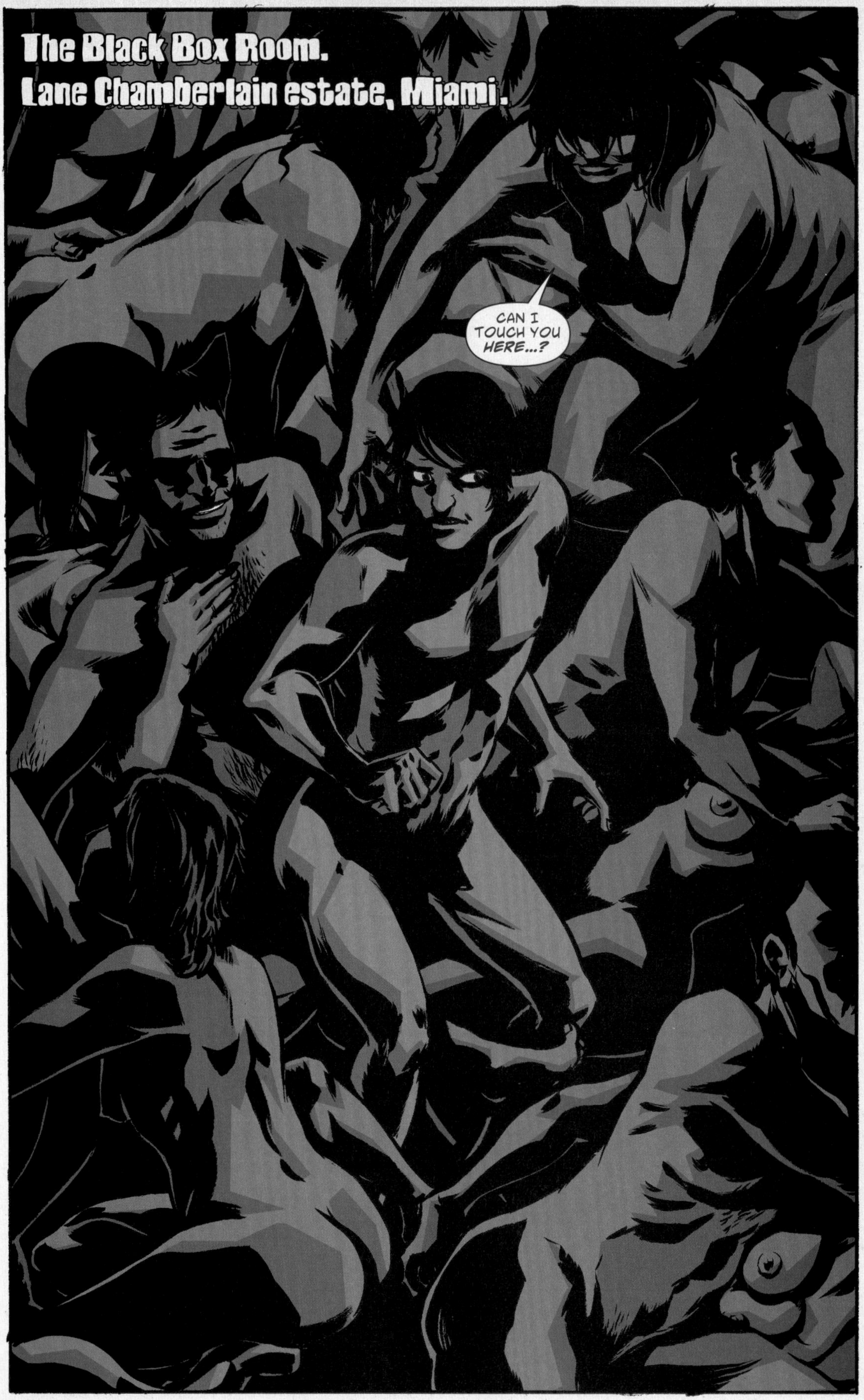
The Black Box Room.
Lane Chamberlain estate, Miami.
CAN I TOUCH YOU HERE...?

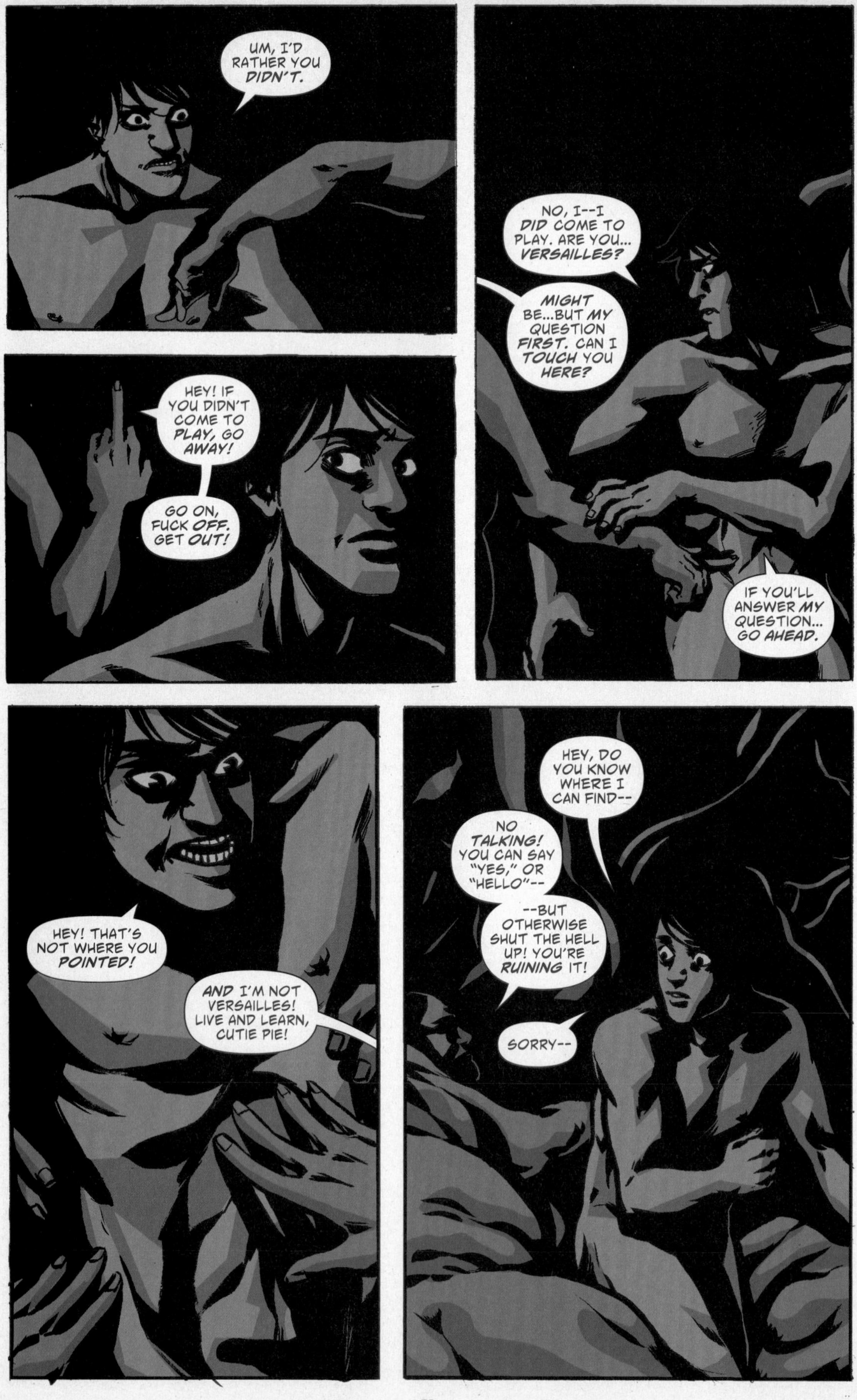
UM, I'D RATHER YOU DIDN'T.
HEY! IF YOU DIDN'T COME TO PLAY, GO AWAY!
GO ON, FUCK OFF. GET OUT!
NO, I--I DID COME TO PLAY. ARE YOU... VERSAILLES?
MIGHT BE...BUT MY QUESTION FIRST. CAN I TOUCH YOU HERE?
IF YOU'LL ANSWER MY QUESTION... GO AHEAD.
HEY! THAT'S NOT WHERE YOU POINTED!
AND I'M NOT VERSAILLES! LIVE AND LEARN, CUTIE PIE!
HEY, DO YOU KNOW WHERE I CAN FIND--
NO TALKING! YOU CAN SAY "YES," OR "HELLO"--
--BUT OTHERWISE SHUT THE HELL UP! YOU'RE RUINING IT!
SORRY--

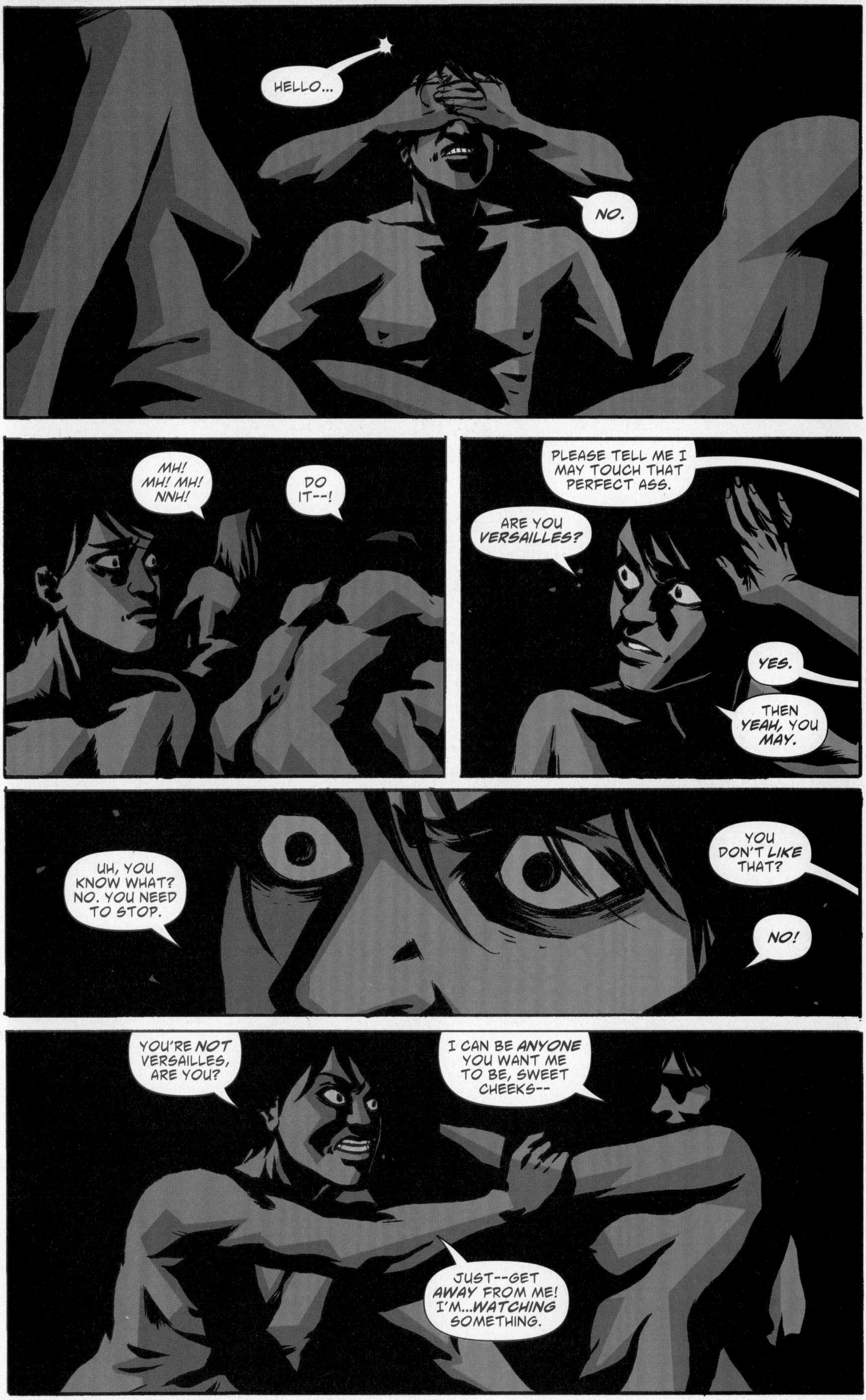
HELLO...
NO.
MH! MH! MH! NNH!
DO IT--!
PLEASE TELL ME I MAY TOUCH THAT PERFECT ASS.
ARE YOU VERSAILLES?
YES.
THEN YEAH, YOU MAY.
UH, YOU KNOW WHAT? NO. YOU NEED TO STOP.
YOU DON'T LIKE THAT?
NO!
YOU'RE NOT VERSAILLES, ARE YOU?
I CAN BE ANYONE YOU WANT ME TO BE, SWEET CHEEKS--
JUST--GET AWAY FROM ME! I'M...WATCHING SOMETHING.

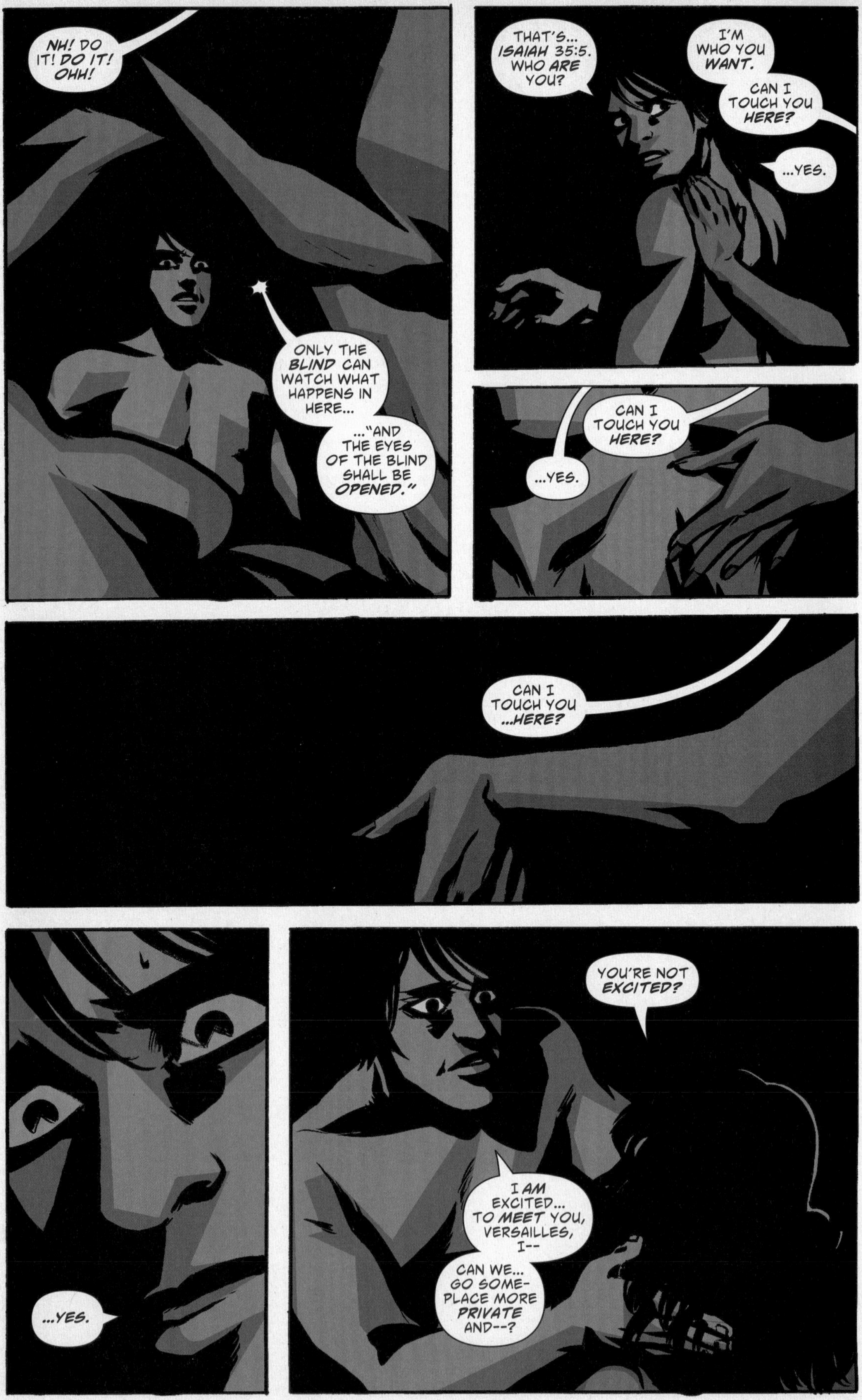
NH! DO IT! DO IT! OHH!
ONLY THE BLIND CAN WATCH WHAT HAPPENS IN HERE...
..."AND THE EYES OF THE BLIND SHALL BE OPENED."
THAT'S... ISAIAH 35:5. WHO ARE YOU?
I'M WHO YOU WANT.
CAN I TOUCH YOU HERE?
...YES.
CAN I TOUCH YOU HERE?
...YES.
CAN I TOUCH YOU ...HERE?
...YES.
YOU'RE NOT EXCITED?
I AM EXCITED... TO MEET YOU, VERSAILLES, I--
CAN WE... GO SOME-PLACE MORE PRIVATE AND--?

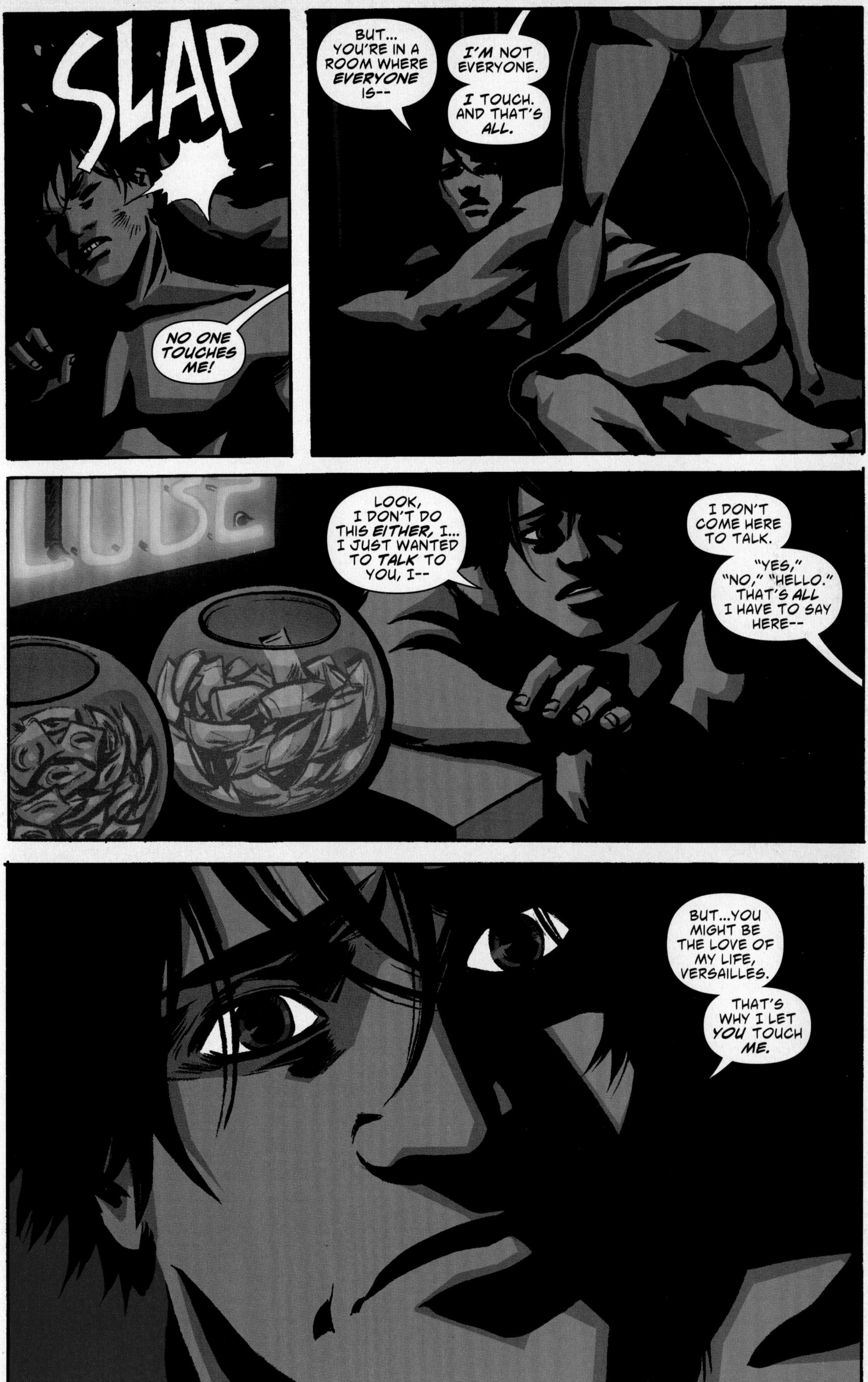
SLAP
NO ONE TOUCHES ME!
BUT... YOU'RE IN A ROOM WHERE EVERYONE IS--
I'M NOT EVERYONE.
I TOUCH. AND THAT'S ALL.
LUBE
LOOK, I DON'T DO THIS EITHER, I... I JUST WANTED TO TALK TO YOU, I--
I DON'T COME HERE TO TALK.
"YES," "NO," "HELLO." THAT'S ALL I HAVE TO SAY HERE--
BUT...YOU MIGHT BE THE LOVE OF MY LIFE, VERSAILLES.
THAT'S WHY I LET YOU TOUCH ME.

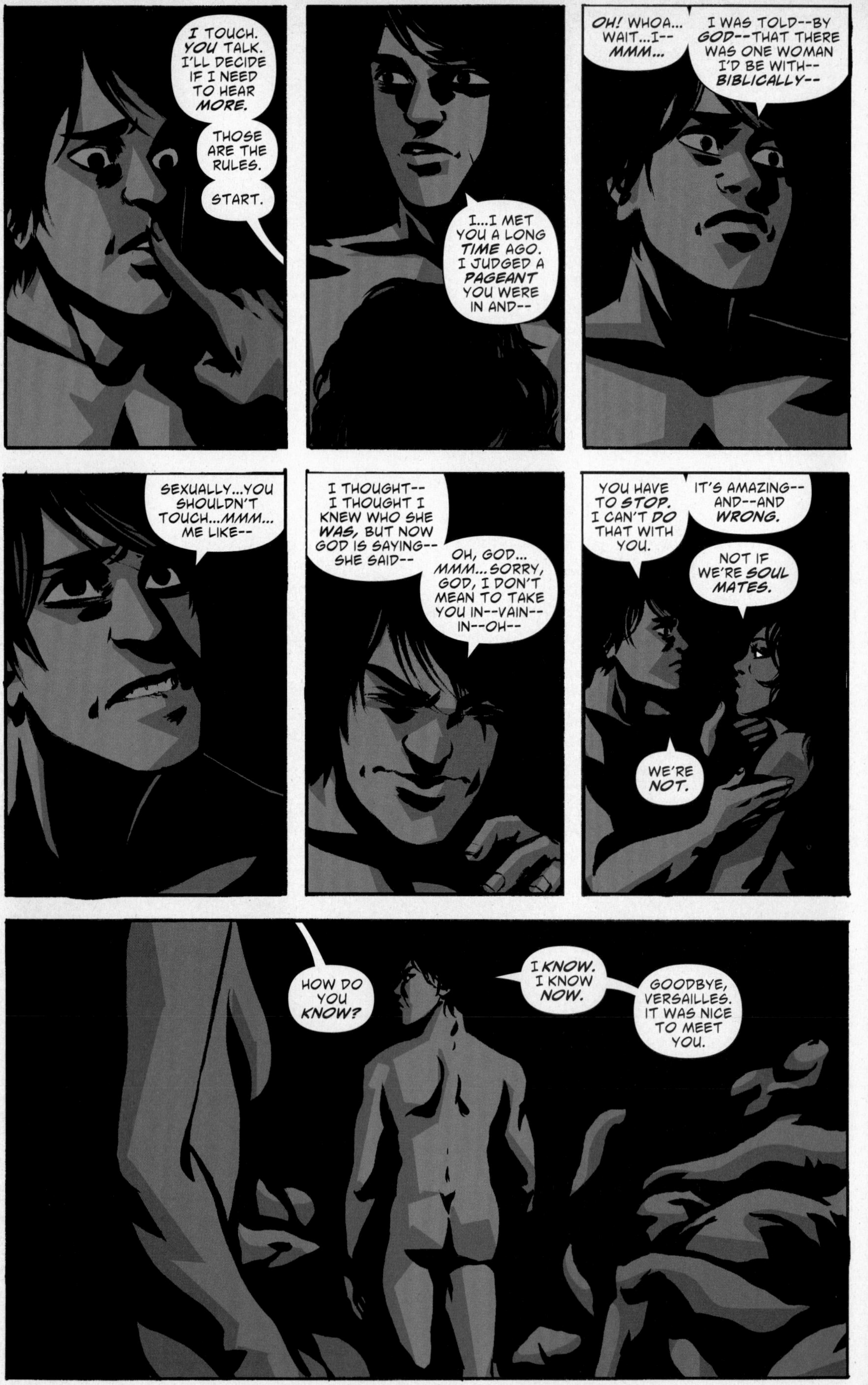
I TOUCH. YOU TALK. I'LL DECIDE IF I NEED TO HEAR MORE.
THOSE ARE THE RULES.
START.
I...I MET YOU A LONG TIME AGO. I JUDGED A PAGEANT YOU WERE IN AND--
OH! WHOA... WAIT...I-- MMM...
I WAS TOLD--BY GOD--THAT THERE WAS ONE WOMAN I'D BE WITH-- BIBLICALLY--
SEXUALLY...YOU SHOULDN'T TOUCH...MMM... ME LIKE--
I THOUGHT-- I THOUGHT I KNEW WHO SHE WAS, BUT NOW GOD IS SAYING-- SHE SAID--
OH, GOD... MMM...SORRY, GOD, I DON'T MEAN TO TAKE YOU IN--VAIN-- IN--OH--
YOU HAVE TO STOP. I CAN'T DO THAT WITH YOU.
IT'S AMAZING-- AND--AND WRONG.
NOT IF WE'RE SOUL MATES.
WE'RE NOT.
HOW DO YOU KNOW?
I KNOW. I KNOW NOW.
GOODBYE, VERSAILLES. IT WAS NICE TO MEET YOU.

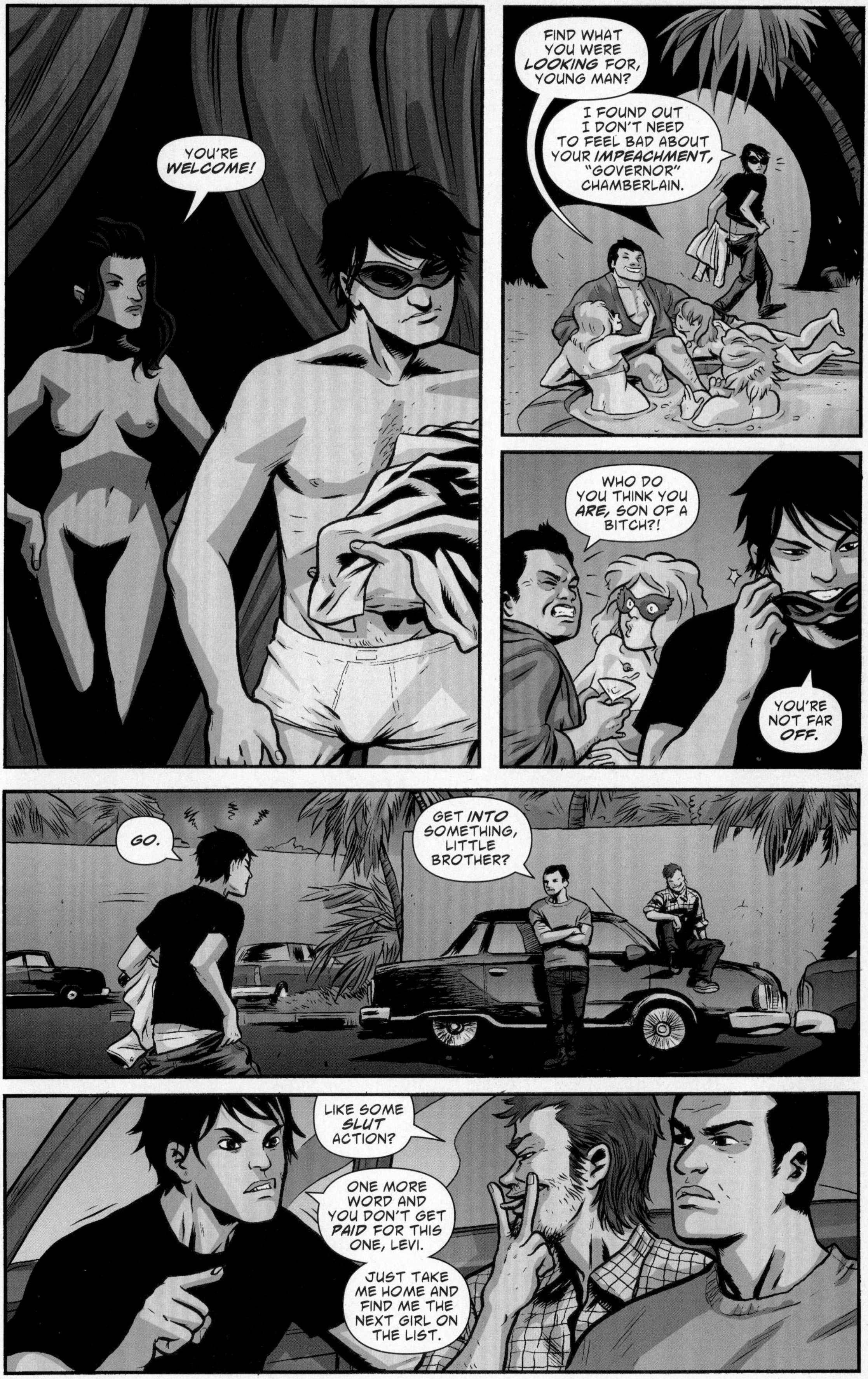
YOU'RE WELCOME!
FIND WHAT YOU WERE LOOKING FOR, YOUNG MAN?
I FOUND OUT I DON'T NEED TO FEEL BAD ABOUT YOUR IMPEACHMENT, "GOVERNOR" CHAMBERLAIN.
WHO DO YOU THINK YOU ARE, SON OF A BITCH?!
YOU'RE NOT FAR OFF.
GO.
GET INTO SOMETHING, LITTLE BROTHER?
LIKE SOME SLUT ACTION?
ONE MORE WORD AND YOU DON'T GET PAID FOR THIS ONE, LEVI.
JUST TAKE ME HOME AND FIND ME THE NEXT GIRL ON THE LIST.

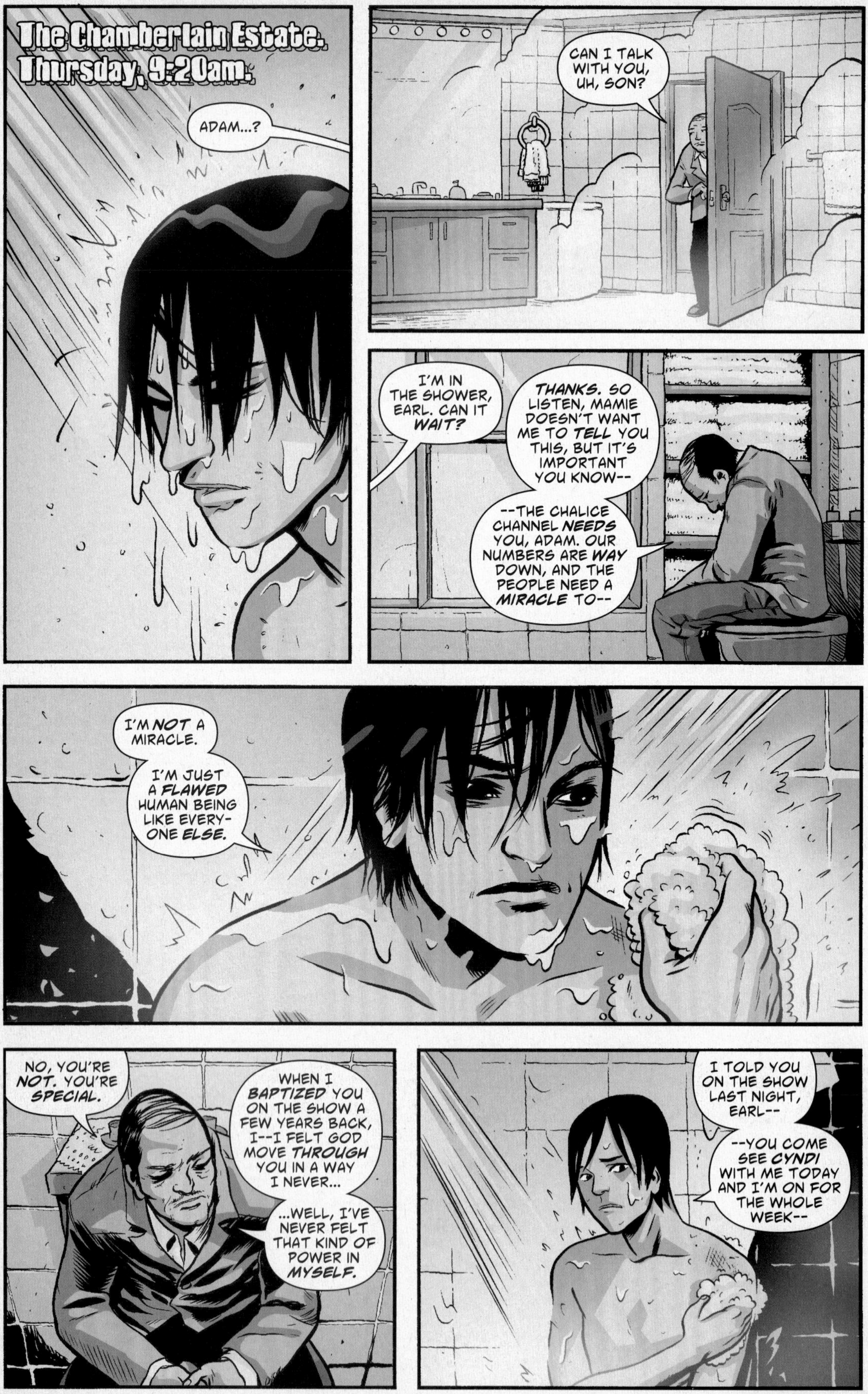
The Chamberlain Estate. Thursday, 9:20am.
ADAM...?
CAN I TALK WITH YOU, UH, SON?
I'M IN THE SHOWER, EARL. CAN IT WAIT?
THANKS. SO LISTEN, MAMIE DOESN'T WANT ME TO TELL YOU THIS, BUT IT'S IMPORTANT YOU KNOW--
--THE CHALICE CHANNEL NEEDS YOU, ADAM. OUR NUMBERS ARE WAY DOWN, AND THE PEOPLE NEED A MIRACLE TO--
I'M NOT A MIRACLE.
I'M JUST A FLAWED HUMAN BEING LIKE EVERY-ONE ELSE.
NO, YOU'RE NOT. YOU'RE SPECIAL.
WHEN I BAPTIZED YOU ON THE SHOW A FEW YEARS BACK, I--I FELT GOD MOVE THROUGH YOU IN A WAY I NEVER...
...WELL, I'VE NEVER FELT THAT KIND OF POWER IN MYSELF.
I TOLD YOU ON THE SHOW LAST NIGHT, EARL--
--YOU COME SEE CYNDI WITH ME TODAY AND I'M ON FOR THE WHOLE WEEK--

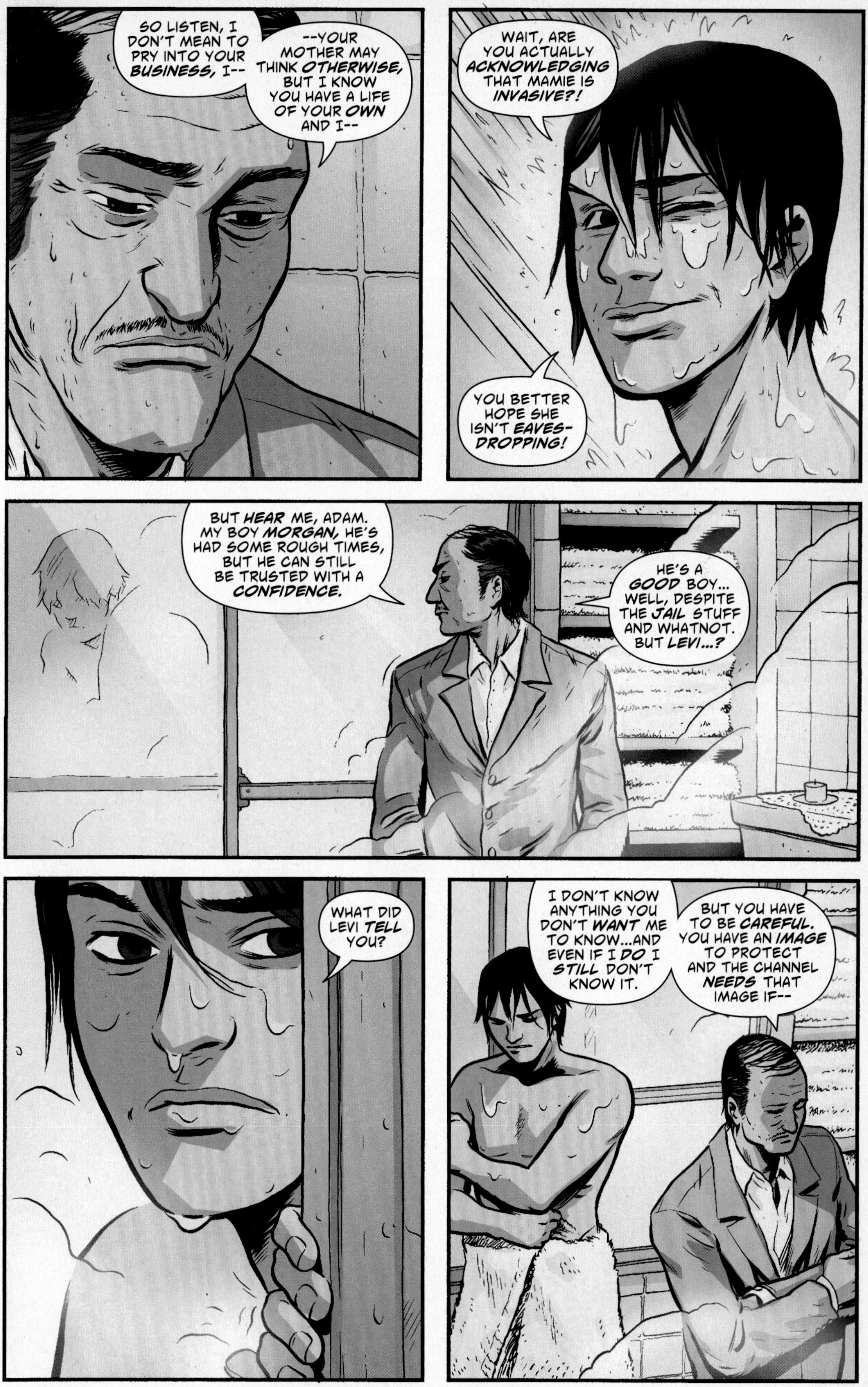
SO LISTEN, I DON'T MEAN TO PRY INTO YOUR BUSINESS, I--
--YOUR MOTHER MAY THINK OTHERWISE, BUT I KNOW YOU HAVE A LIFE OF YOUR OWN AND I--
WAIT, ARE YOU ACTUALLY ACKNOWLEDGING THAT MAMIE IS INVASIVE?!
YOU BETTER HOPE SHE ISN'T EAVES-DROPPING!
BUT HEAR ME, ADAM. MY BOY MORGAN, HE'S HAD SOME ROUGH TIMES, BUT HE CAN STILL BE TRUSTED WITH A CONFIDENCE.
HE'S A GOOD BOY... WELL, DESPITE THE JAIL STUFF AND WHATNOT. BUT LEVI...?
WHAT DID LEVI TELL YOU?
I DON'T KNOW ANYTHING YOU DON'T WANT ME TO KNOW...AND EVEN IF I DO I STILL DON'T KNOW IT.
BUT YOU HAVE TO BE CAREFUL. YOU HAVE AN IMAGE TO PROTECT AND THE CHANNEL NEEDS THAT IMAGE IF--

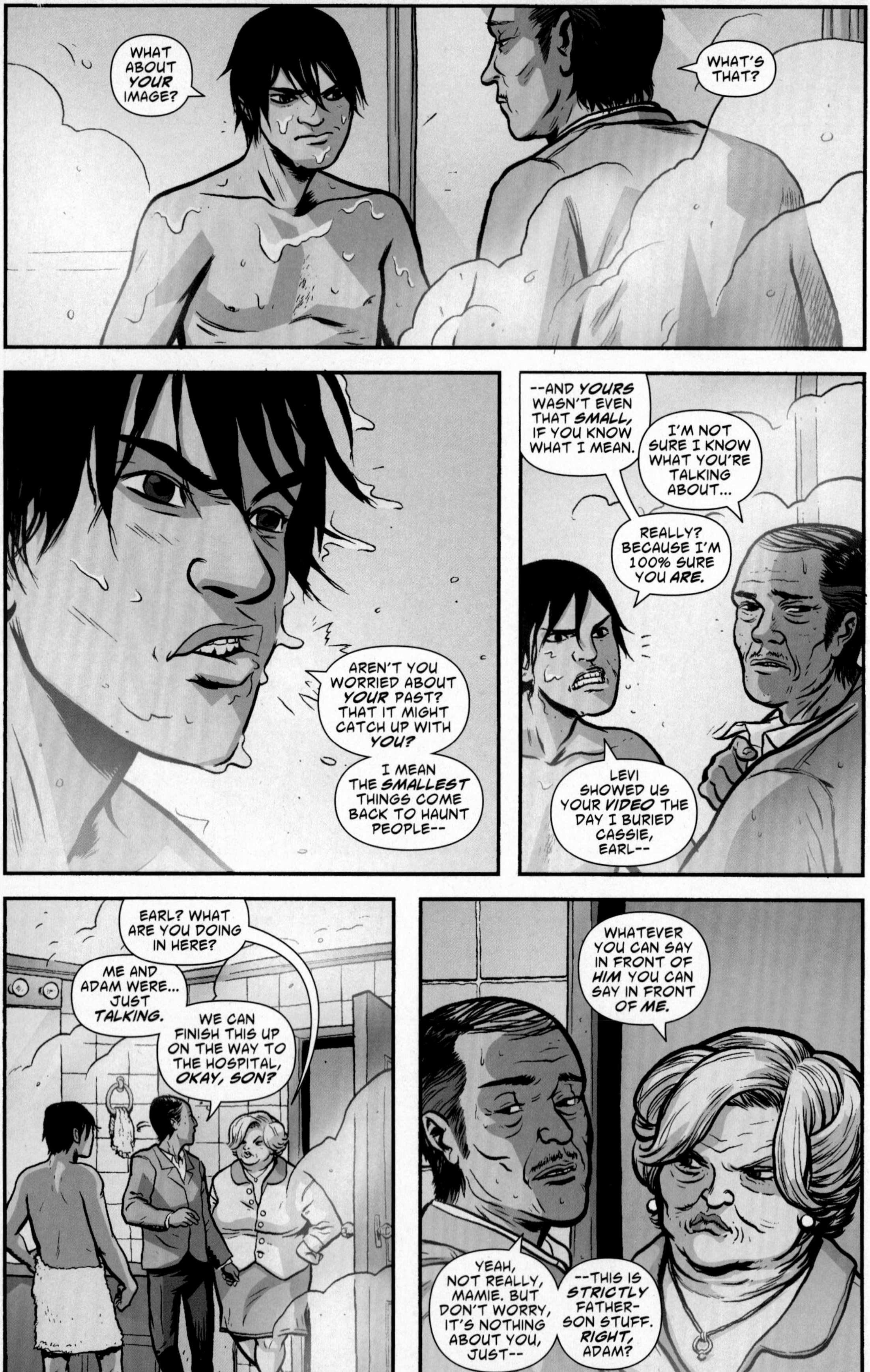
WHAT ABOUT YOUR IMAGE?
WHAT'S THAT?
AREN'T YOU WORRIED ABOUT YOUR PAST? THAT IT MIGHT CATCH UP WITH YOU?
I MEAN THE SMALLEST THINGS COME BACK TO HAUNT PEOPLE--
--AND YOURS WASN'T EVEN THAT SMALL, IF YOU KNOW WHAT I MEAN.
I'M NOT SURE I KNOW WHAT YOU'RE TALKING ABOUT...
REALLY? BECAUSE I'M 100% SURE YOU ARE.
LEVI SHOWED US YOUR VIDEO THE DAY I BURIED CASSIE, EARL--
EARL? WHAT ARE YOU DOING IN HERE?
ME AND ADAM WERE... JUST TALKING.
WE CAN FINISH THIS UP ON THE WAY TO THE HOSPITAL, OKAY, SON?
WHATEVER YOU CAN SAY IN FRONT OF HIM YOU CAN SAY IN FRONT OF ME.
YEAH, NOT REALLY, MAMIE. BUT DON'T WORRY, IT'S NOTHING ABOUT YOU, JUST--
--THIS IS STRICTLY FATHER-SON STUFF. RIGHT, ADAM?

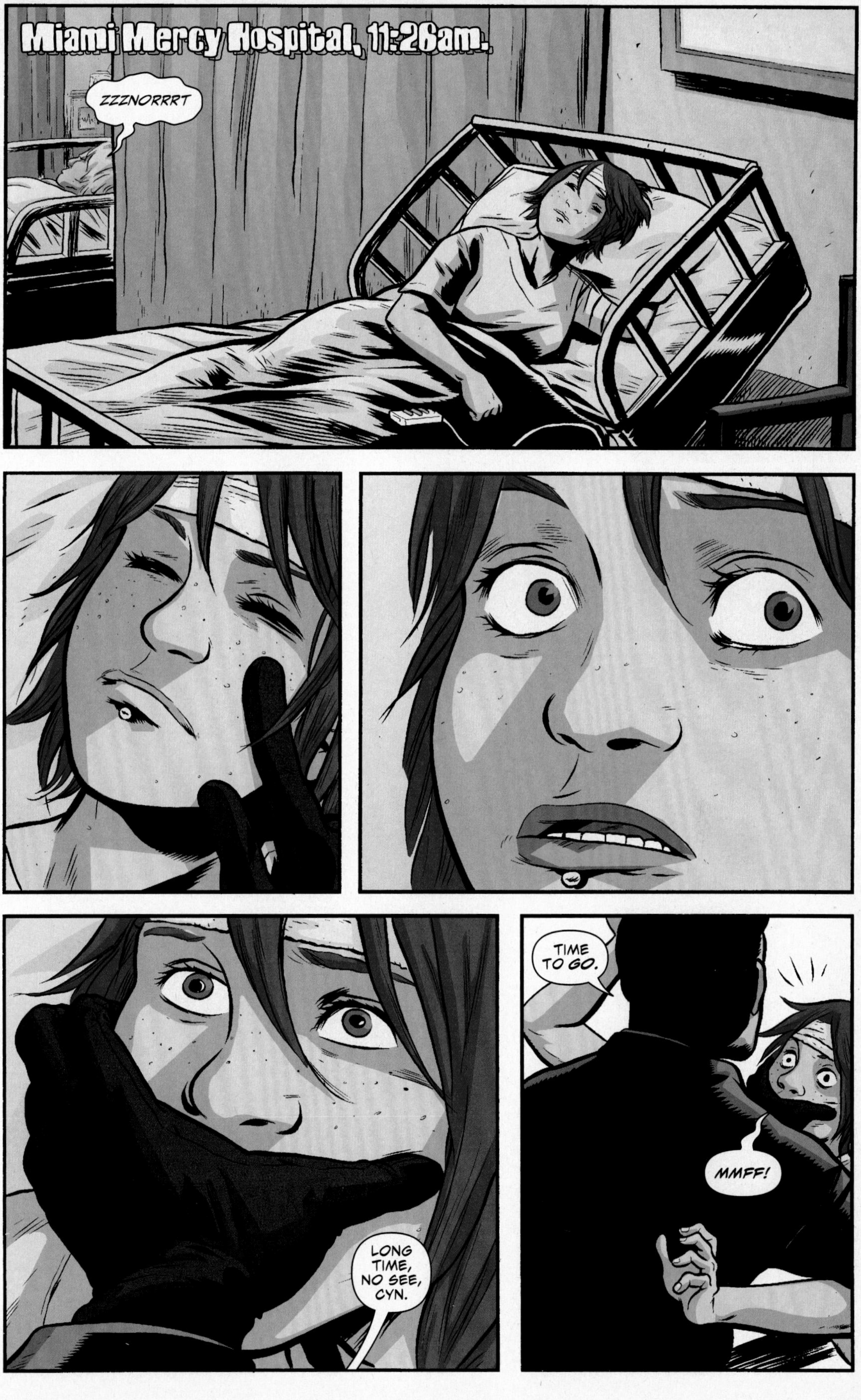
Miami Mercy Hospital, 11:26am.
ZZZNORRRT
LONG TIME, NO SEE, CYN.
TIME TO GO.
MMFF!

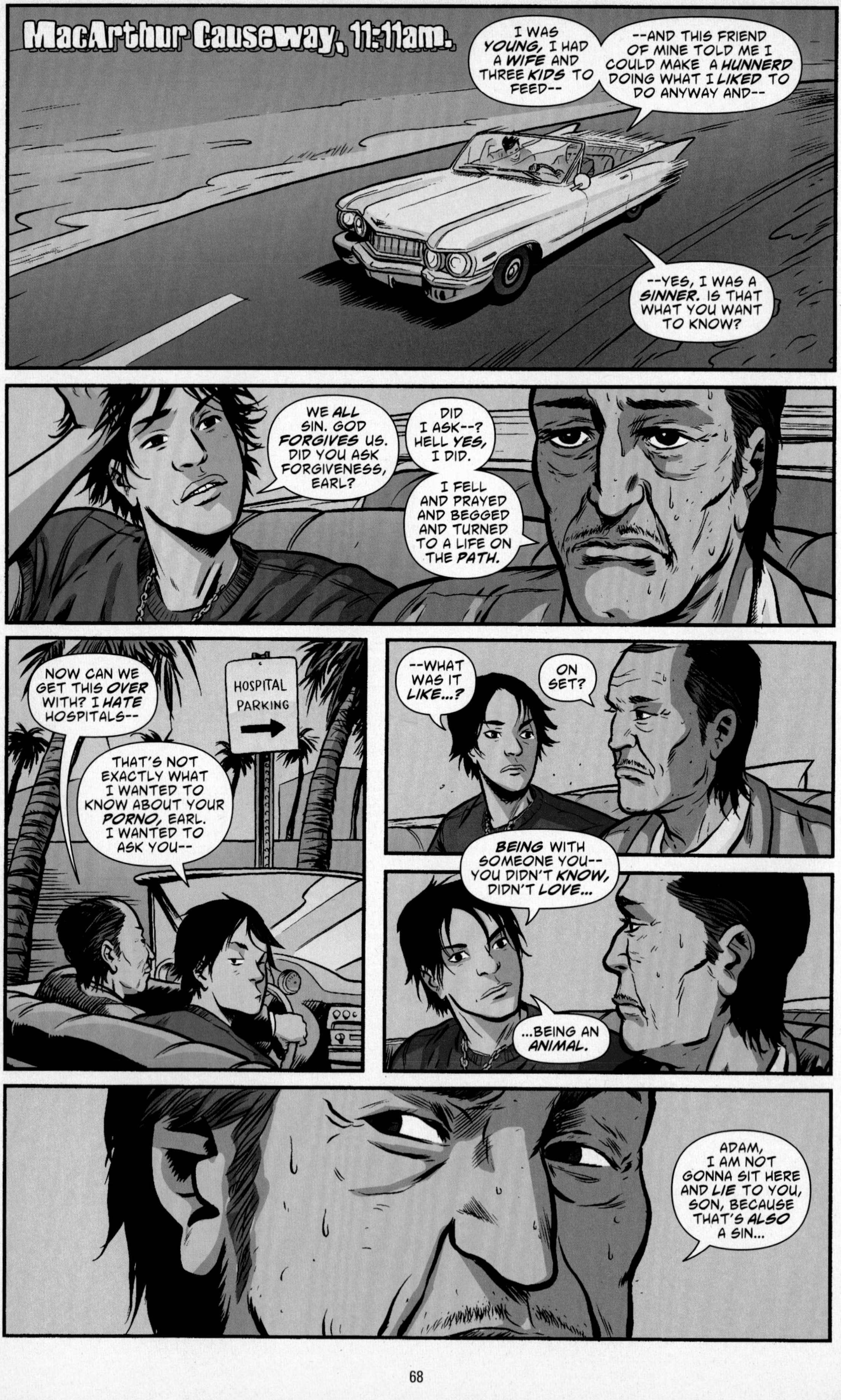
MacArthur Causeway, 11:11am.
I WAS YOUNG, I HAD A WIFE AND THREE KIDS TO FEED--
--AND THIS FRIEND OF MINE TOLD ME I COULD MAKE A HUNNERD DOING WHAT I LIKED TO DO ANYWAY AND--
--YES, I WAS A SINNER. IS THAT WHAT YOU WANT TO KNOW?
WE ALL SIN. GOD FORGIVES US. DID YOU ASK FORGIVENESS, EARL?
DID I ASK--? HELL YES, I DID.
I FELL AND PRAYED AND BEGGED AND TURNED TO A LIFE ON THE PATH.
NOW CAN WE GET THIS OVER WITH? I HATE HOSPITALS--
HOSPITAL PARKING
THAT'S NOT EXACTLY WHAT I WANTED TO KNOW ABOUT YOUR PORNO, EARL. I WANTED TO ASK YOU--
--WHAT WAS IT LIKE...?
ON SET?
BEING WITH SOMEONE YOU-- YOU DIDN'T KNOW, DIDN'T LOVE...
...BEING AN ANIMAL.
ADAM, I AM NOT GONNA SIT HERE AND LIE TO YOU, SON, BECAUSE THAT'S ALSO A SIN...

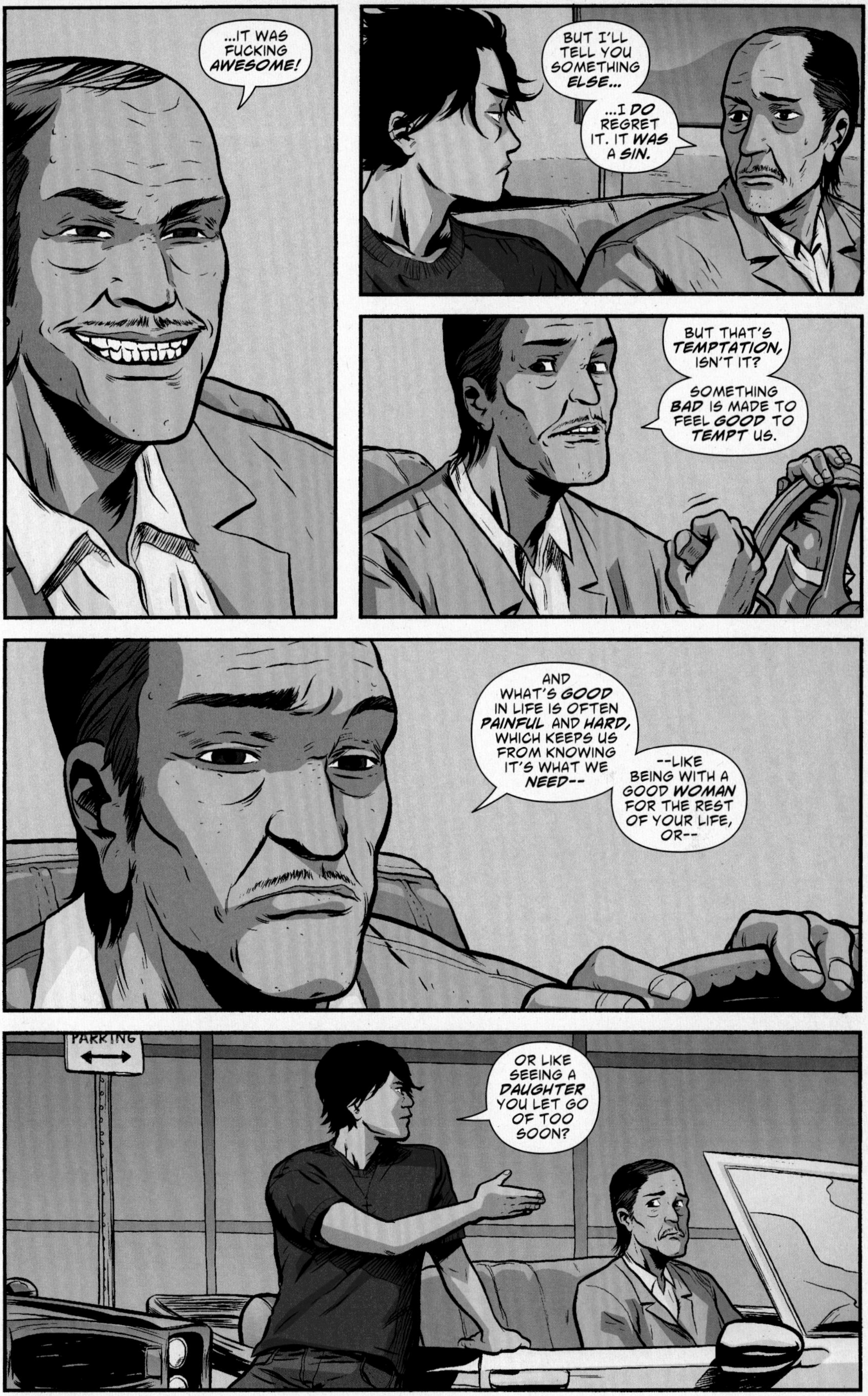
...IT WAS FUCKING AWESOME!
BUT I'LL TELL YOU SOMETHING ELSE...
...I DO REGRET IT. IT WAS A SIN.
BUT THAT'S TEMPTATION, ISN'T IT?
SOMETHING BAD IS MADE TO FEEL GOOD TO TEMPT US.
AND WHAT'S GOOD IN LIFE IS OFTEN PAINFUL AND HARD, WHICH KEEPS US FROM KNOWING IT'S WHAT WE NEED--
--LIKE BEING WITH A GOOD WOMAN FOR THE REST OF YOUR LIFE, OR--
PARKING
OR LIKE SEEING A DAUGHTER YOU LET GO OF TOO SOON?

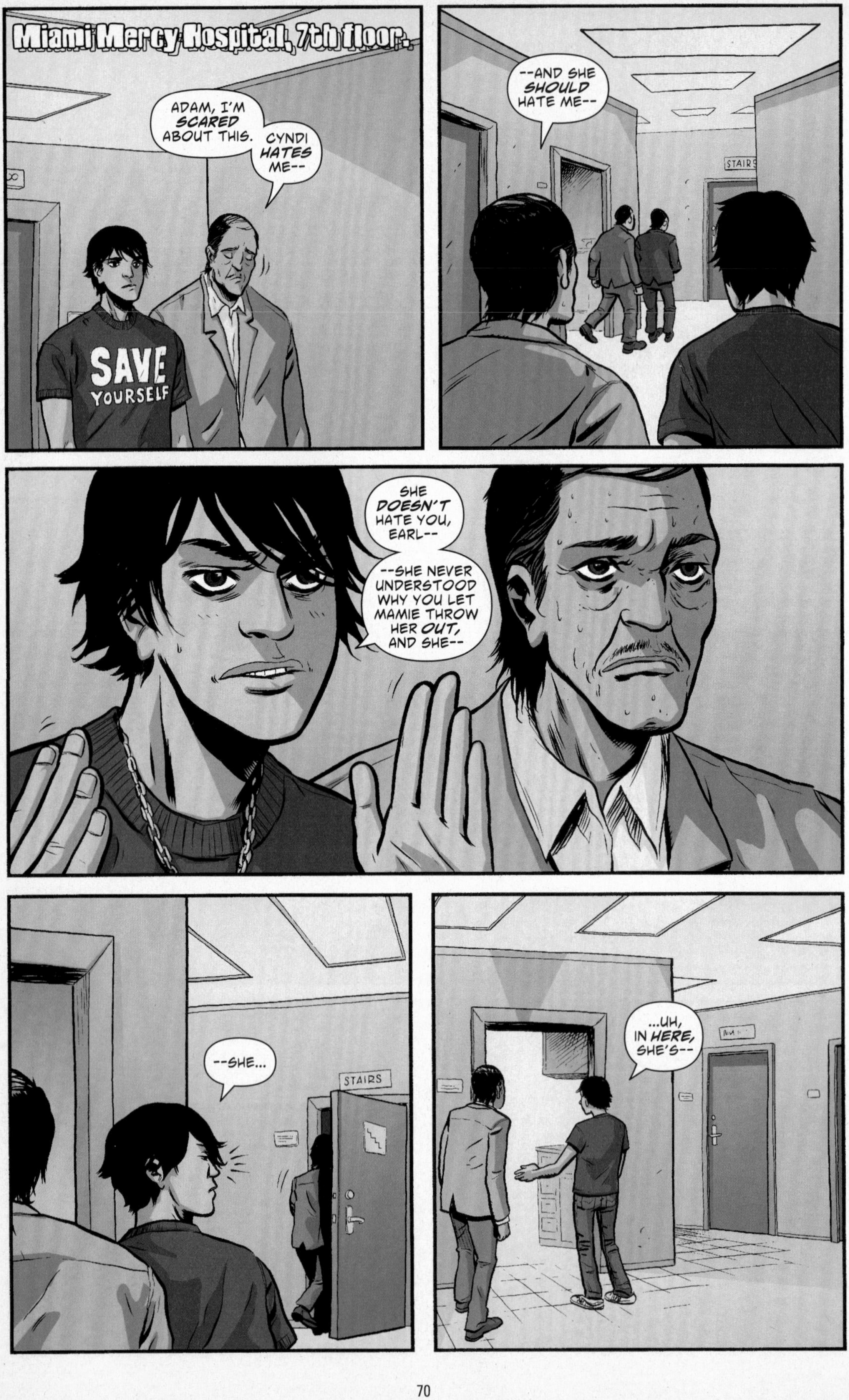

Miami Mercy Hospital, 7th floor.
ADAM, I'M SCARED ABOUT THIS.
CYNDI HATES ME--
SAVE YOURSELF
--AND SHE SHOULD HATE ME--
STAIRS
SHE DOESN'T HATE YOU, EARL--
--SHE NEVER UNDERSTOOD WHY YOU LET MAMIE THROW HER OUT, AND SHE--
--SHE...
STAIRS
...UH, IN HERE, SHE'S--

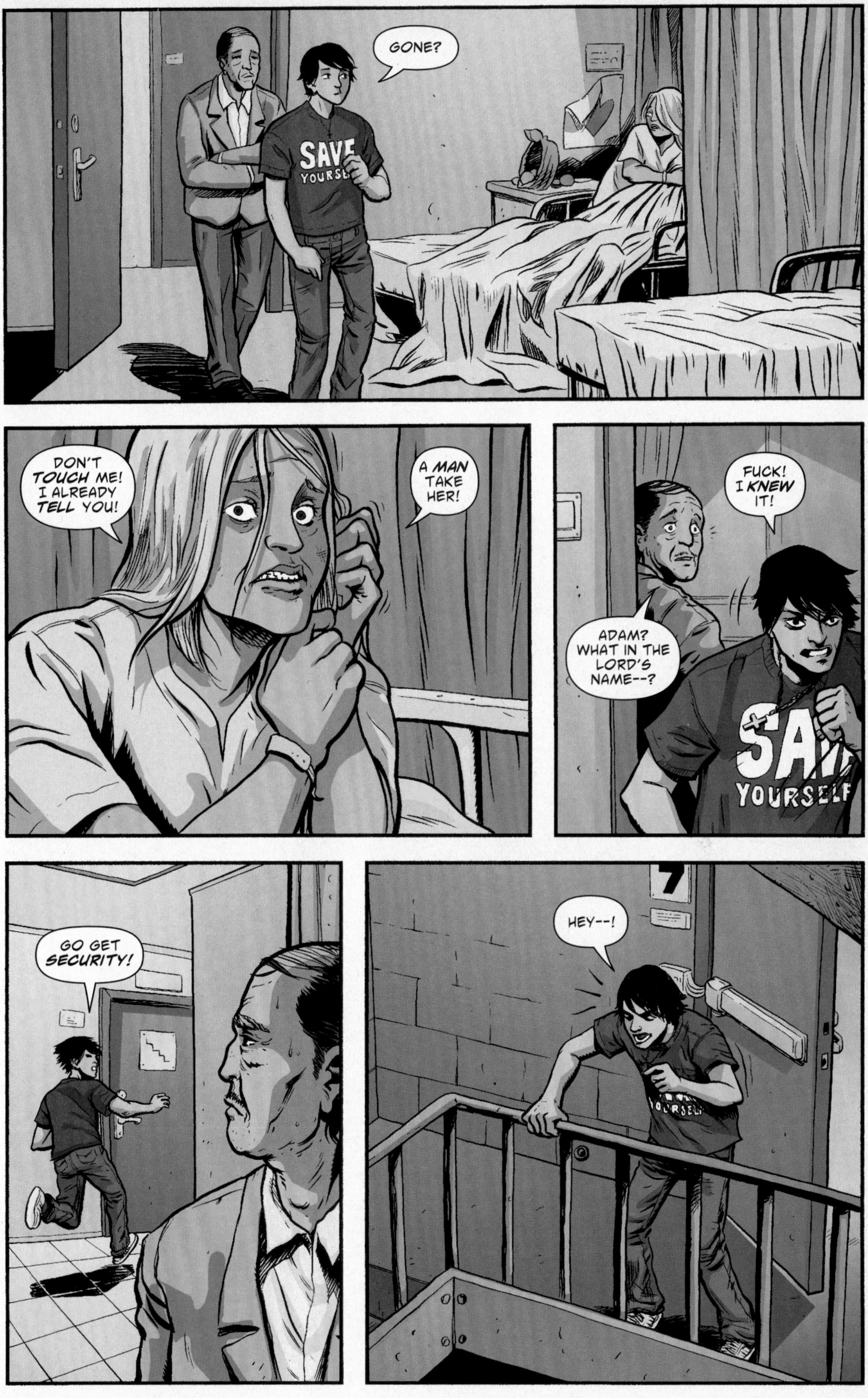
GONE?
DON'T TOUCH ME! I ALREADY TELL YOU!
A MAN TAKE HER!
FUCK! I KNEW IT!
ADAM? WHAT IN THE LORD'S NAME--?
GO GET SECURITY!
HEY--!

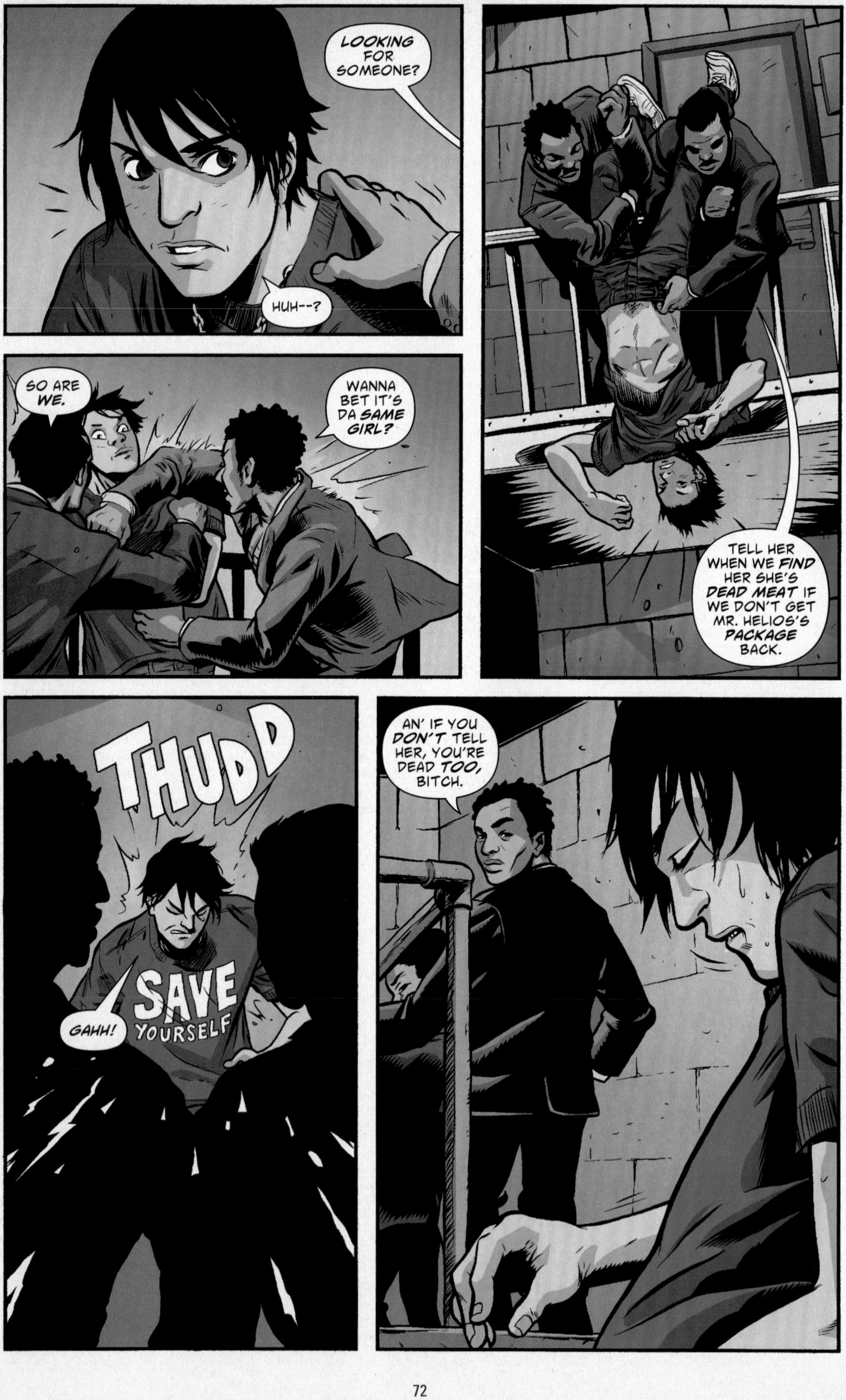

LOOKING FOR SOMEONE?
HUH--?
SO ARE WE.
WANNA BET IT'S DA SAME GIRL?
TELL HER WHEN WE FIND HER SHE'S DEAD MEAT IF WE DON'T GET MR. HELIOS'S PACKAGE BACK.
THUDD
SAVE YOURSELF
GAHH!
AN' IF YOU DON'T TELL HER, YOU'RE DEAD TOO, BITCH.

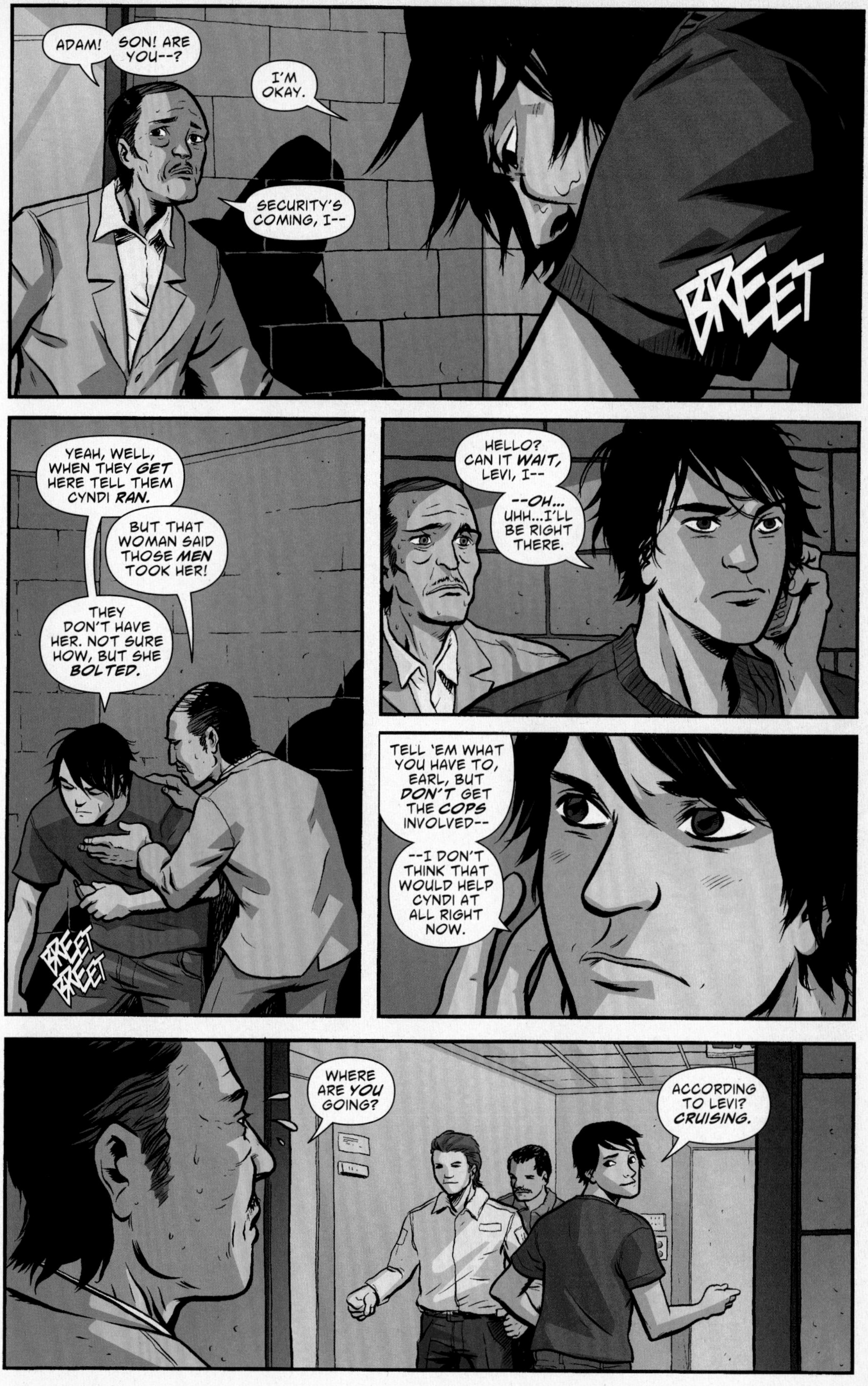
ADAM!
SON! ARE YOU--?
I'M OKAY.
SECURITY'S COMING, I--
BREET
YEAH, WELL, WHEN THEY GET HERE TELL THEM CYNDI RAN.
BUT THAT WOMAN SAID THOSE MEN TOOK HER!
THEY DON'T HAVE HER. NOT SURE HOW, BUT SHE BOLTED.
BREET BREET
HELLO? CAN IT WAIT, LEVI, I--
--OH... UHH...I'LL BE RIGHT THERE.
TELL 'EM WHAT YOU HAVE TO, EARL, BUT DON'T GET THE COPS INVOLVED--
--I DON'T THINK THAT WOULD HELP CYNDI AT ALL RIGHT NOW.
WHERE ARE YOU GOING?
ACCORDING TO LEVI? CRUISING.

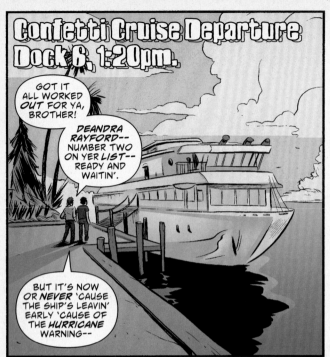

Confetti Cruise Departure Dock 6, 1:20pm.

GOT IT ALL WORKED *OUT* FOR YA, BROTHER!

DEANDRA RAYFORD-- NUMBER TWO ON YER *LIST*-- READY AND WAITIN'.

BUT IT'S NOW OR *NEVER* 'CAUSE THE SHIP'S LEAVIN' EARLY 'CAUSE OF THE *HURRICANE* WARNING--

THERE'S A *HURRICANE* WARNING?

WHERE THE FUCK YOU *BEEN*? IT'S ALL OVER CNN!

YOU WATCH CNN?

NO...BUT FROM WHAT I *HEAR* IT'S ALL *OVER* IT.

AN' YOU CAN PAY ME DIRECTLY FOR *THIS* 'N! MORGAN DIDN'T DO *SHIT* ON THIS!

NOW WALK THE *BLANK*, MATEY!

THAT'S "PLANK," DUMBASS. "WALK THE *PLANK*."

IT SHORE AS SHIT *AIN'T!* WHAT THE HELL SENSE WOULD *THAT* MAKE?

WHAT THE FUCK'S A *PLANK*?

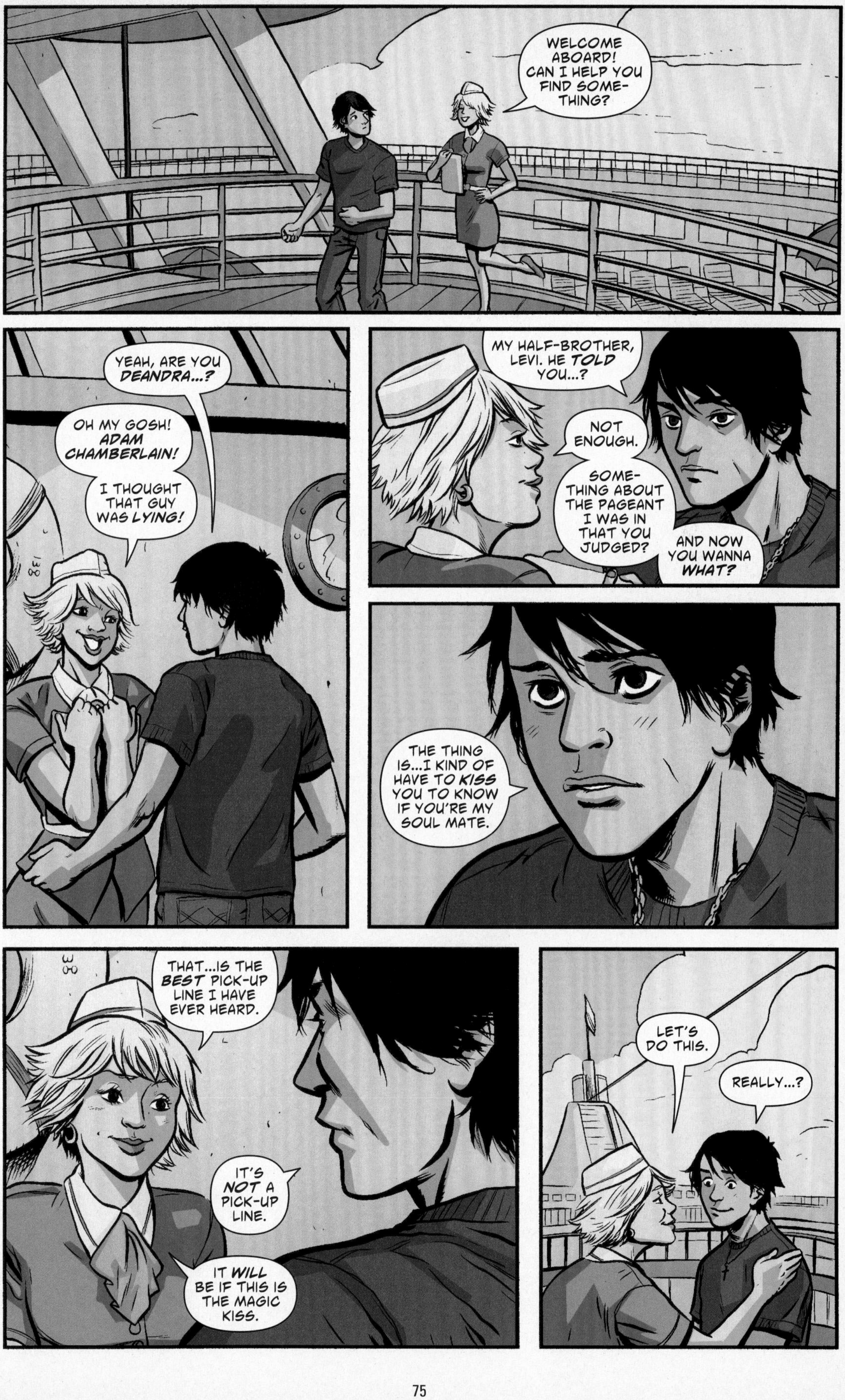
WELCOME ABOARD! CAN I HELP YOU FIND SOME-THING?
YEAH, ARE YOU DEANDRA...?
OH MY GOSH! ADAM CHAMBERLAIN!
I THOUGHT THAT GUY WAS LYING!
MY HALF-BROTHER, LEVI. HE TOLD YOU...?
NOT ENOUGH.
SOME-THING ABOUT THE PAGEANT I WAS IN THAT YOU JUDGED?
AND NOW YOU WANNA WHAT?
THE THING IS...I KIND OF HAVE TO KISS YOU TO KNOW IF YOU'RE MY SOUL MATE.
THAT...IS THE BEST PICK-UP LINE I HAVE EVER HEARD.
IT'S NOT A PICK-UP LINE.
IT WILL BE IF THIS IS THE MAGIC KISS.
LET'S DO THIS.
REALLY...?

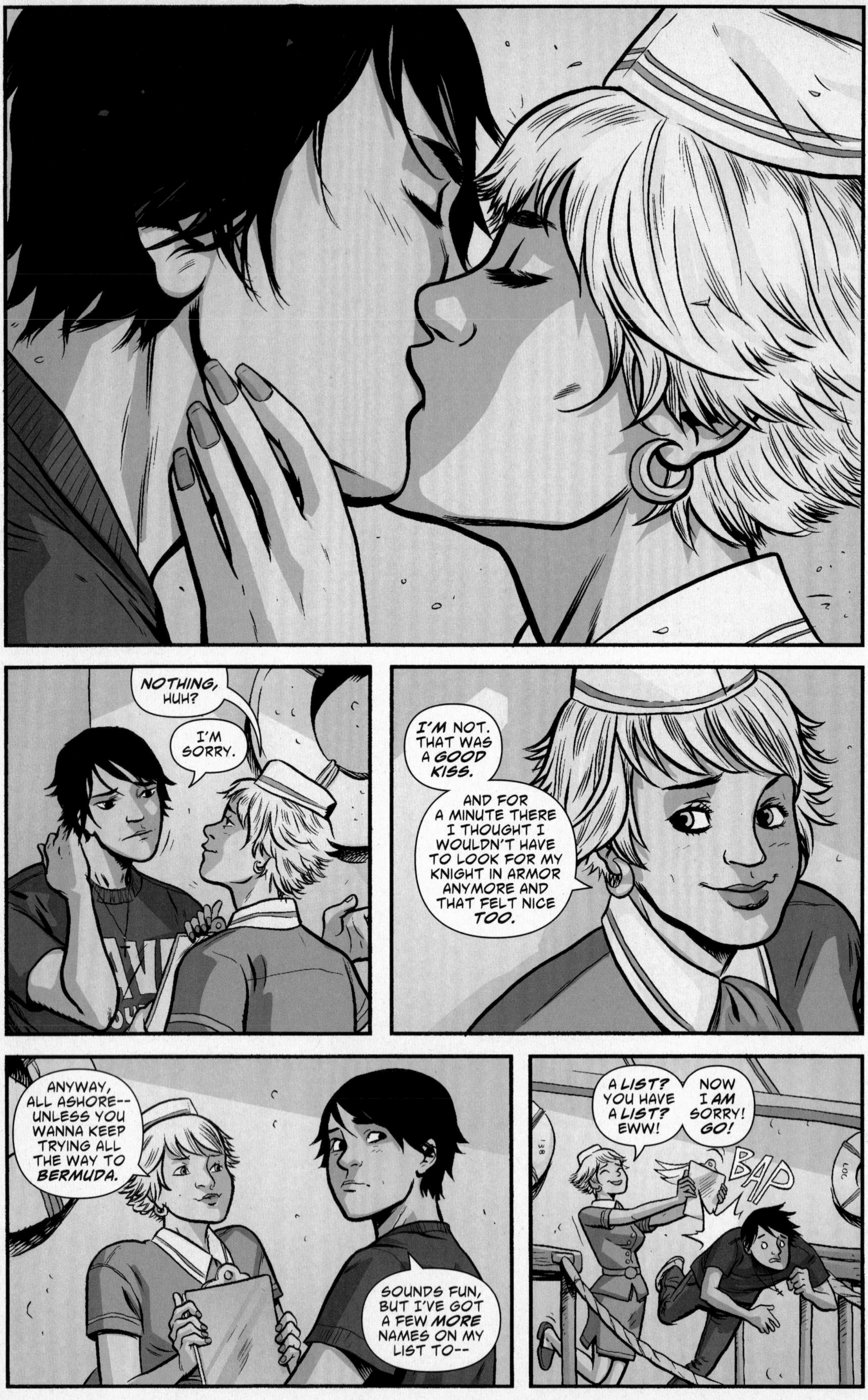
NOTHING, HUH?
I'M SORRY.
I'M NOT. THAT WAS A GOOD KISS.
AND FOR A MINUTE THERE I THOUGHT I WOULDN'T HAVE TO LOOK FOR MY KNIGHT IN ARMOR ANYMORE AND THAT FELT NICE TOO.
ANYWAY, ALL ASHORE-- UNLESS YOU WANNA KEEP TRYING ALL THE WAY TO BERMUDA.
SOUNDS FUN, BUT I'VE GOT A FEW MORE NAMES ON MY LIST TO--
A LIST? YOU HAVE A LIST? EWW!
NOW I AM SORRY! GO!
BAP

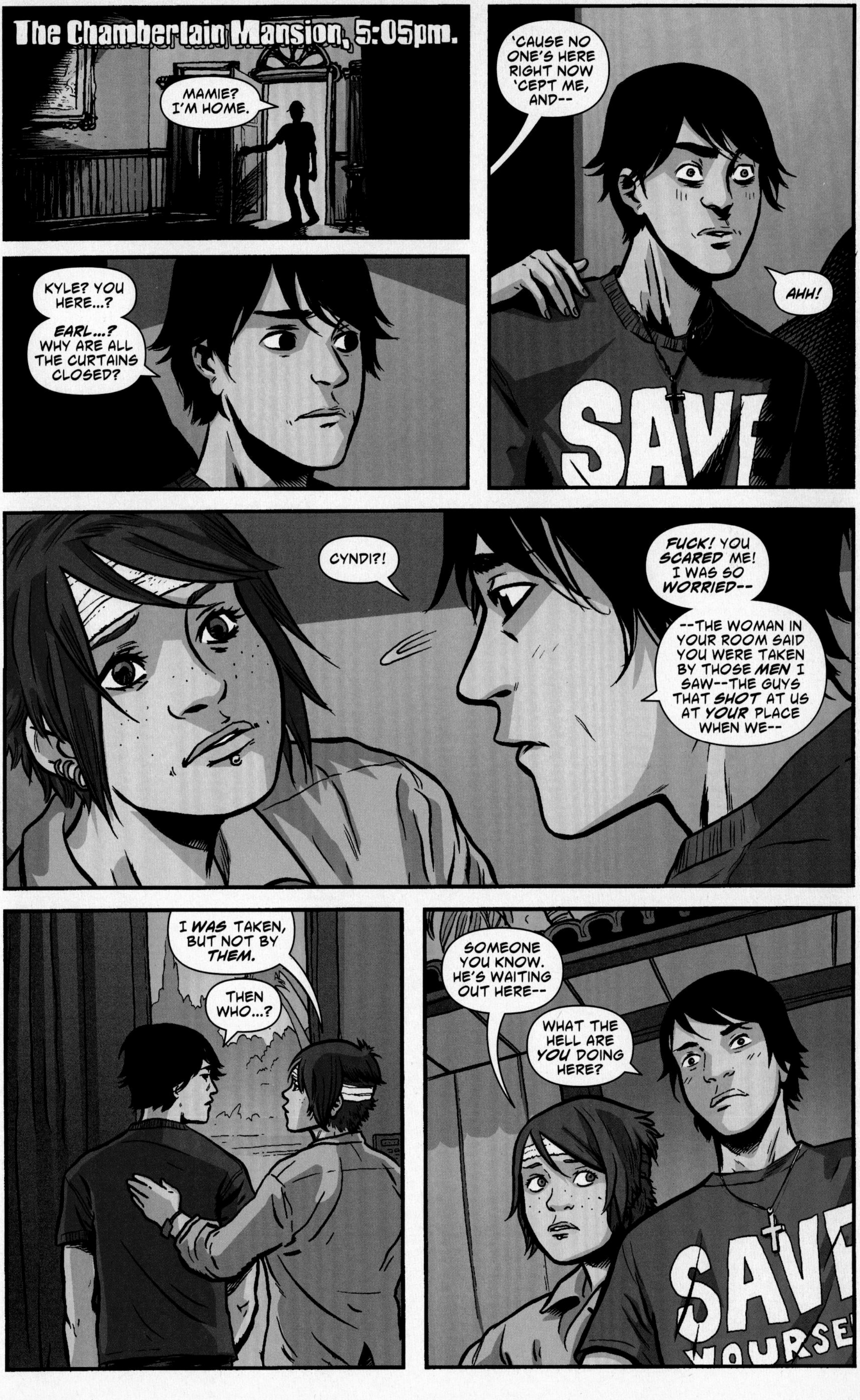
The Chamberlain Mansion, 5:05pm.
MAMIE? I'M HOME.
KYLE? YOU HERE...? EARL...? WHY ARE ALL THE CURTAINS CLOSED?
'CAUSE NO ONE'S HERE RIGHT NOW 'CEPT ME, AND--
AHH!
SAVE
CYNDI?!
FUCK! YOU SCARED ME! I WAS SO WORRIED--
--THE WOMAN IN YOUR ROOM SAID YOU WERE TAKEN BY THOSE MEN I SAW--THE GUYS THAT SHOT AT US AT YOUR PLACE WHEN WE--
I WAS TAKEN, BUT NOT BY THEM.
THEN WHO...?
SOMEONE YOU KNOW. HE'S WAITING OUT HERE--
WHAT THE HELL ARE YOU DOING HERE?

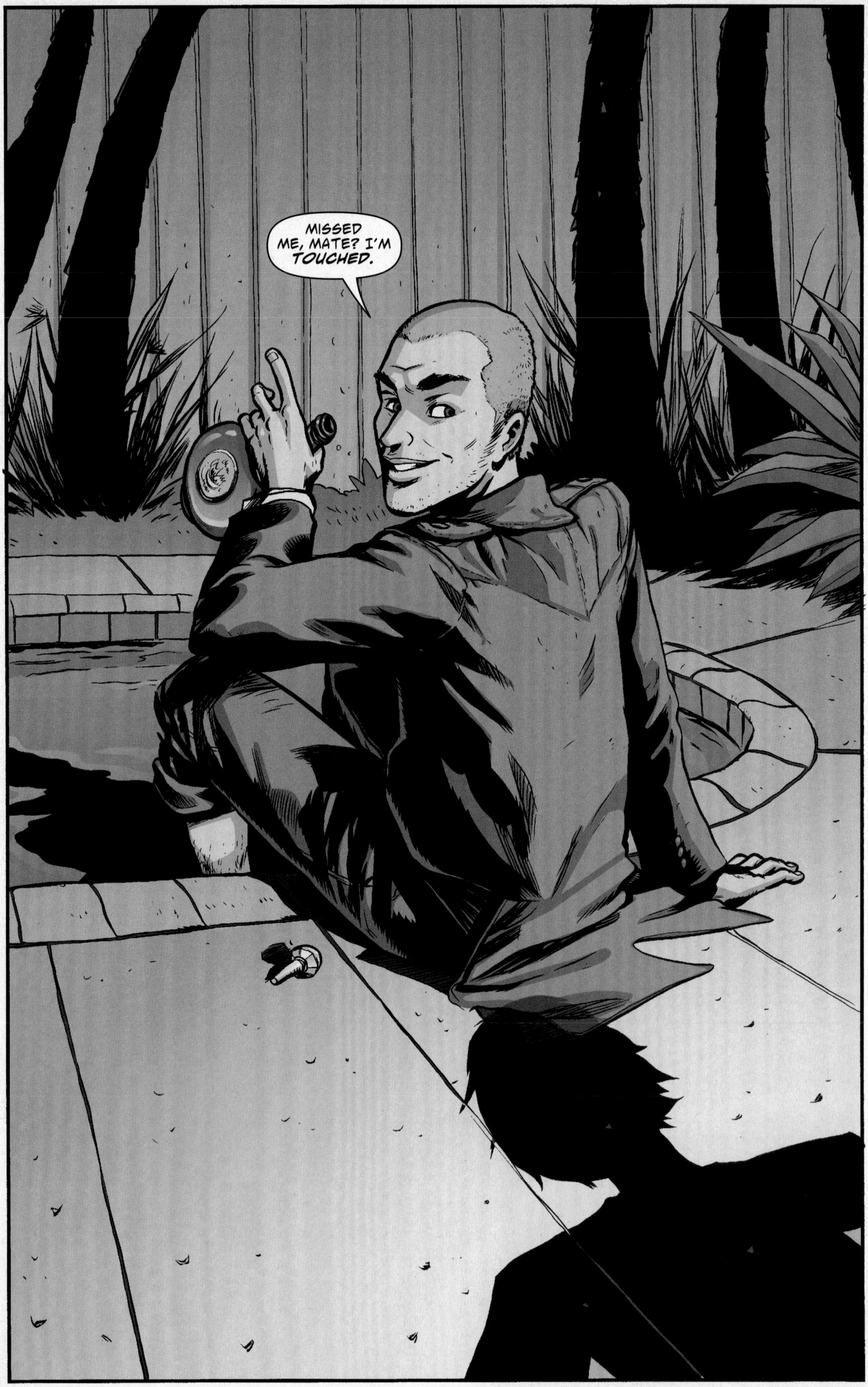
MISSED ME, MATE? I'M *TOUCHED.*

CHAPTER FOUR

Chapter pencils by Becky Cloonan, inks by Jim Rugg

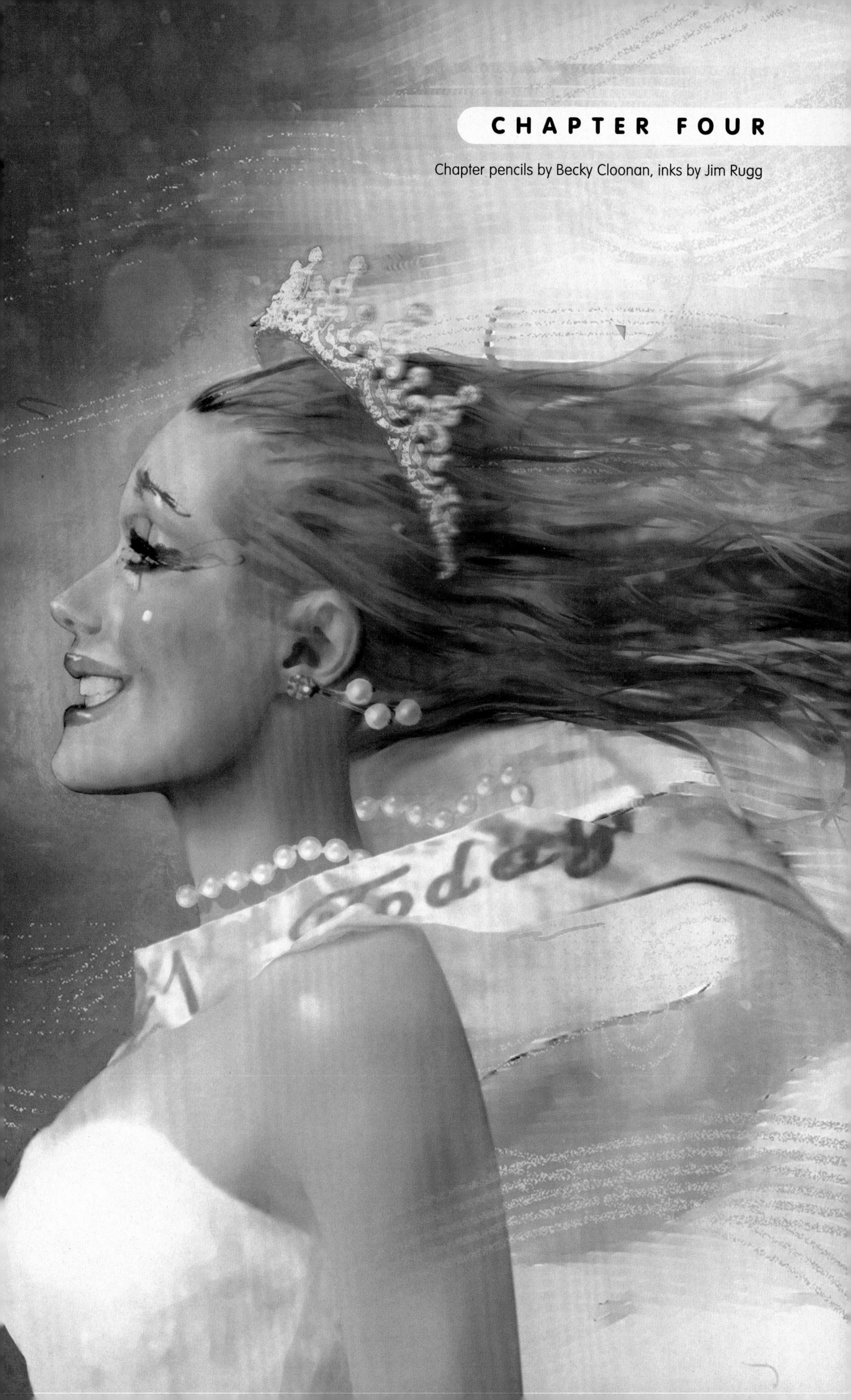

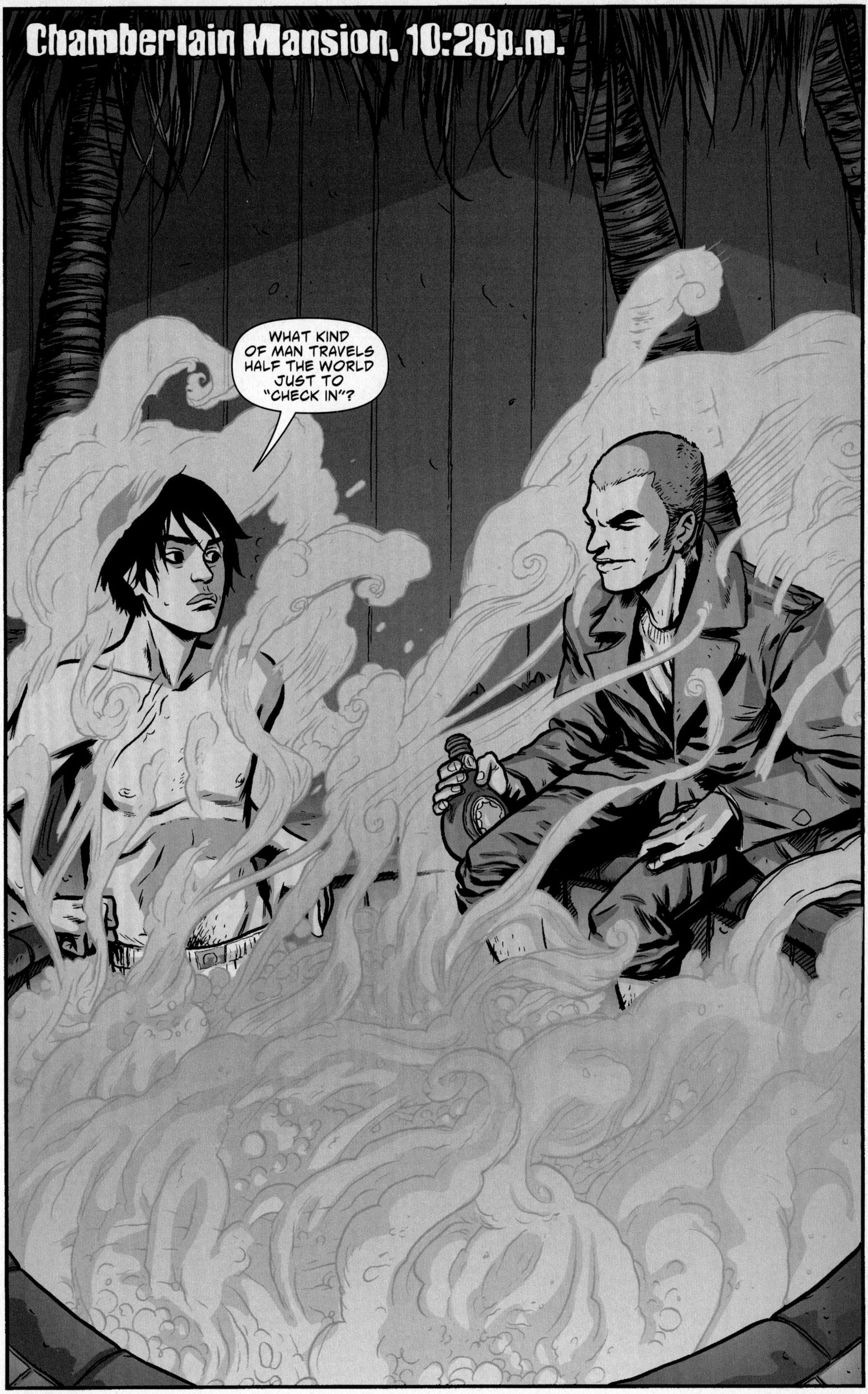
Chamberlain Mansion, 10:26p.m.
WHAT KIND OF MAN TRAVELS HALF THE WORLD JUST TO "CHECK IN"?

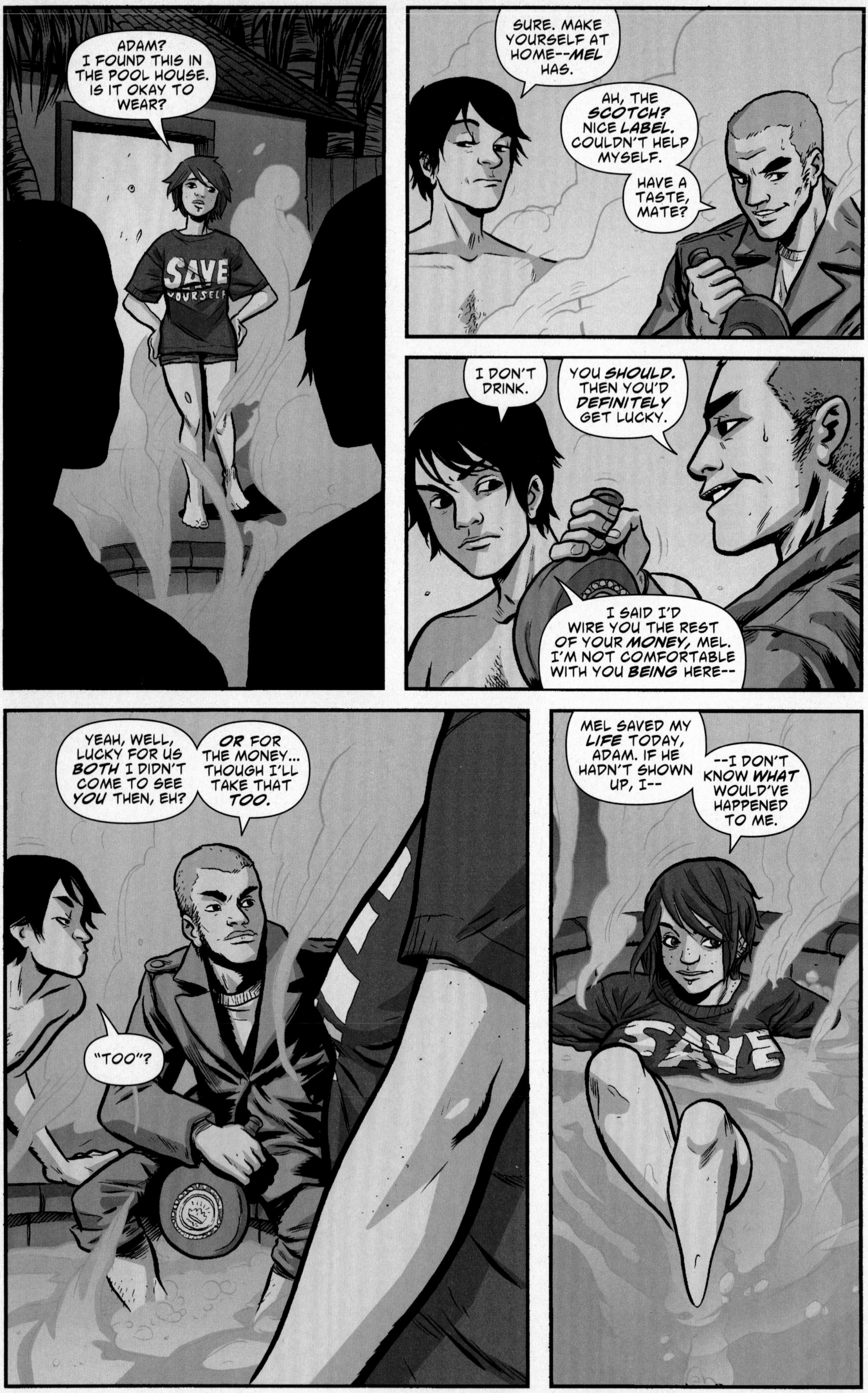
ADAM? I FOUND THIS IN THE POOL HOUSE. IS IT OKAY TO WEAR?
SAVE YOURSELF
SURE. MAKE YOURSELF AT HOME--*MEL* HAS.
AH, THE *SCOTCH?* NICE *LABEL.* COULDN'T HELP MYSELF.
HAVE A TASTE, MATE?
I DON'T DRINK.
YOU *SHOULD.* THEN YOU'D *DEFINITELY* GET LUCKY.
I SAID I'D WIRE YOU THE REST OF YOUR *MONEY,* MEL. I'M NOT COMFORTABLE WITH YOU *BEING* HERE--
YEAH, WELL, LUCKY FOR US *BOTH* I DIDN'T COME TO SEE *YOU* THEN, EH?
OR FOR THE MONEY... THOUGH I'LL TAKE THAT *TOO.*
"TOO"?
MEL SAVED MY *LIFE* TODAY, ADAM. IF HE HADN'T SHOWN UP, I--
--I DON'T KNOW *WHAT* WOULD'VE HAPPENED TO ME.
SAVE

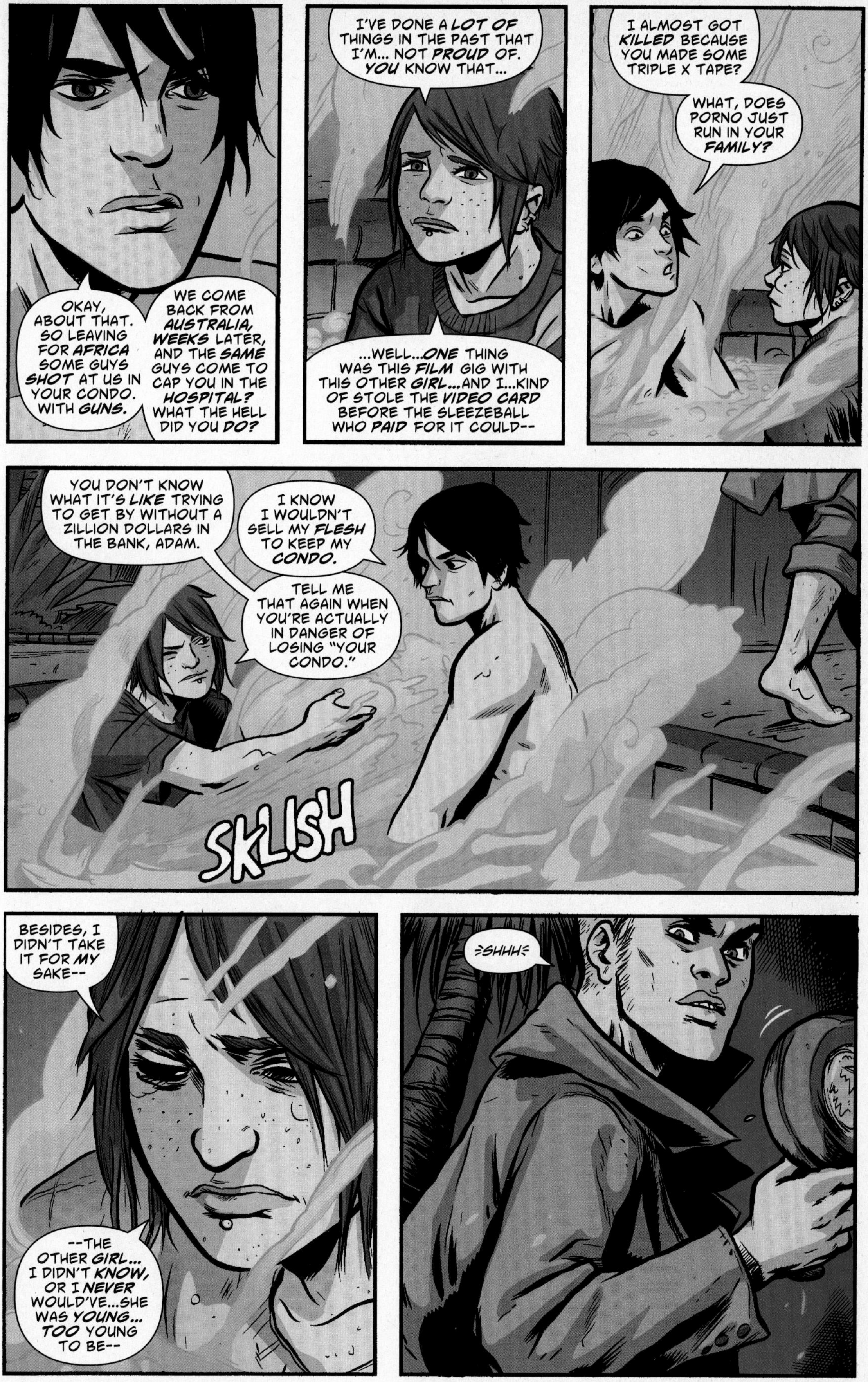
OKAY, ABOUT THAT. SO LEAVING FOR AFRICA SOME GUYS SHOT AT US IN YOUR CONDO. WITH GUNS.
WE COME BACK FROM AUSTRALIA, WEEKS LATER, AND THE SAME GUYS COME TO CAP YOU IN THE HOSPITAL? WHAT THE HELL DID YOU DO?
I'VE DONE A LOT OF THINGS IN THE PAST THAT I'M... NOT PROUD OF. YOU KNOW THAT...
...WELL...ONE THING WAS THIS FILM GIG WITH THIS OTHER GIRL...AND I...KIND OF STOLE THE VIDEO CARD BEFORE THE SLEEZEBALL WHO PAID FOR IT COULD--
I ALMOST GOT KILLED BECAUSE YOU MADE SOME TRIPLE X TAPE?
WHAT, DOES PORNO JUST RUN IN YOUR FAMILY?
YOU DON'T KNOW WHAT IT'S LIKE TRYING TO GET BY WITHOUT A ZILLION DOLLARS IN THE BANK, ADAM.
I KNOW I WOULDN'T SELL MY FLESH TO KEEP MY CONDO.
TELL ME THAT AGAIN WHEN YOU'RE ACTUALLY IN DANGER OF LOSING "YOUR CONDO."
SKLISH
BESIDES, I DIDN'T TAKE IT FOR MY SAKE--
--THE OTHER GIRL... I DIDN'T KNOW, OR I NEVER WOULD'VE...SHE WAS YOUNG... TOO YOUNG TO BE--
SHHH

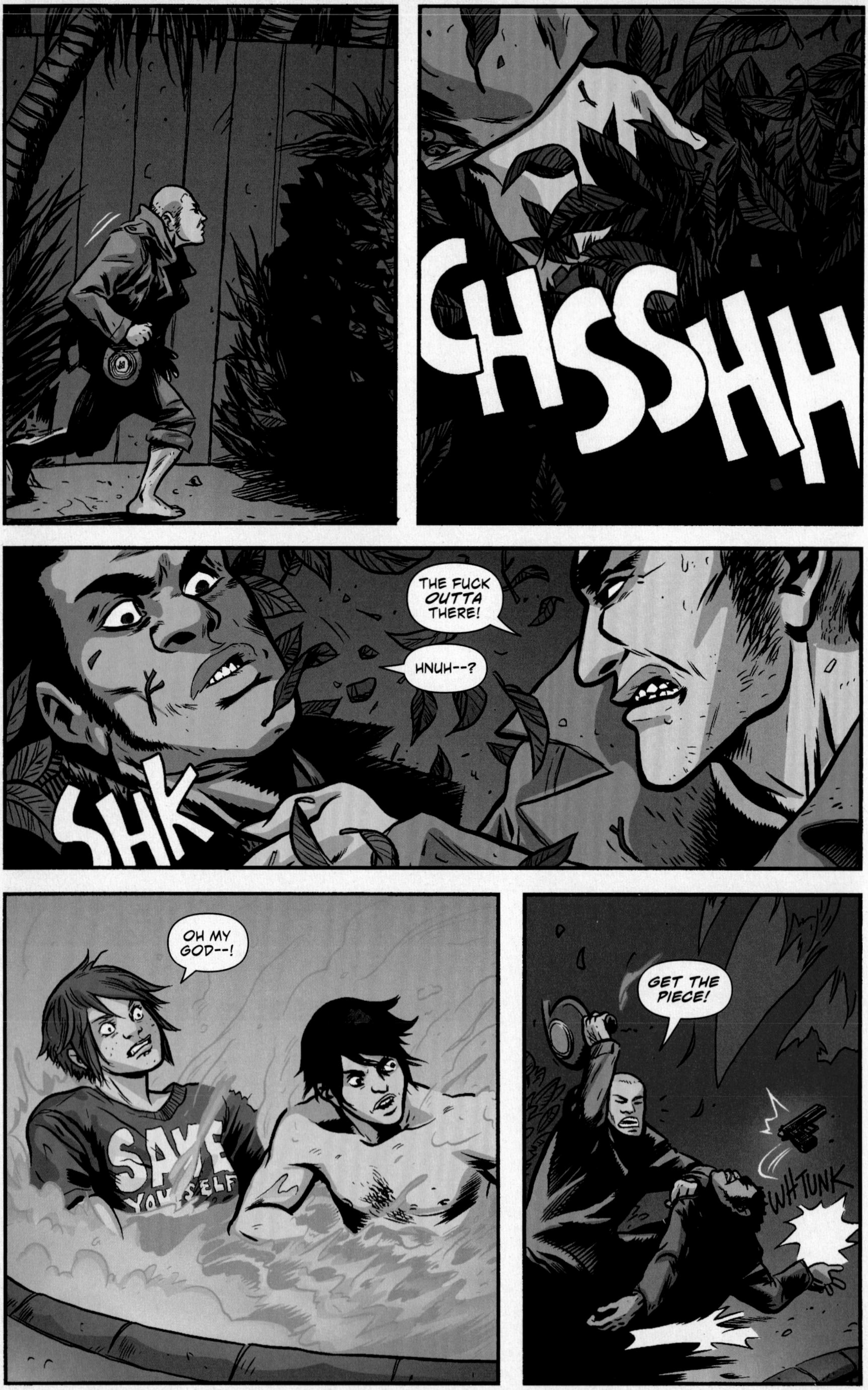
CHSSHH
THE FUCK OUTTA THERE!
HNUH--?
SHK
OH MY GOD--!
SAVE YOURSELF
GET THE PIECE!
WHTUNK

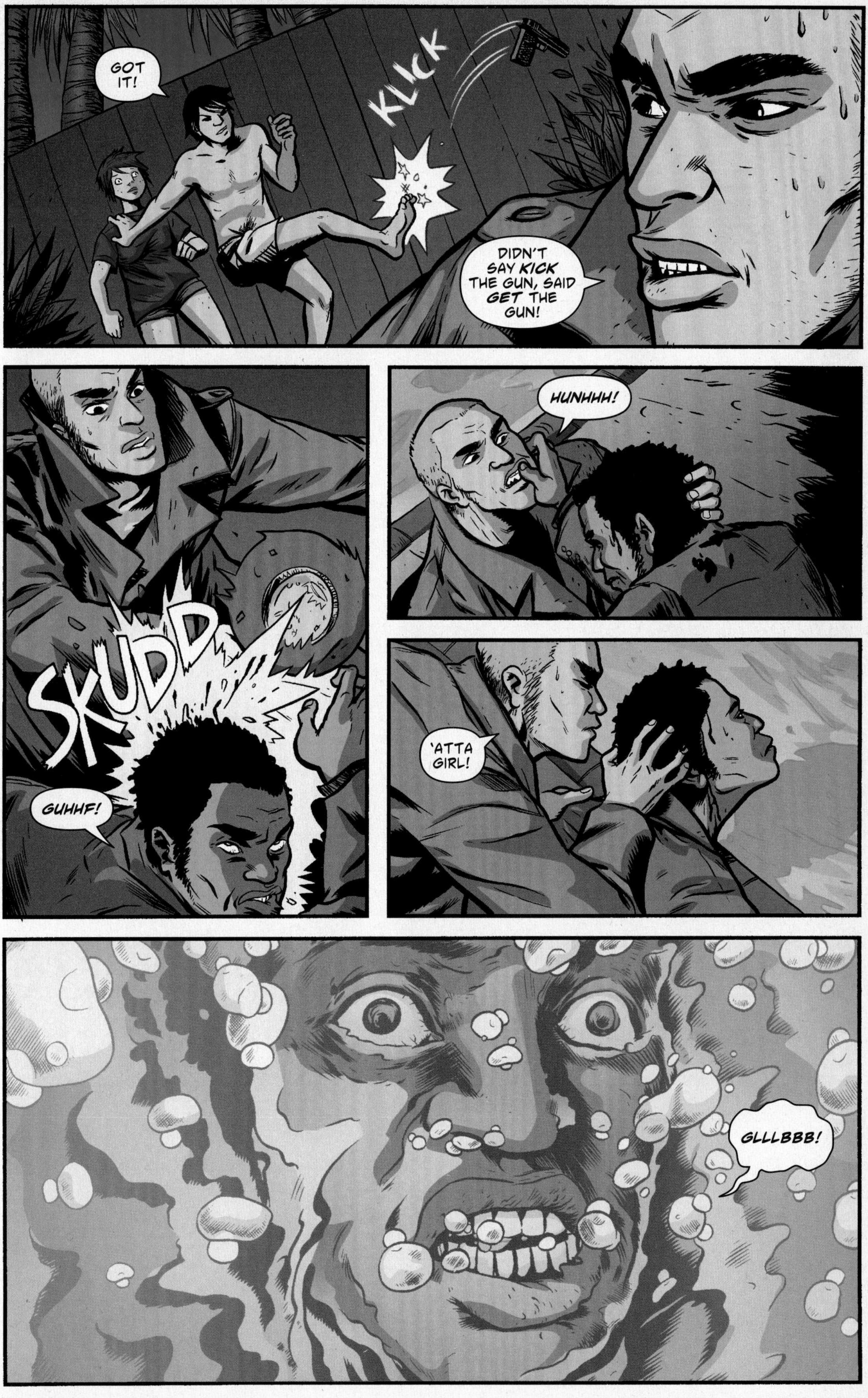
GOT IT!
KLICK
DIDN'T SAY KICK THE GUN, SAID GET THE GUN!
SKUDD
GUHHF!
HUNHHH!
'ATTA GIRL!
GLLLBBB!

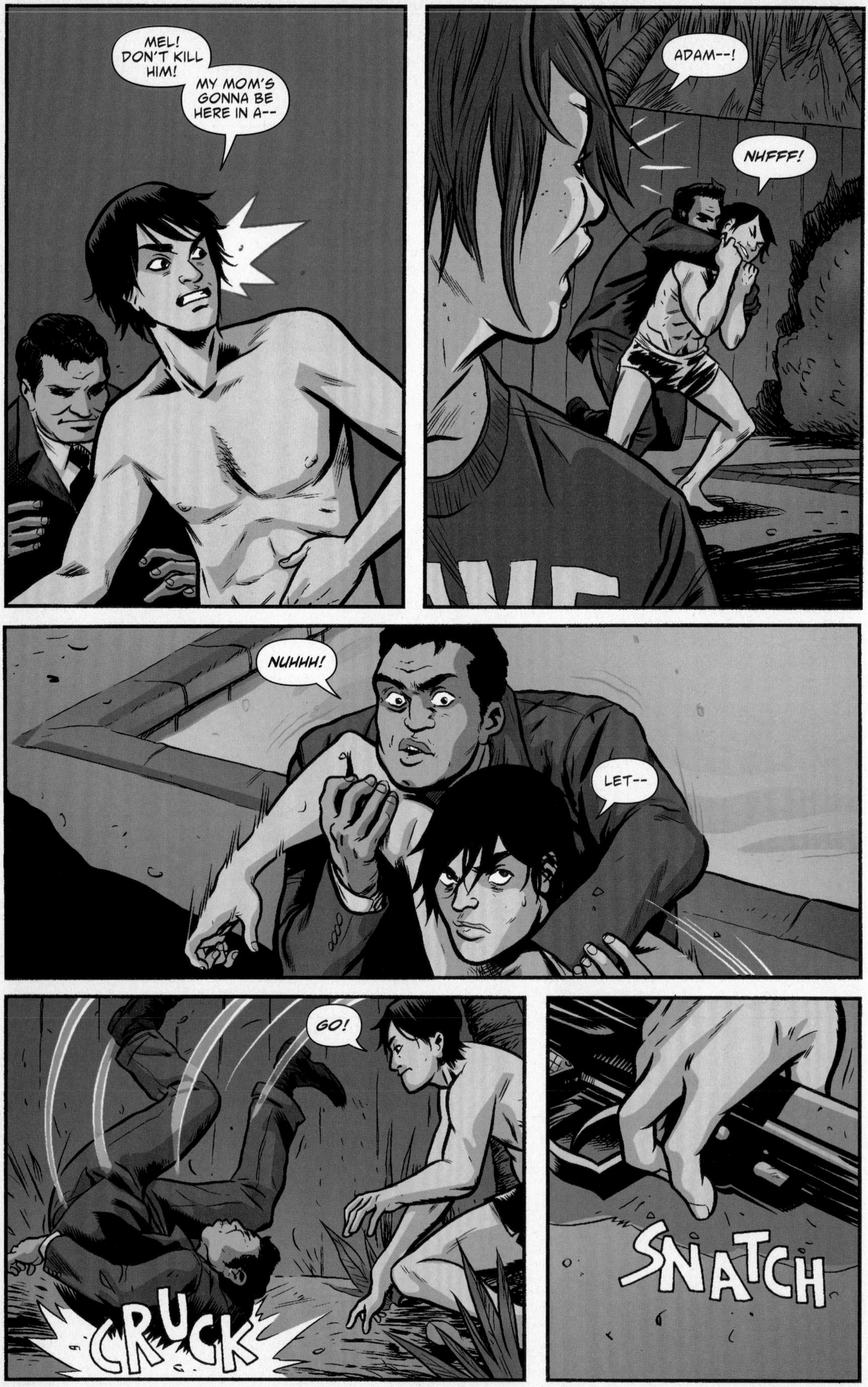
MEL! DON'T KILL HIM!
MY MOM'S GONNA BE HERE IN A--
ADAM--!
NHFFF!
NUHHH!
LET--
GO!
CRUCK
SNATCH

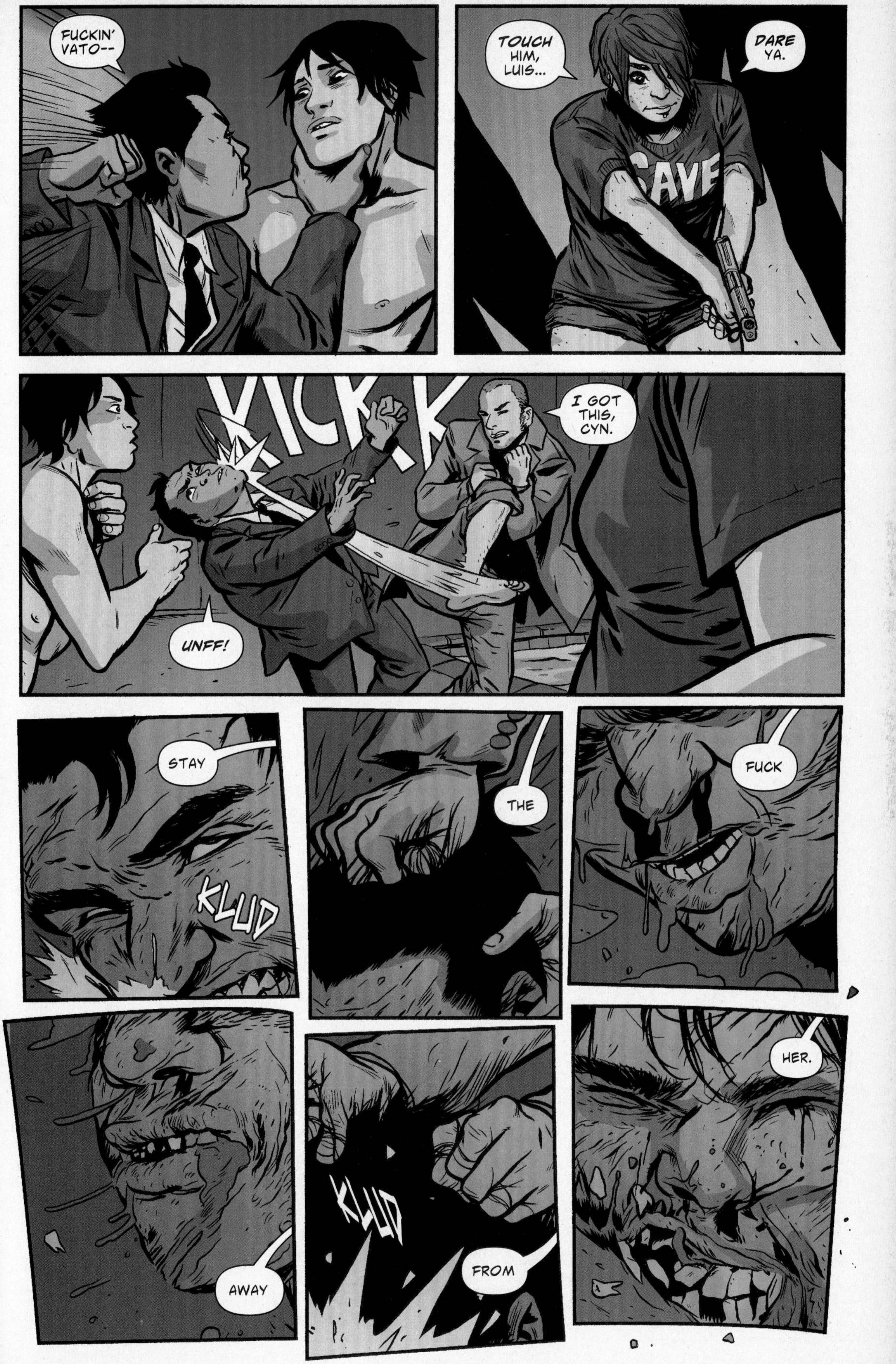
FUCKIN' VATO--
TOUCH HIM, LUIS...
DARE YA.
SAVE
KICK-K
I GOT THIS, CYN.
UNFF!
STAY
KLUD
THE
FUCK
AWAY
KLUD
FROM
HER.

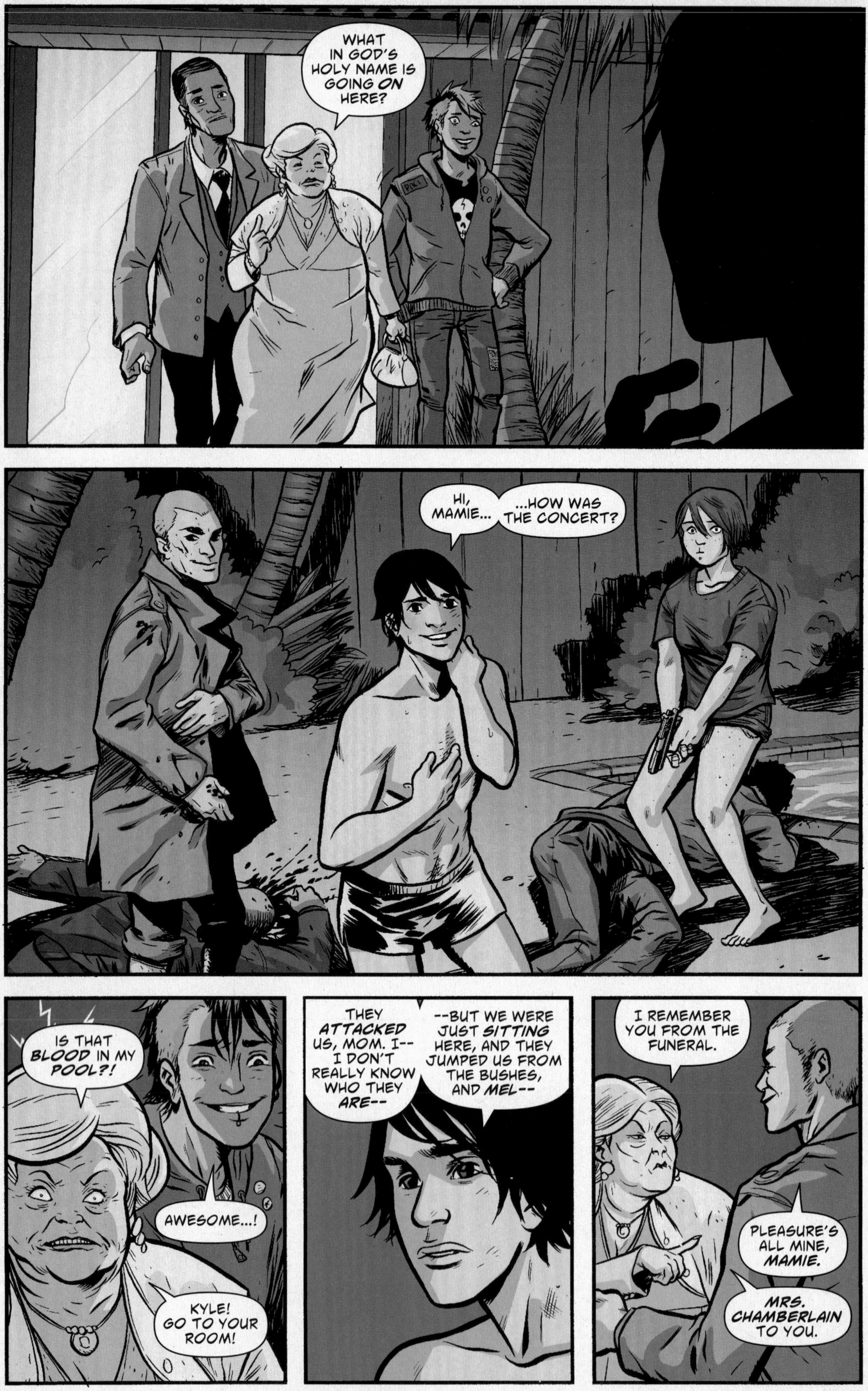
WHAT IN GOD'S HOLY NAME IS GOING ON HERE?
HI, MAMIE...
...HOW WAS THE CONCERT?
IS THAT BLOOD IN MY POOL?!
AWESOME...!
KYLE! GO TO YOUR ROOM!
THEY ATTACKED US, MOM. I-- I DON'T REALLY KNOW WHO THEY ARE--
--BUT WE WERE JUST SITTING HERE, AND THEY JUMPED US FROM THE BUSHES, AND MEL--
I REMEMBER YOU FROM THE FUNERAL.
PLEASURE'S ALL MINE, MAMIE.
MRS. CHAMBERLAIN TO YOU.

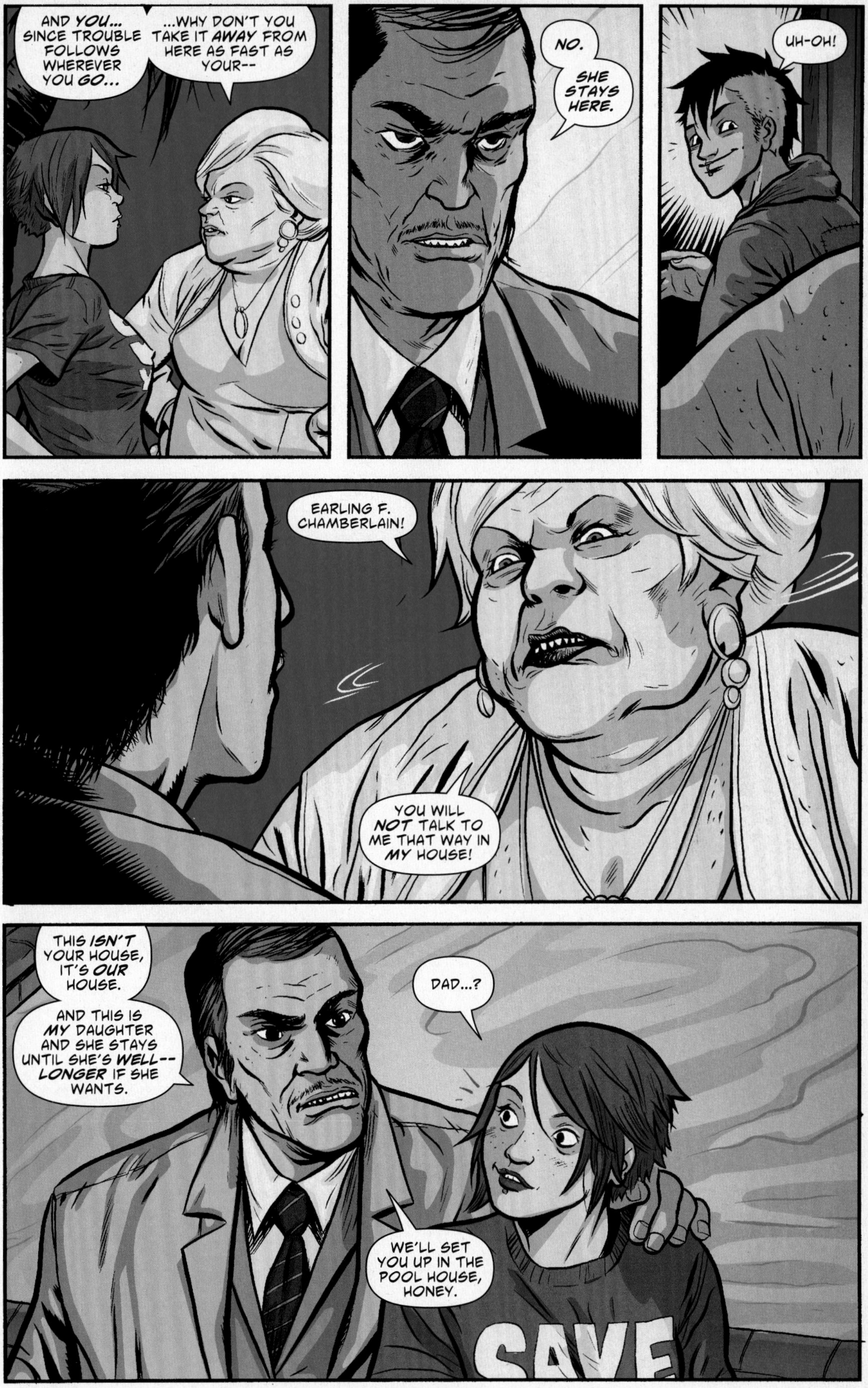
AND YOU... SINCE TROUBLE FOLLOWS WHEREVER YOU GO...
...WHY DON'T YOU TAKE IT AWAY FROM HERE AS FAST AS YOUR--
NO.
SHE STAYS HERE.
UH-OH!
EARLING F. CHAMBERLAIN!
YOU WILL NOT TALK TO ME THAT WAY IN MY HOUSE!
THIS ISN'T YOUR HOUSE, IT'S OUR HOUSE.
AND THIS IS MY DAUGHTER AND SHE STAYS UNTIL SHE'S WELL-- LONGER IF SHE WANTS.
DAD...?
WE'LL SET YOU UP IN THE POOL HOUSE, HONEY.
SAVE

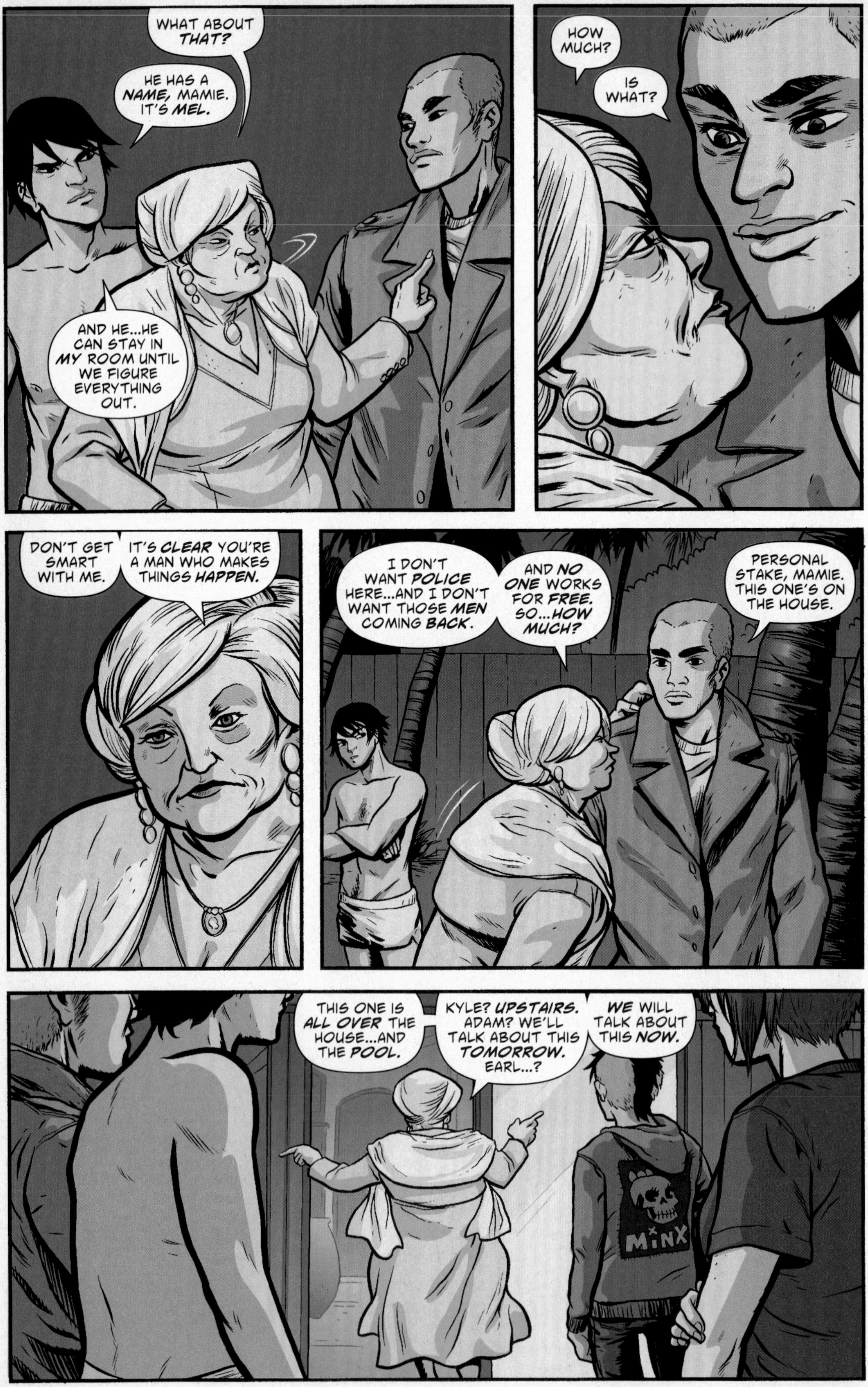
WHAT ABOUT THAT?
HE HAS A NAME, MAMIE. IT'S MEL.
AND HE...HE CAN STAY IN MY ROOM UNTIL WE FIGURE EVERYTHING OUT.
HOW MUCH?
IS WHAT?
DON'T GET SMART WITH ME.
IT'S CLEAR YOU'RE A MAN WHO MAKES THINGS HAPPEN.
I DON'T WANT POLICE HERE...AND I DON'T WANT THOSE MEN COMING BACK.
AND NO ONE WORKS FOR FREE. SO...HOW MUCH?
PERSONAL STAKE, MAMIE. THIS ONE'S ON THE HOUSE.
THIS ONE IS ALL OVER THE HOUSE...AND THE POOL.
KYLE? UPSTAIRS. ADAM? WE'LL TALK ABOUT THIS TOMORROW. EARL...?
WE WILL TALK ABOUT THIS NOW.
MINX

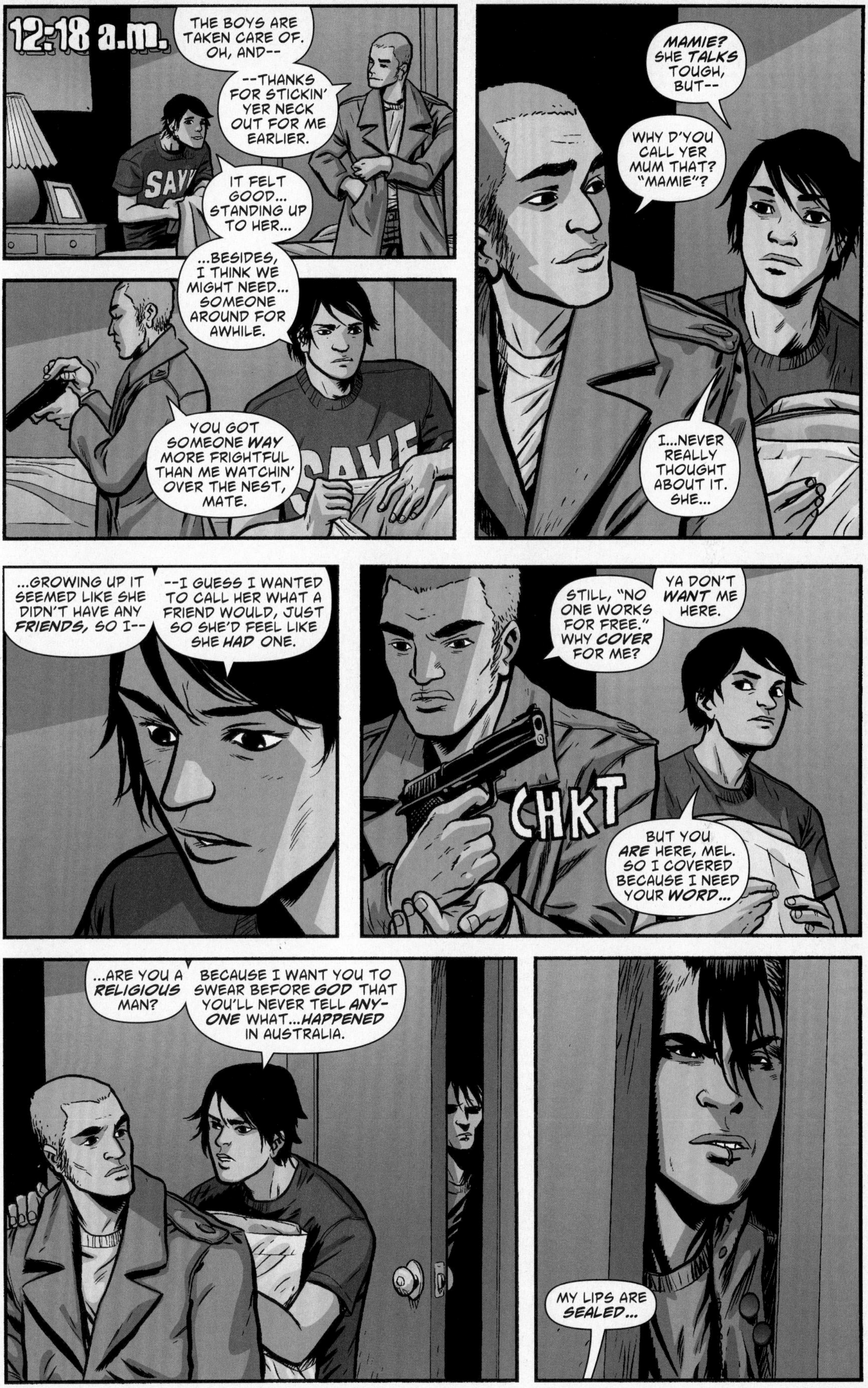
12:18 a.m.
THE BOYS ARE TAKEN CARE OF. OH, AND--
--THANKS FOR STICKIN' YER NECK OUT FOR ME EARLIER.
IT FELT GOOD... STANDING UP TO HER...
...BESIDES, I THINK WE MIGHT NEED... SOMEONE AROUND FOR AWHILE.
YOU GOT SOMEONE WAY MORE FRIGHTFUL THAN ME WATCHIN' OVER THE NEST, MATE.
MAMIE? SHE TALKS TOUGH, BUT--
WHY D'YOU CALL YER MUM THAT? "MAMIE"?
I...NEVER REALLY THOUGHT ABOUT IT. SHE...
...GROWING UP IT SEEMED LIKE SHE DIDN'T HAVE ANY FRIENDS, SO I--
--I GUESS I WANTED TO CALL HER WHAT A FRIEND WOULD, JUST SO SHE'D FEEL LIKE SHE HAD ONE.
YA DON'T WANT ME HERE.
STILL, "NO ONE WORKS FOR FREE." WHY COVER FOR ME?
CHKT
BUT YOU ARE HERE, MEL. SO I COVERED BECAUSE I NEED YOUR WORD...
...ARE YOU A RELIGIOUS MAN?
BECAUSE I WANT YOU TO SWEAR BEFORE GOD THAT YOU'LL NEVER TELL ANY-ONE WHAT...HAPPENED IN AUSTRALIA.
MY LIPS ARE SEALED...

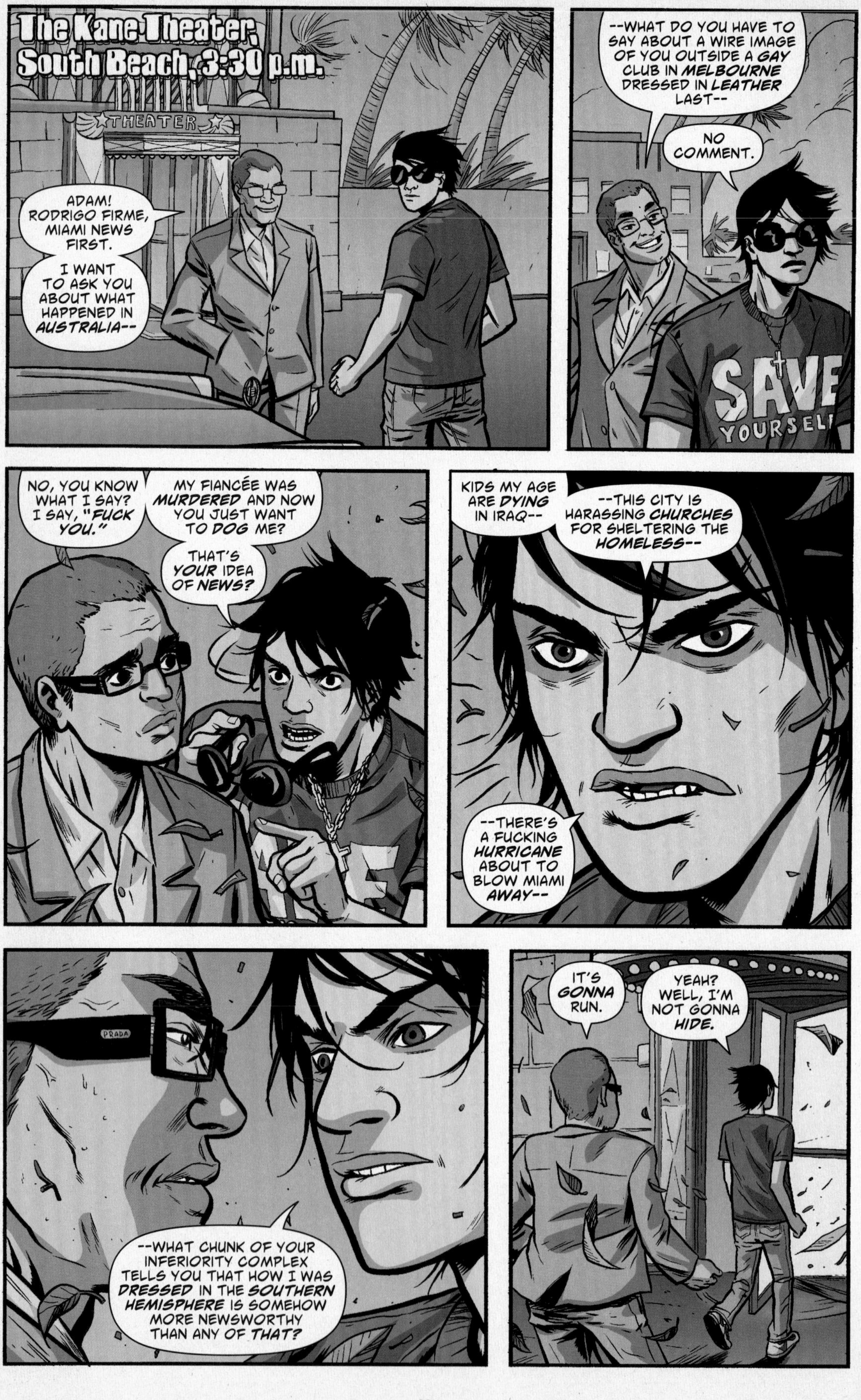
The Kane Theater, South Beach, 3:30 p.m.
THEATER
ADAM! RODRIGO FIRME, MIAMI NEWS FIRST.
I WANT TO ASK YOU ABOUT WHAT HAPPENED IN AUSTRALIA--
--WHAT DO YOU HAVE TO SAY ABOUT A WIRE IMAGE OF YOU OUTSIDE A GAY CLUB IN MELBOURNE DRESSED IN LEATHER LAST--
NO COMMENT.
SAVE YOURSELF
NO, YOU KNOW WHAT I SAY? I SAY, "FUCK YOU."
MY FIANCÉE WAS MURDERED AND NOW YOU JUST WANT TO DOG ME?
THAT'S YOUR IDEA OF NEWS?
KIDS MY AGE ARE DYING IN IRAQ--
--THIS CITY IS HARASSING CHURCHES FOR SHELTERING THE HOMELESS--
--THERE'S A FUCKING HURRICANE ABOUT TO BLOW MIAMI AWAY--
PRADA
--WHAT CHUNK OF YOUR INFERIORITY COMPLEX TELLS YOU THAT HOW I WAS DRESSED IN THE SOUTHERN HEMISPHERE IS SOMEHOW MORE NEWSWORTHY THAN ANY OF THAT?
IT'S GONNA RUN.
YEAH? WELL, I'M NOT GONNA HIDE.

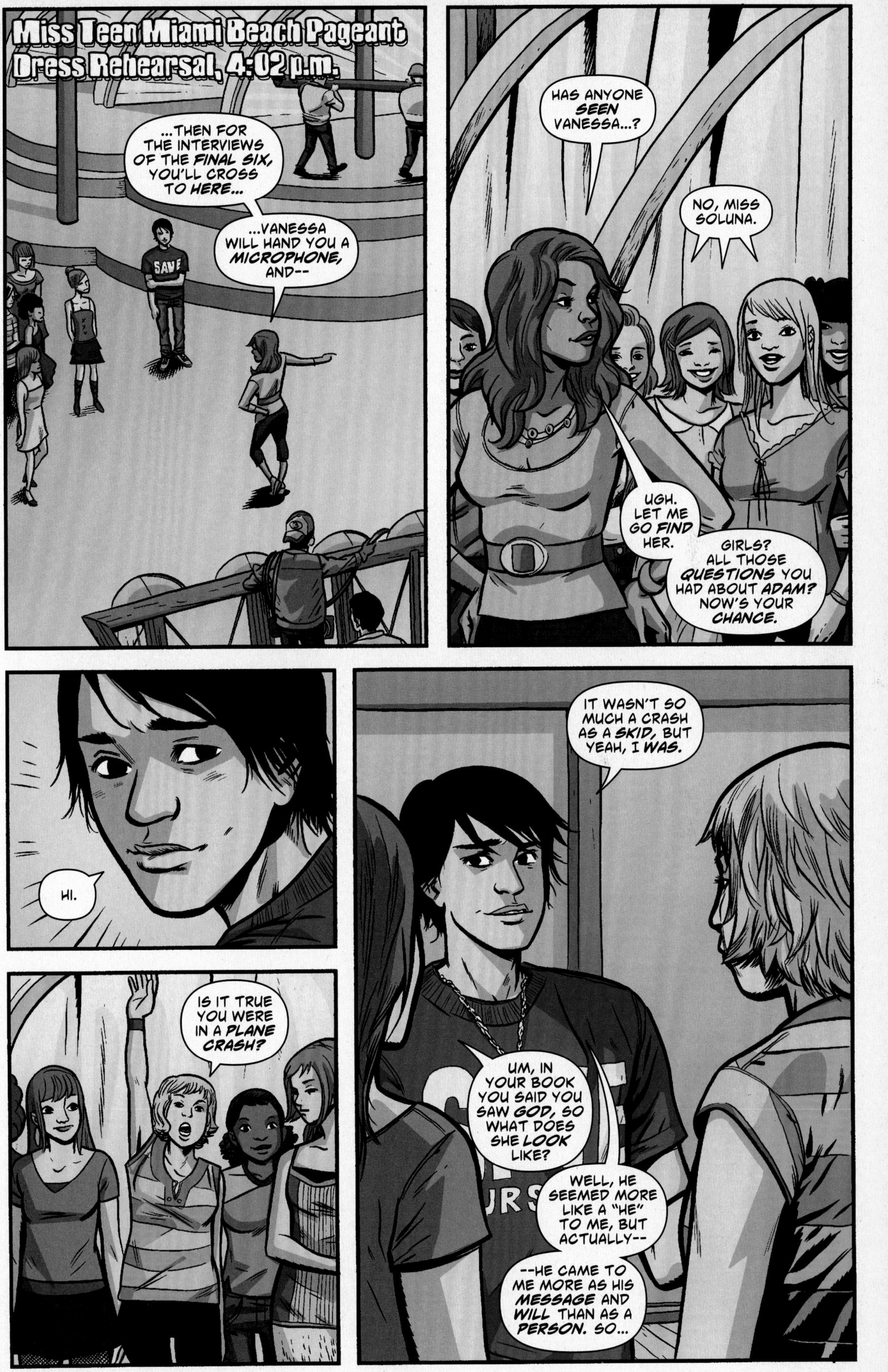
Miss Teen Miami Beach Pageant
Dress Rehearsal, 4:02 p.m.
...THEN FOR THE INTERVIEWS OF THE FINAL SIX, YOU'LL CROSS TO HERE...
...VANESSA WILL HAND YOU A MICROPHONE, AND--
HAS ANYONE SEEN VANESSA...?
NO, MISS SOLUNA.
UGH. LET ME GO FIND HER.
GIRLS? ALL THOSE QUESTIONS YOU HAD ABOUT ADAM? NOW'S YOUR CHANCE.
HI.
IS IT TRUE YOU WERE IN A PLANE CRASH?
IT WASN'T SO MUCH A CRASH AS A SKID, BUT YEAH, I WAS.
UM, IN YOUR BOOK YOU SAID YOU SAW GOD, SO WHAT DOES SHE LOOK LIKE?
WELL, HE SEEMED MORE LIKE A "HE" TO ME, BUT ACTUALLY--
--HE CAME TO ME MORE AS HIS MESSAGE AND WILL THAN AS A PERSON. SO...

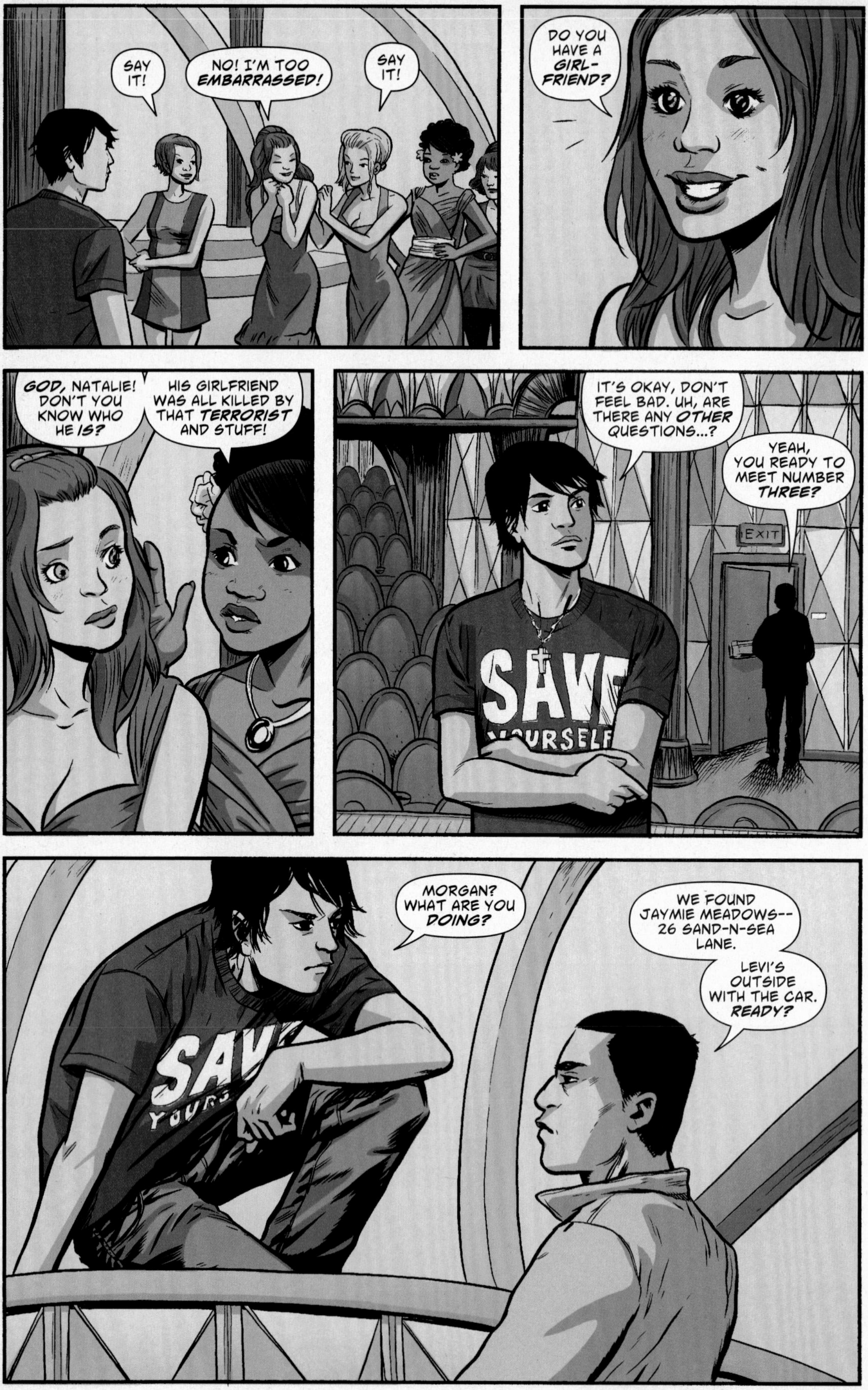
SAY IT!
NO! I'M TOO EMBARRASSED!
SAY IT!
DO YOU HAVE A GIRL-FRIEND?
GOD, NATALIE! DON'T YOU KNOW WHO HE IS?
HIS GIRLFRIEND WAS ALL KILLED BY THAT TERRORIST AND STUFF!
IT'S OKAY, DON'T FEEL BAD. UH, ARE THERE ANY OTHER QUESTIONS...?
YEAH, YOU READY TO MEET NUMBER THREE?
EXIT
SAVE YOURSELF
MORGAN? WHAT ARE YOU DOING?
WE FOUND JAYMIE MEADOWS-- 26 SAND-N-SEA LANE.
LEVI'S OUTSIDE WITH THE CAR. READY?

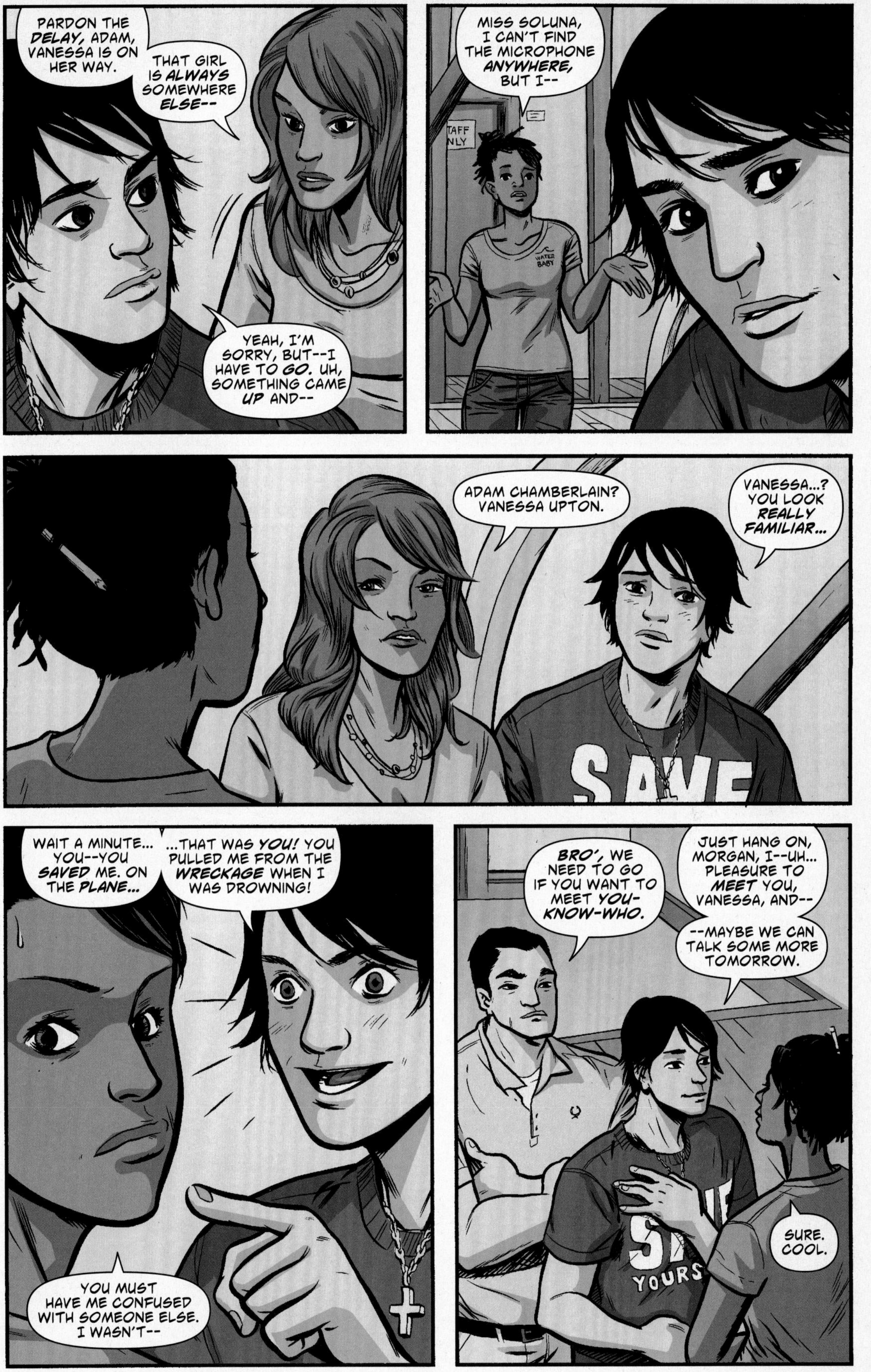
PARDON THE DELAY, ADAM, VANESSA IS ON HER WAY.
THAT GIRL IS ALWAYS SOMEWHERE ELSE--
YEAH, I'M SORRY, BUT--I HAVE TO GO. UH, SOMETHING CAME UP AND--
MISS SOLUNA, I CAN'T FIND THE MICROPHONE ANYWHERE, BUT I--
TAFF NLY
WATER BABY
ADAM CHAMBERLAIN? VANESSA UPTON.
VANESSA...? YOU LOOK REALLY FAMILIAR...
SAVE
WAIT A MINUTE... YOU--YOU SAVED ME. ON THE PLANE...
...THAT WAS YOU! YOU PULLED ME FROM THE WRECKAGE WHEN I WAS DROWNING!
YOU MUST HAVE ME CONFUSED WITH SOMEONE ELSE. I WASN'T--
BRO', WE NEED TO GO IF YOU WANT TO MEET YOU-KNOW-WHO.
JUST HANG ON, MORGAN, I--UH... PLEASURE TO MEET YOU, VANESSA, AND--
--MAYBE WE CAN TALK SOME MORE TOMORROW.
SURE. COOL.
YOURS

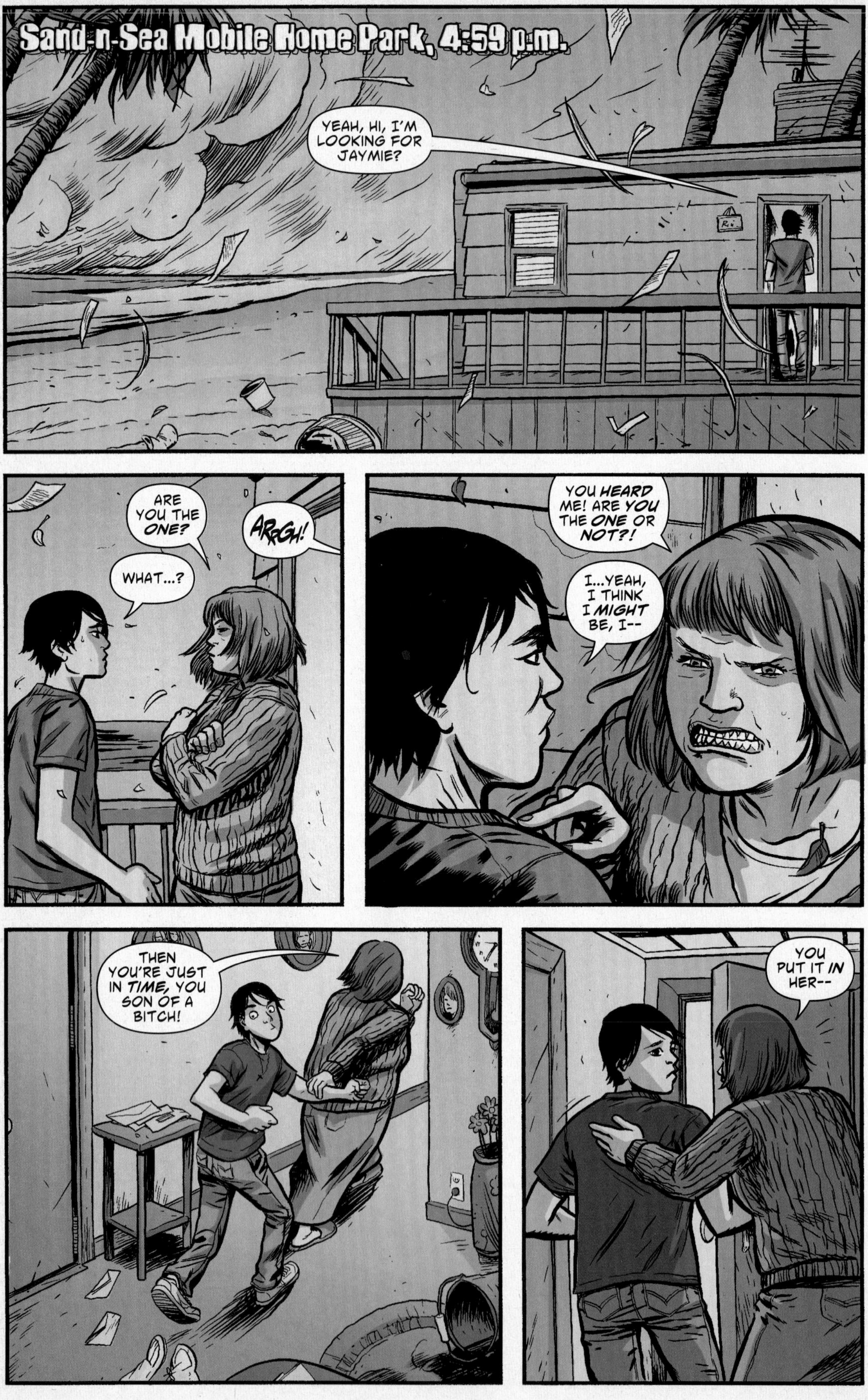

Sand-n-Sea Mobile Home Park, 4:59 p.m.
YEAH, HI, I'M LOOKING FOR JAYMIE?
ARE YOU THE ONE?
WHAT...?
ARRGH!
YOU HEARD ME! ARE YOU THE ONE OR NOT?!
I...YEAH, I THINK I MIGHT BE, I--
THEN YOU'RE JUST IN TIME, YOU SON OF A BITCH!
YOU PUT IT IN HER--

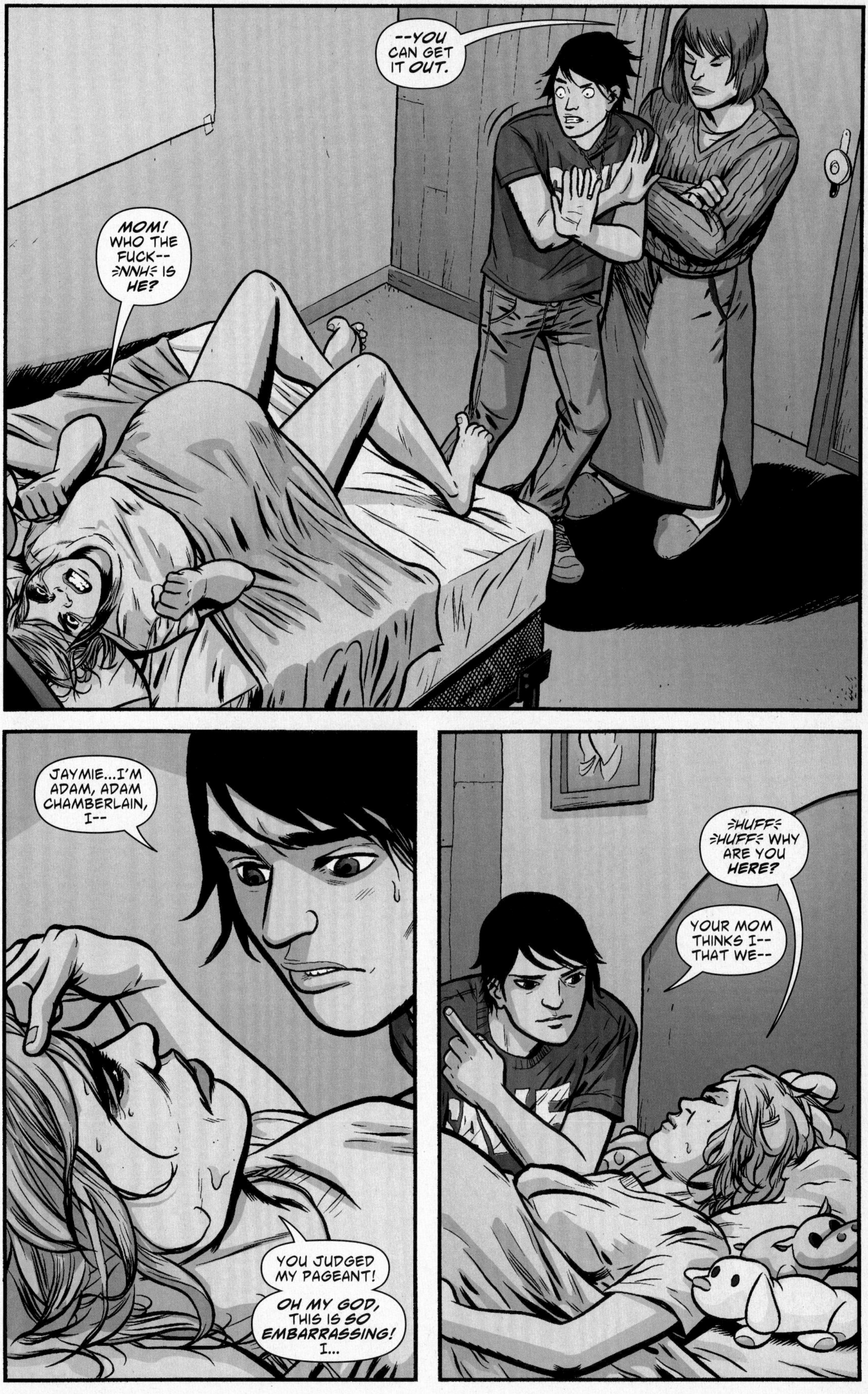
--YOU CAN GET IT OUT.
MOM! WHO THE FUCK-- =NNH= IS HE?
JAYMIE...I'M ADAM, ADAM CHAMBERLAIN, I--
YOU JUDGED MY PAGEANT!
OH MY GOD, THIS IS SO EMBARRASSING! I...
=HUFF= =HUFF= WHY ARE YOU HERE?
YOUR MOM THINKS I-- THAT WE--

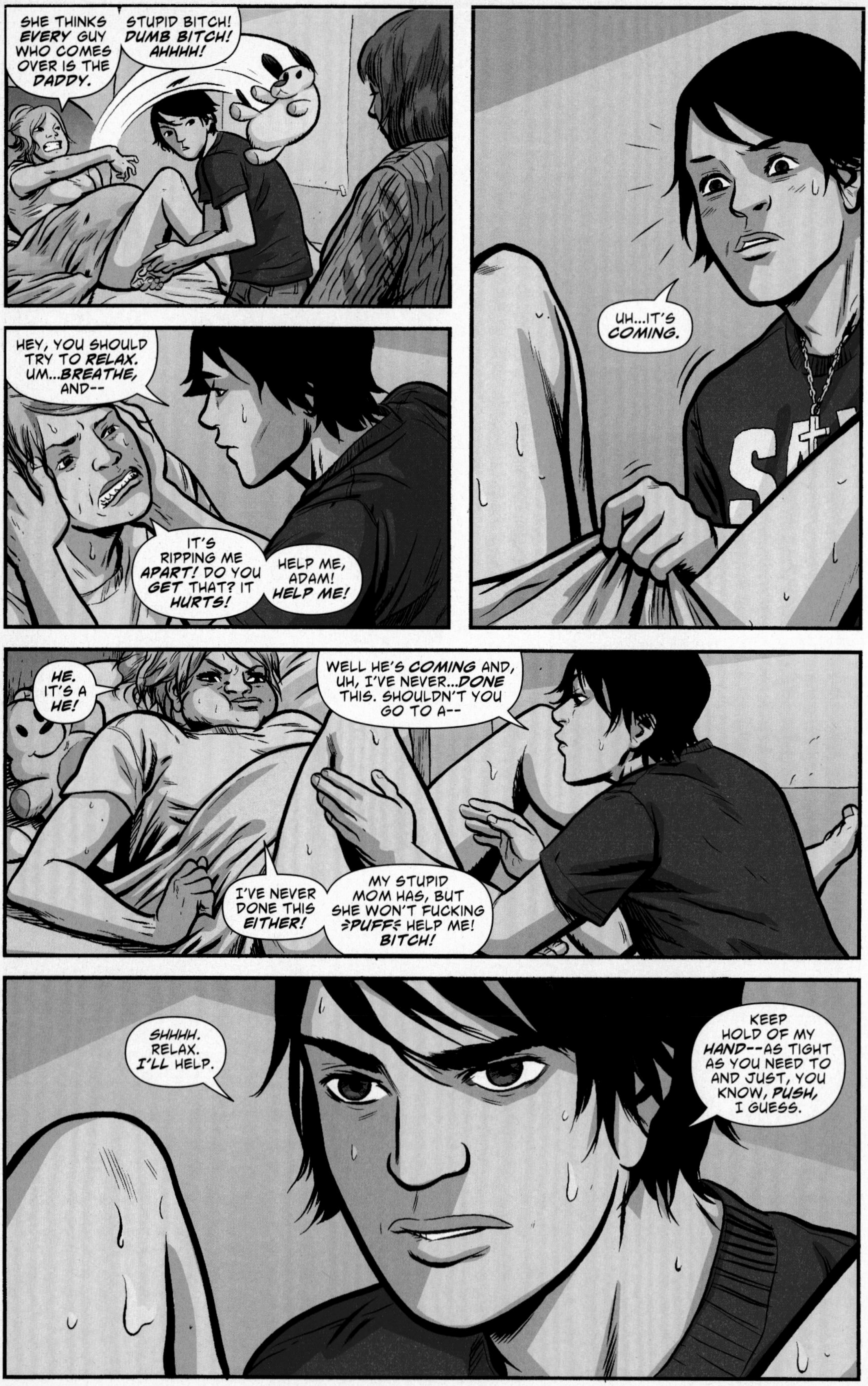

SHE THINKS EVERY GUY WHO COMES OVER IS THE DADDY.
STUPID BITCH! DUMB BITCH! AHHHH!
UH...IT'S COMING.
HEY, YOU SHOULD TRY TO RELAX. UM...BREATHE, AND--
IT'S RIPPING ME APART! DO YOU GET THAT? IT HURTS!
HELP ME, ADAM! HELP ME!
HE. IT'S A HE!
WELL HE'S COMING AND, UH, I'VE NEVER...DONE THIS. SHOULDN'T YOU GO TO A--
I'VE NEVER DONE THIS EITHER!
MY STUPID MOM HAS, BUT SHE WON'T FUCKING =PUFF= HELP ME! BITCH!
SHHHH. RELAX. I'LL HELP.
KEEP HOLD OF MY HAND--AS TIGHT AS YOU NEED TO AND JUST, YOU KNOW, PUSH, I GUESS.

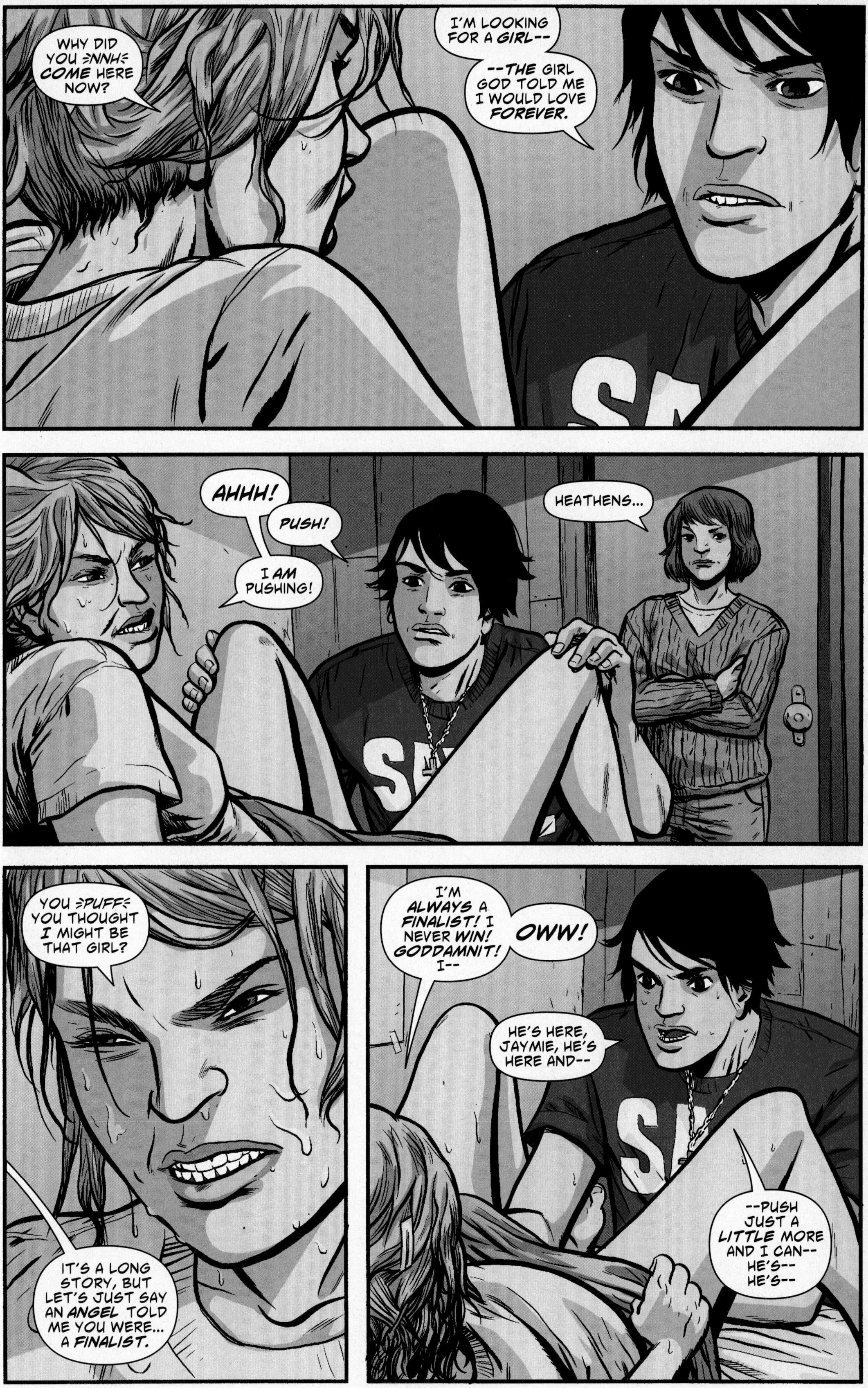
WHY DID YOU ≡NNH≡ COME HERE NOW?
I'M LOOKING FOR A GIRL--
--THE GIRL GOD TOLD ME I WOULD LOVE FOREVER.
AHHH!
PUSH!
I AM PUSHING!
HEATHENS...
YOU ≡PUFF≡ YOU THOUGHT I MIGHT BE THAT GIRL?
IT'S A LONG STORY, BUT LET'S JUST SAY AN ANGEL TOLD ME YOU WERE... A FINALIST.
I'M ALWAYS A FINALIST! I NEVER WIN! GODDAMNIT! I--
OWW!
HE'S HERE, JAYMIE, HE'S HERE AND--
--PUSH JUST A LITTLE MORE AND I CAN-- HE'S-- HE'S--

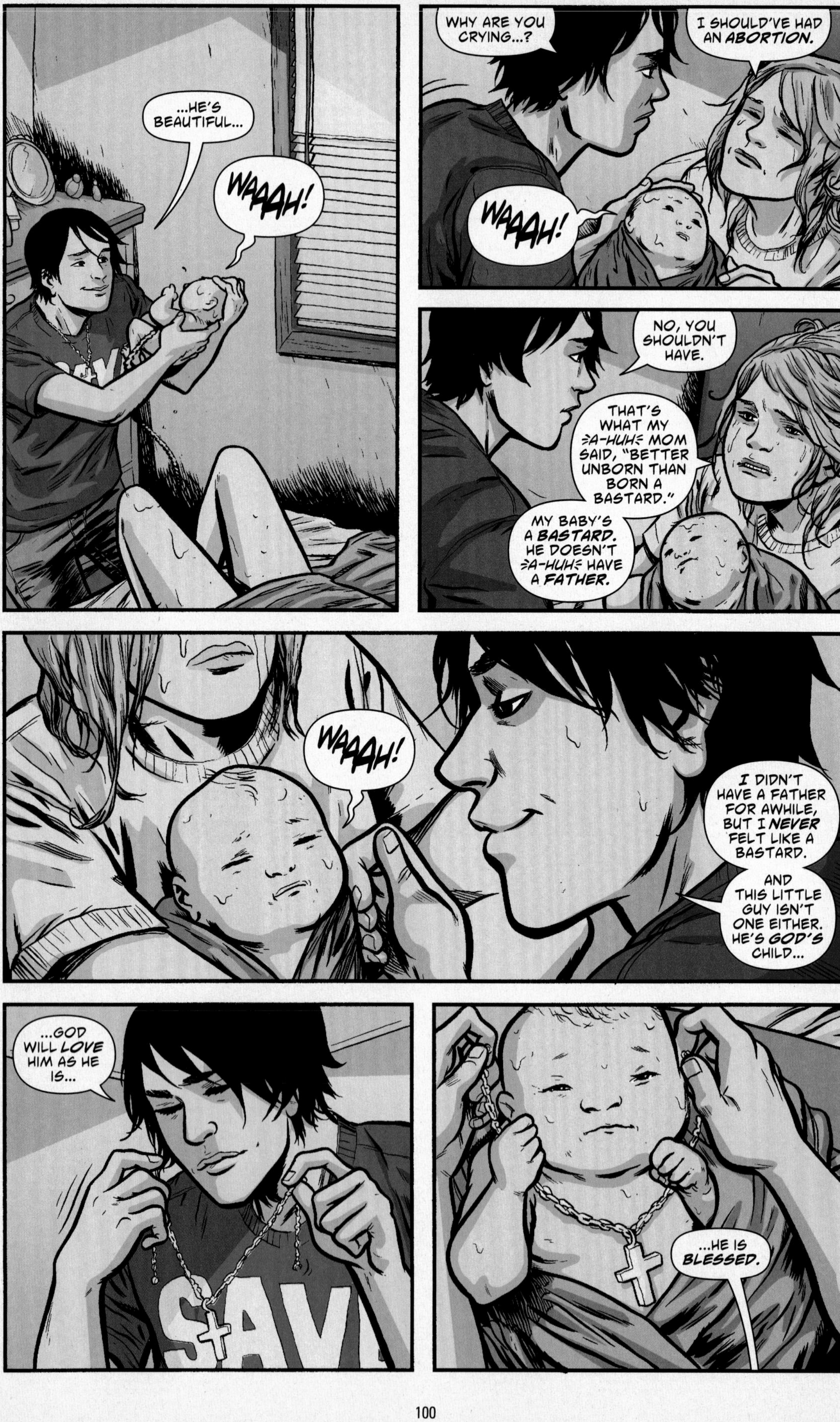
...HE'S BEAUTIFUL...
WAAAH!
WHY ARE YOU CRYING...?
I SHOULD'VE HAD AN ABORTION.
WAAAH!
NO, YOU SHOULDN'T HAVE.
THAT'S WHAT MY =A-HUH= MOM SAID, "BETTER UNBORN THAN BORN A BASTARD."
MY BABY'S A BASTARD. HE DOESN'T =A-HUH= HAVE A FATHER.
WAAAH!
I DIDN'T HAVE A FATHER FOR AWHILE, BUT I NEVER FELT LIKE A BASTARD.
AND THIS LITTLE GUY ISN'T ONE EITHER. HE'S GOD'S CHILD...
...GOD WILL LOVE HIM AS HE IS...
...HE IS BLESSED.

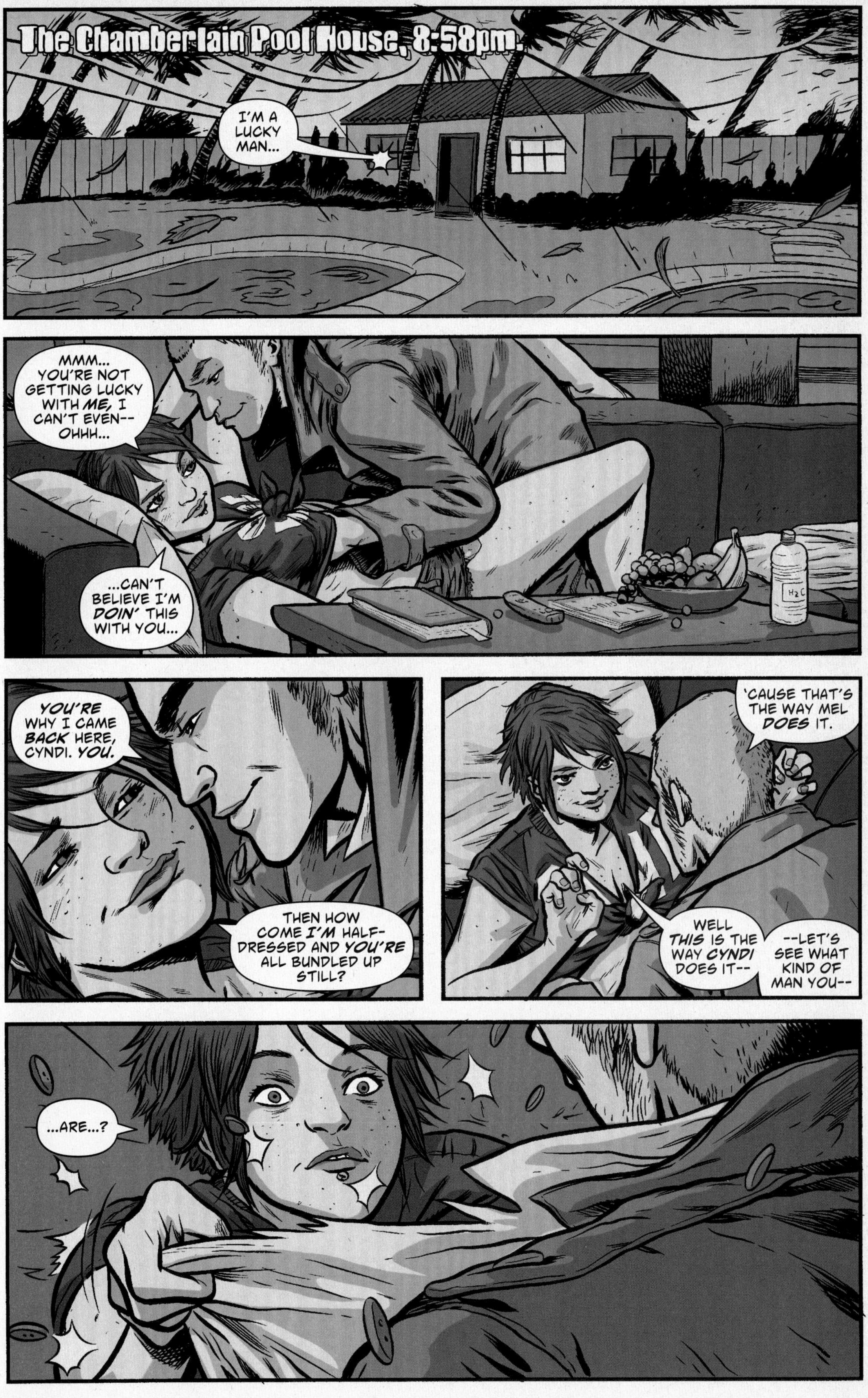
The Chamberlain Pool House, 8:58pm.
I'M A LUCKY MAN...
MMM... YOU'RE NOT GETTING LUCKY WITH ME, I CAN'T EVEN-- OHHH...
...CAN'T BELIEVE I'M DOIN' THIS WITH YOU...
YOU'RE WHY I CAME BACK HERE, CYNDI. YOU.
THEN HOW COME I'M HALF-DRESSED AND YOU'RE ALL BUNDLED UP STILL?
'CAUSE THAT'S THE WAY MEL DOES IT.
WELL THIS IS THE WAY CYNDI DOES IT--
--LET'S SEE WHAT KIND OF MAN YOU--
...ARE...?

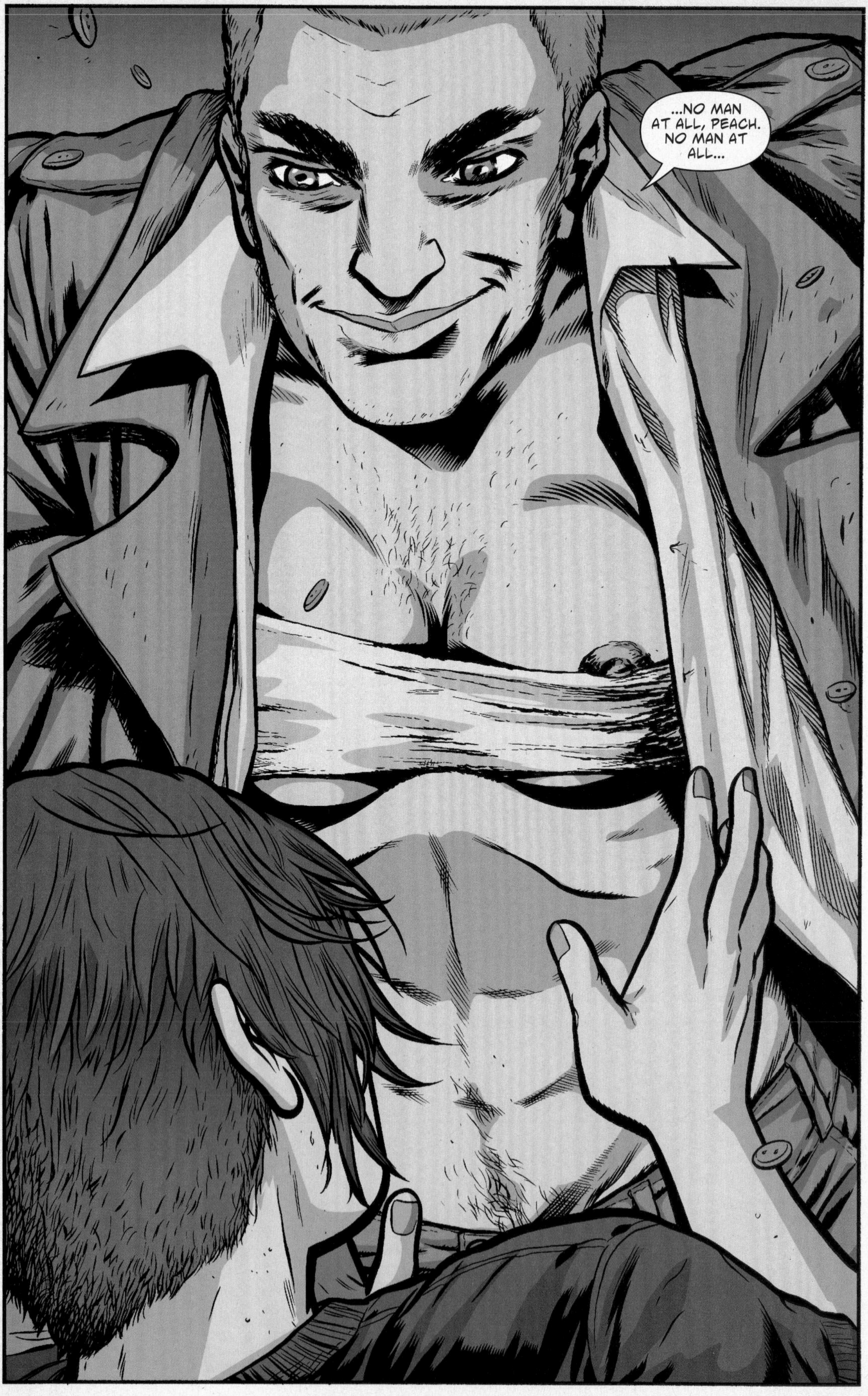
...NO MAN AT ALL, PEACH. NO MAN AT ALL...

CHAPTER FIVE

Chapter pencils by Becky Cloonan, inks by Jim Rugg

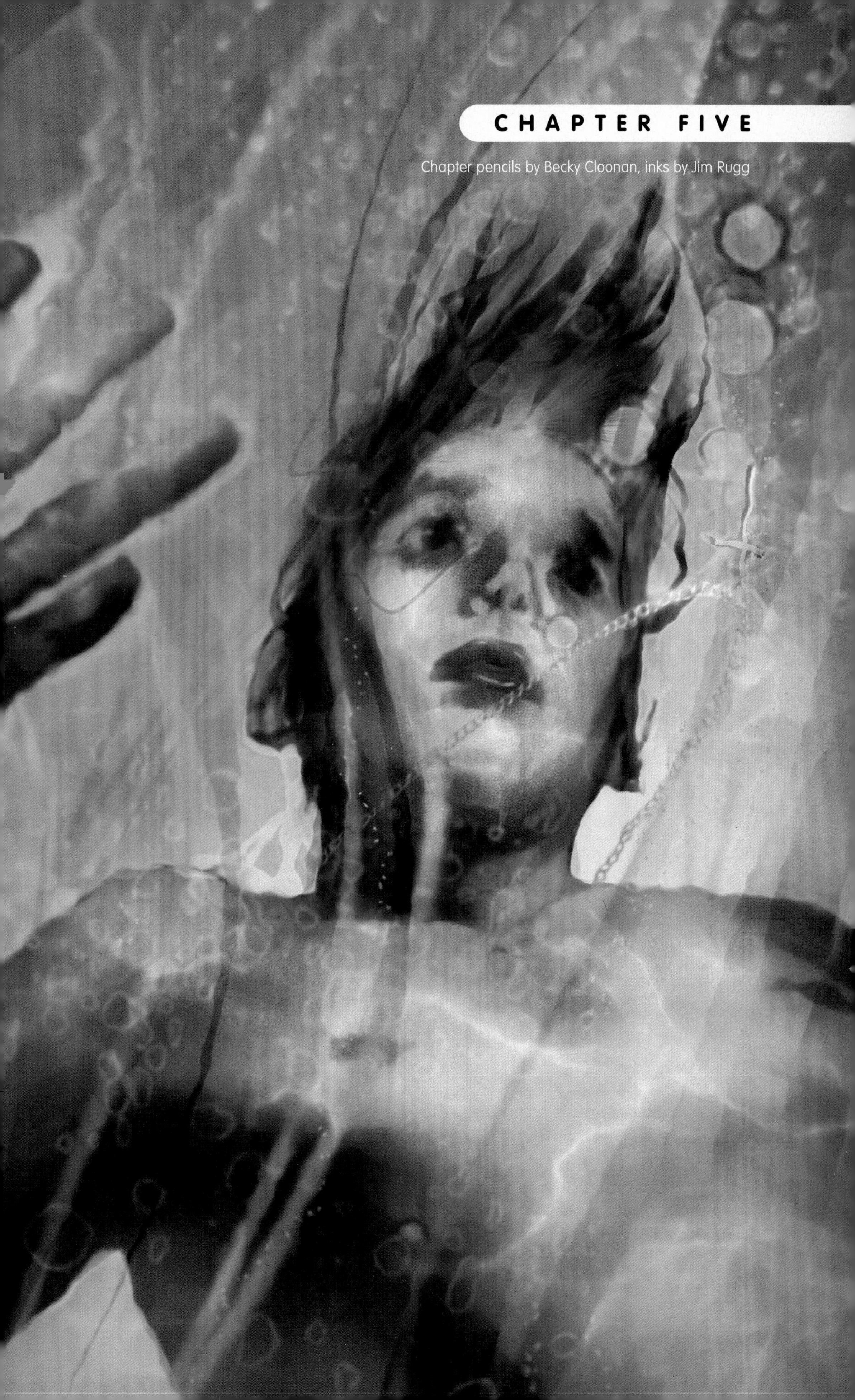

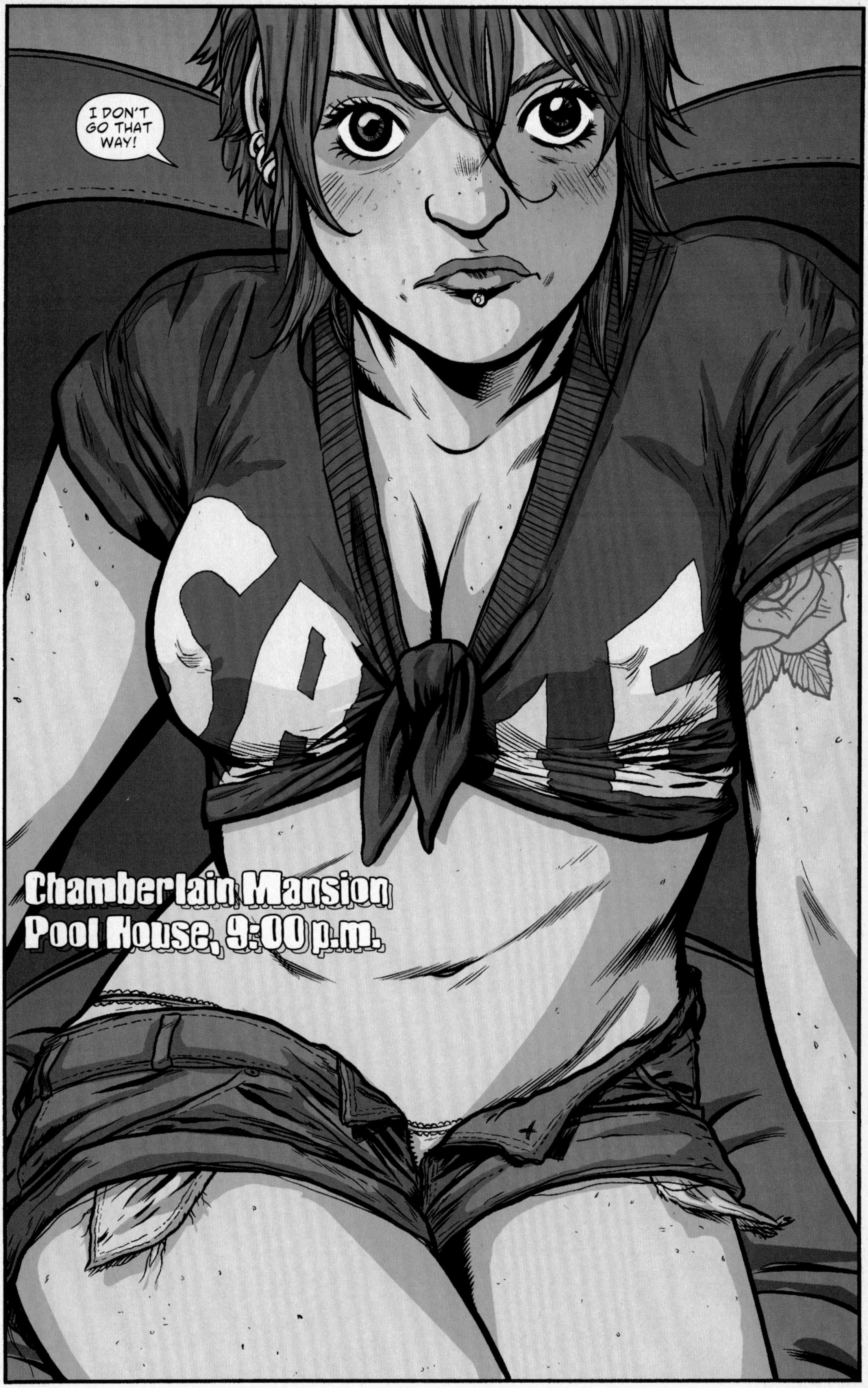
I DON'T GO THAT WAY!
Chamberlain Mansion
Pool House, 9:00 p.m.

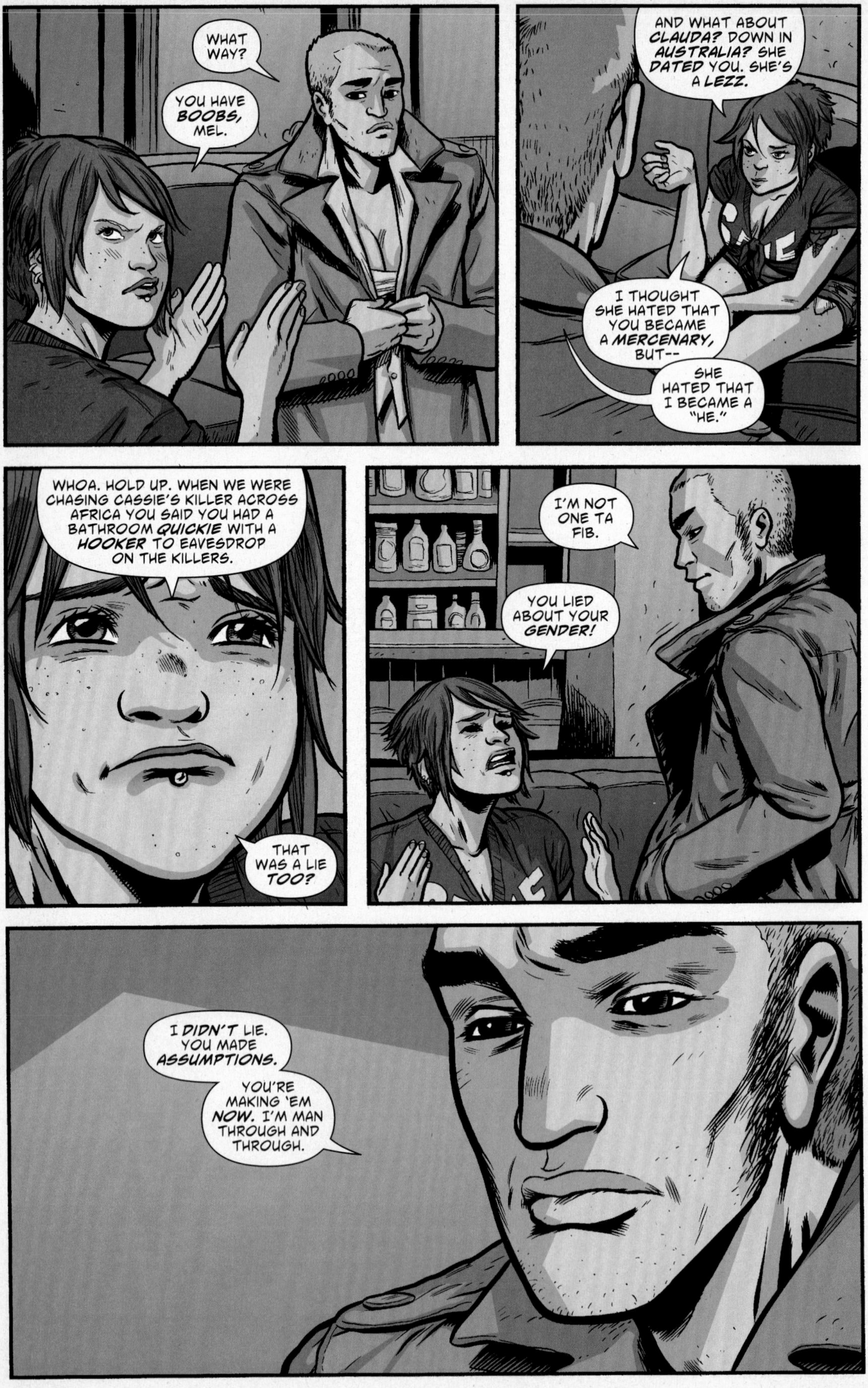
WHAT WAY?
YOU HAVE BOOBS, MEL.
AND WHAT ABOUT CLAUDA? DOWN IN AUSTRALIA? SHE DATED YOU. SHE'S A LEZZ.
I THOUGHT SHE HATED THAT YOU BECAME A MERCENARY, BUT--
SHE HATED THAT I BECAME A "HE."
WHOA. HOLD UP. WHEN WE WERE CHASING CASSIE'S KILLER ACROSS AFRICA YOU SAID YOU HAD A BATHROOM QUICKIE WITH A HOOKER TO EAVESDROP ON THE KILLERS.
THAT WAS A LIE TOO?
I'M NOT ONE TA FIB.
YOU LIED ABOUT YOUR GENDER!
I DIDN'T LIE. YOU MADE ASSUMPTIONS.
YOU'RE MAKING 'EM NOW. I'M MAN THROUGH AND THROUGH.

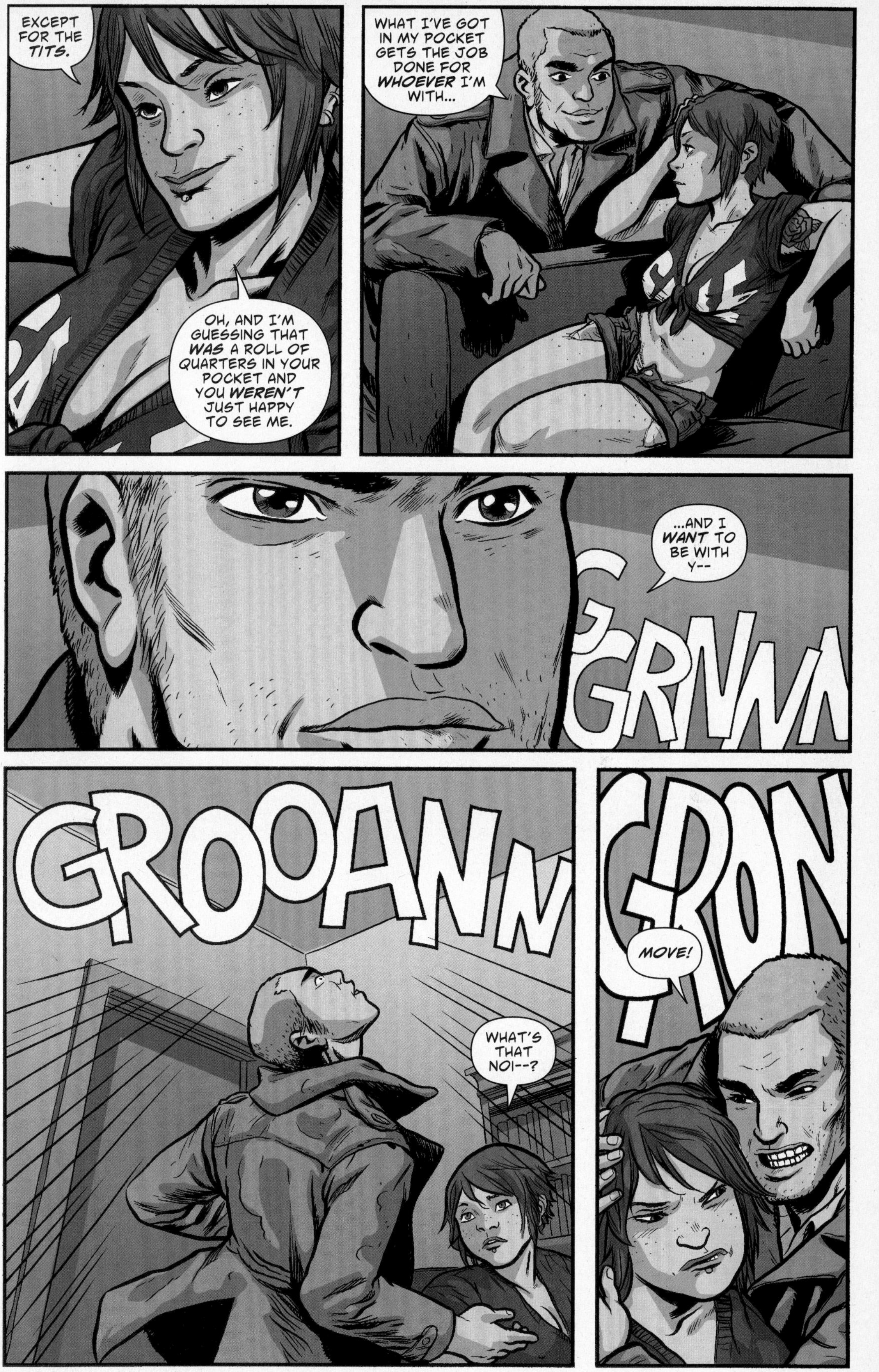
EXCEPT FOR THE TITS.
OH, AND I'M GUESSING THAT WAS A ROLL OF QUARTERS IN YOUR POCKET AND YOU WEREN'T JUST HAPPY TO SEE ME.
WHAT I'VE GOT IN MY POCKET GETS THE JOB DONE FOR WHOEVER I'M WITH...
...AND I WANT TO BE WITH Y--
GRNNN
GROOANNN
WHAT'S THAT NOI--?
GRON
MOVE!

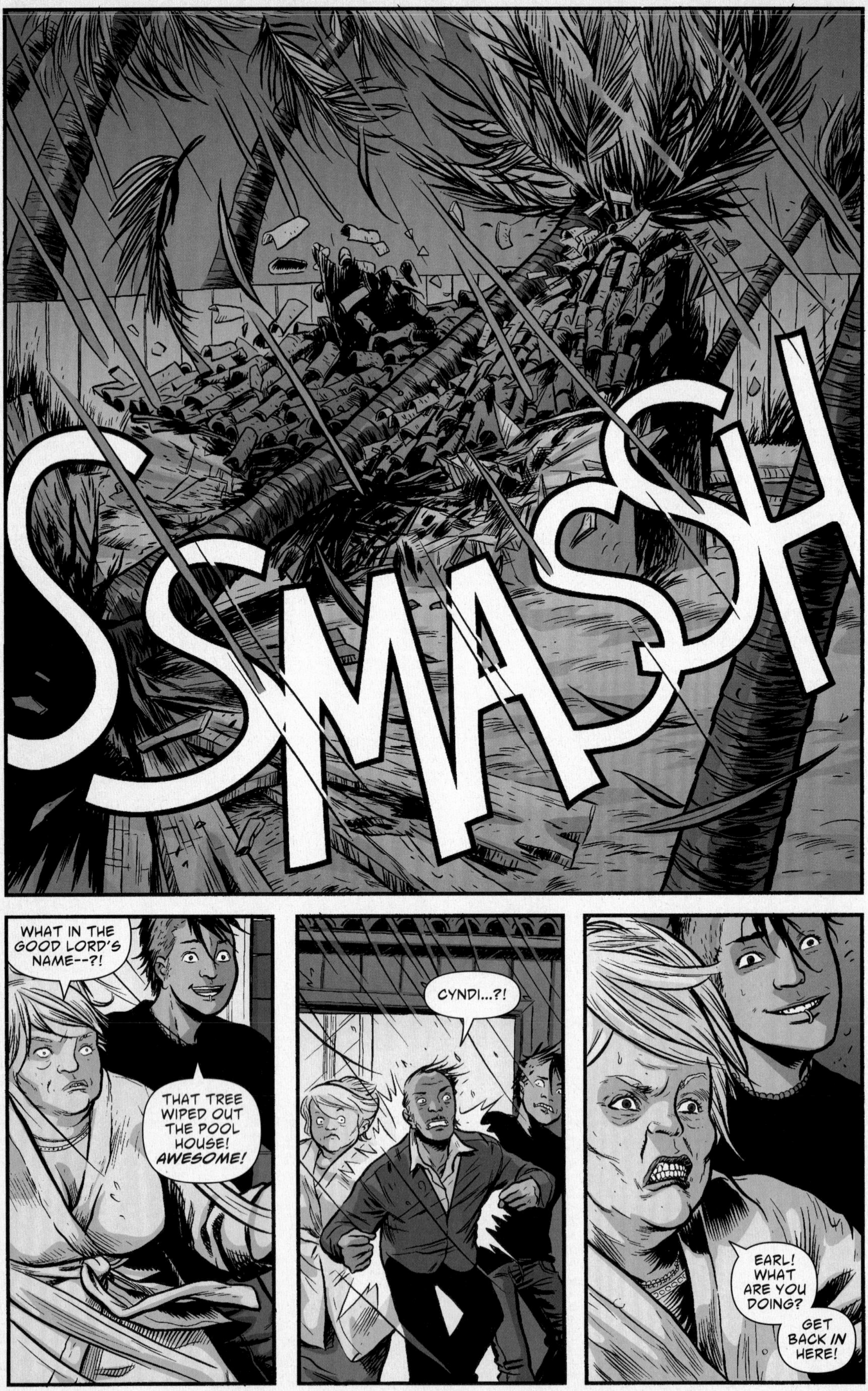
SMASH
WHAT IN THE GOOD LORD'S NAME--?!
THAT TREE WIPED OUT THE POOL HOUSE! *AWESOME!*
CYNDI...?!
EARL! WHAT ARE YOU DOING?
GET BACK *IN* HERE!

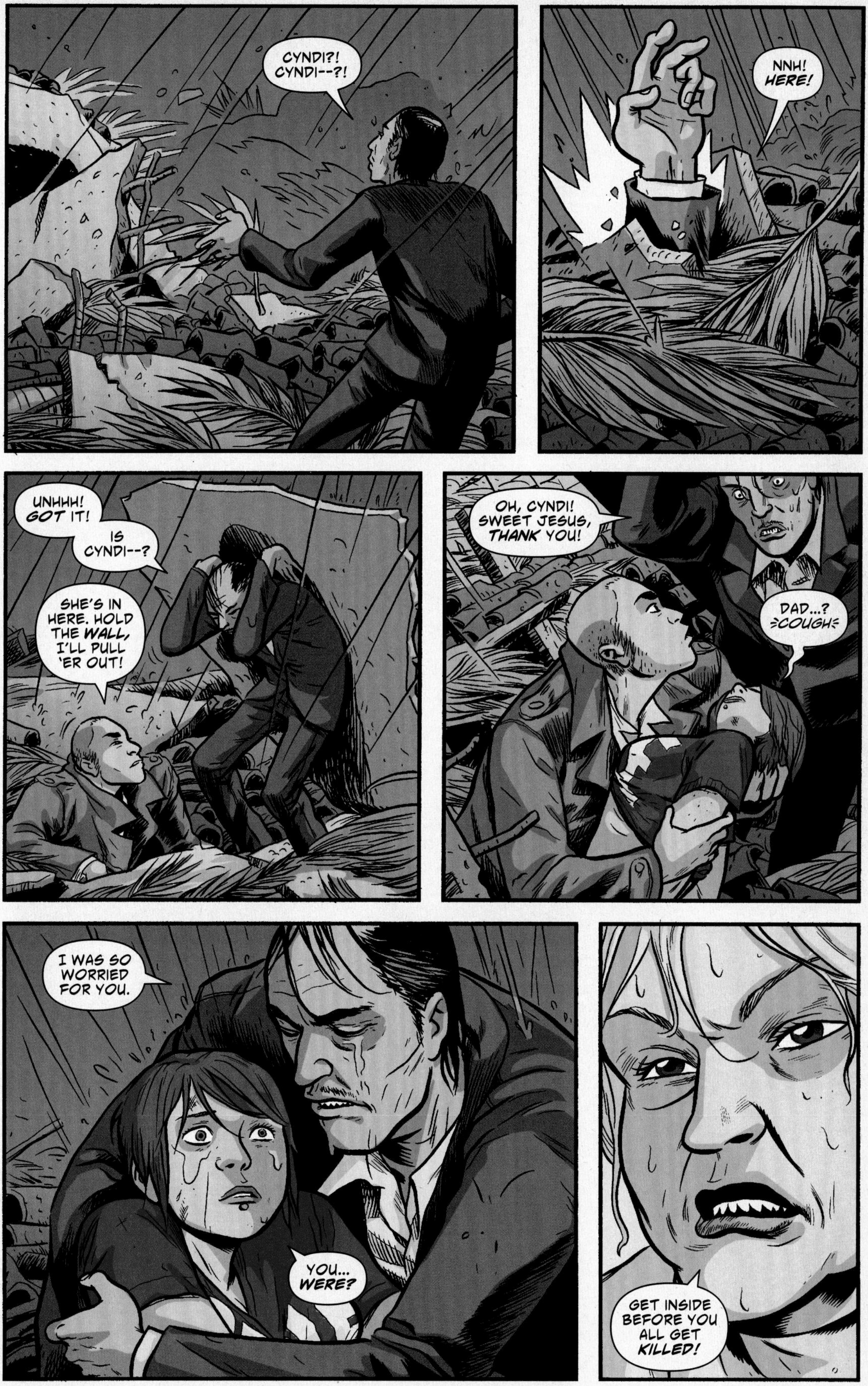
CYNDI?! CYNDI--?!
NNH! HERE!
UNHHH! GOT IT!
IS CYNDI--?
SHE'S IN HERE. HOLD THE WALL, I'LL PULL 'ER OUT!
OH, CYNDI! SWEET JESUS, THANK YOU!
DAD...? COUGH
I WAS SO WORRIED FOR YOU.
YOU... WERE?
GET INSIDE BEFORE YOU ALL GET KILLED!

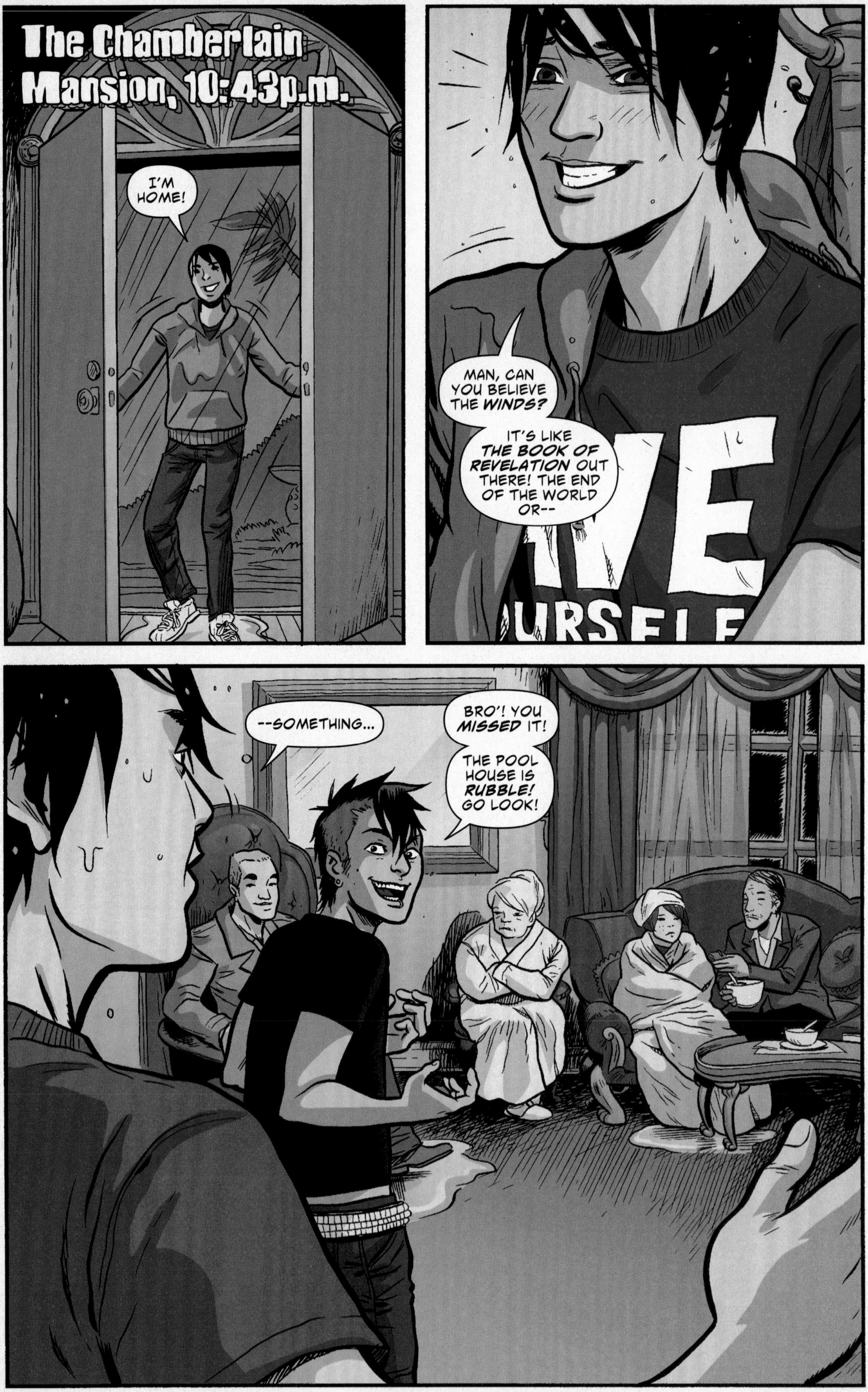
The Chamberlain Mansion, 10:43p.m.
I'M HOME!
MAN, CAN YOU BELIEVE THE *WINDS?*
IT'S LIKE *THE BOOK OF REVELATION* OUT THERE! THE END OF THE WORLD OR--
--SOMETHING...
BRO'! YOU *MISSED* IT!
THE POOL HOUSE IS *RUBBLE!* GO LOOK!

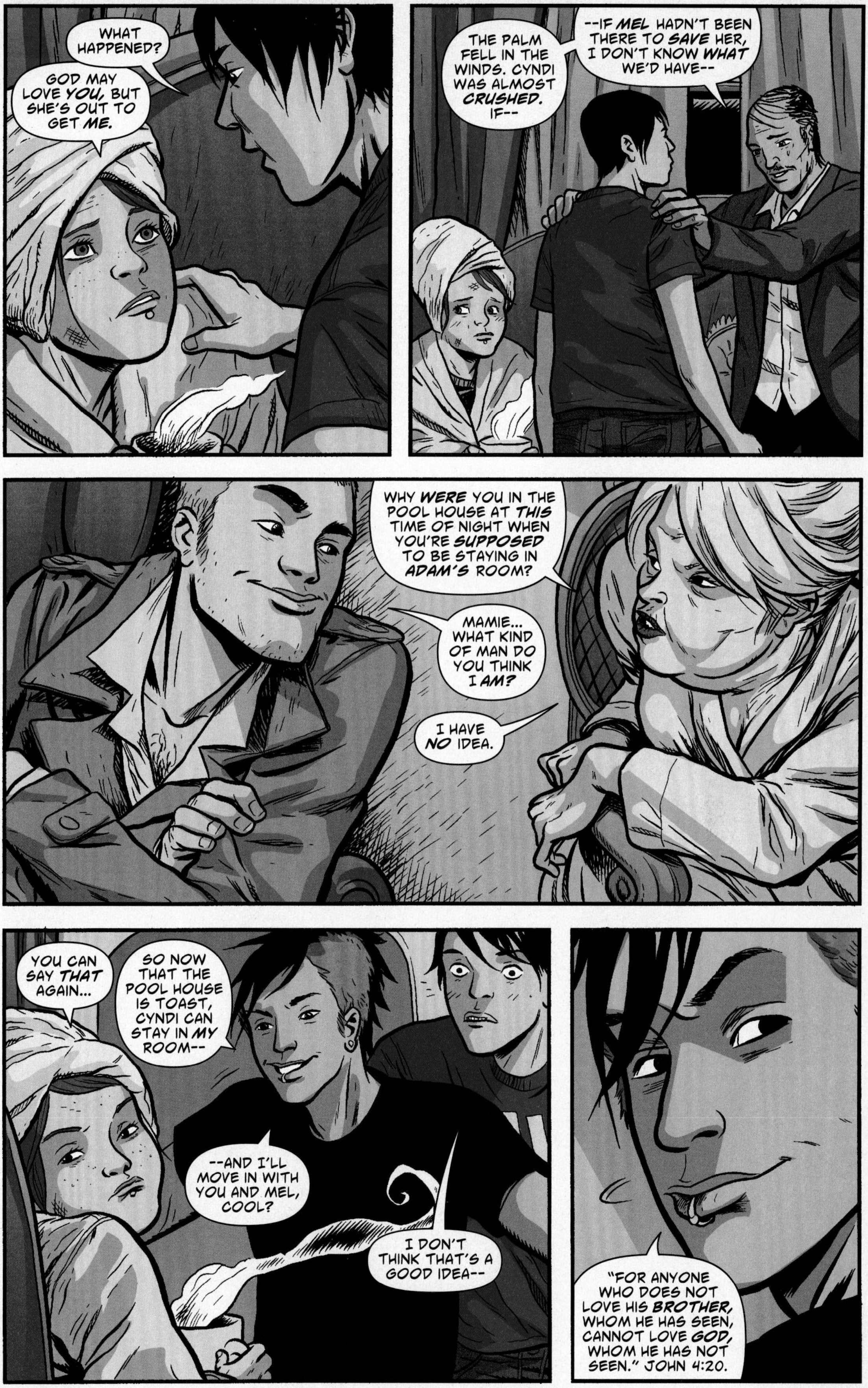
WHAT HAPPENED?
GOD MAY LOVE YOU, BUT SHE'S OUT TO GET ME.
THE PALM FELL IN THE WINDS. CYNDI WAS ALMOST CRUSHED. IF--
--IF MEL HADN'T BEEN THERE TO SAVE HER, I DON'T KNOW WHAT WE'D HAVE--
WHY WERE YOU IN THE POOL HOUSE AT THIS TIME OF NIGHT WHEN YOU'RE SUPPOSED TO BE STAYING IN ADAM'S ROOM?
MAMIE... WHAT KIND OF MAN DO YOU THINK I AM?
I HAVE NO IDEA.
YOU CAN SAY THAT AGAIN...
SO NOW THAT THE POOL HOUSE IS TOAST, CYNDI CAN STAY IN MY ROOM--
--AND I'LL MOVE IN WITH YOU AND MEL, COOL?
I DON'T THINK THAT'S A GOOD IDEA--
"FOR ANYONE WHO DOES NOT LOVE HIS BROTHER, WHOM HE HAS SEEN, CANNOT LOVE GOD, WHOM HE HAS NOT SEEN." JOHN 4:20.

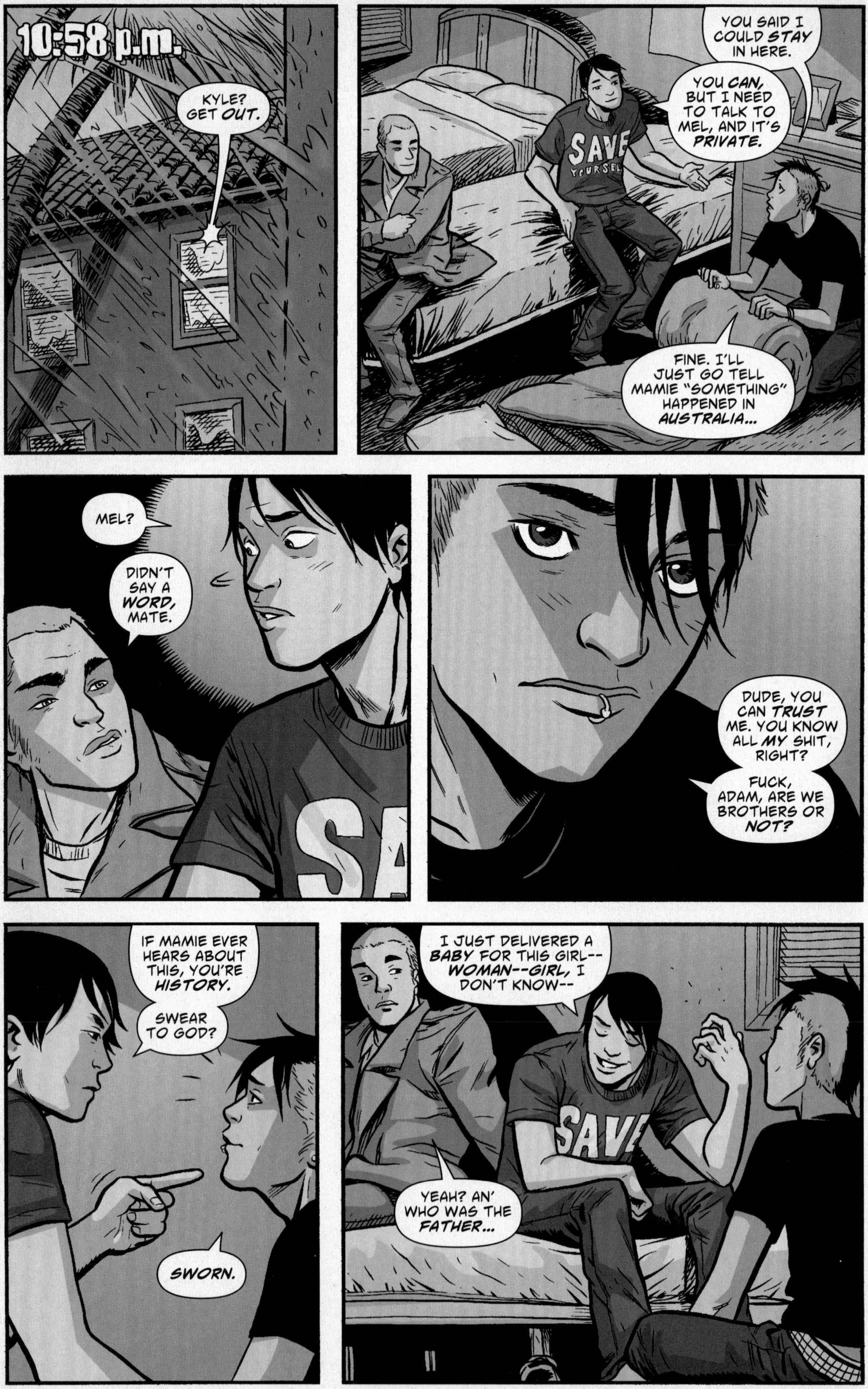
10:58 p.m.
KYLE? GET OUT.
YOU SAID I COULD STAY IN HERE.
YOU CAN, BUT I NEED TO TALK TO MEL, AND IT'S PRIVATE.
FINE. I'LL JUST GO TELL MAMIE "SOMETHING" HAPPENED IN AUSTRALIA...
MEL?
DIDN'T SAY A WORD, MATE.
DUDE, YOU CAN TRUST ME. YOU KNOW ALL MY SHIT, RIGHT?
FUCK, ADAM, ARE WE BROTHERS OR NOT?
IF MAMIE EVER HEARS ABOUT THIS, YOU'RE HISTORY.
SWEAR TO GOD?
SWORN.
I JUST DELIVERED A BABY FOR THIS GIRL--WOMAN--GIRL, I DON'T KNOW--
YEAH? AN' WHO WAS THE FATHER...

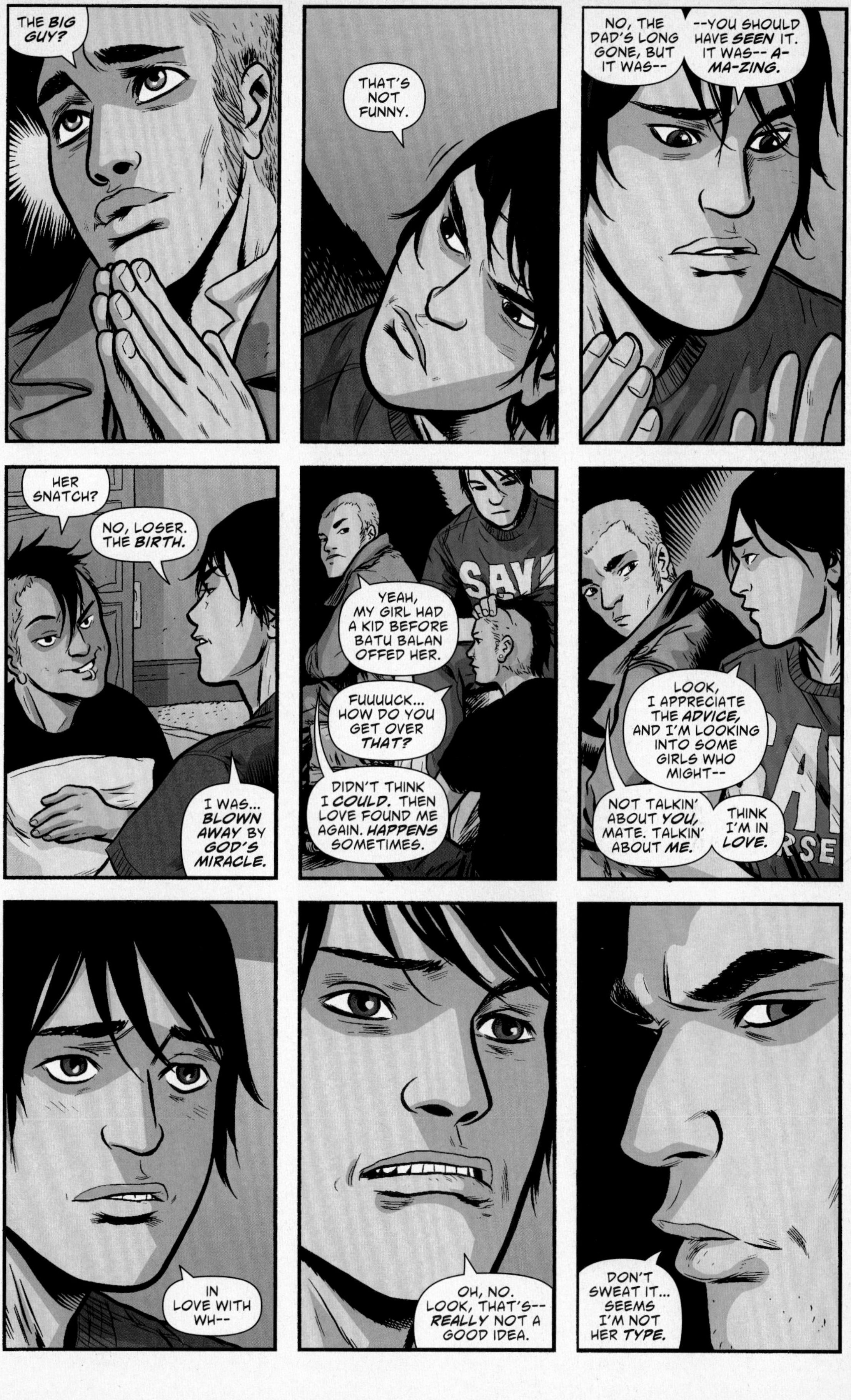
THE BIG GUY?
THAT'S NOT FUNNY.
NO, THE DAD'S LONG GONE, BUT IT WAS--
--YOU SHOULD HAVE SEEN IT. IT WAS-- A-MA-ZING.
HER SNATCH?
NO, LOSER. THE BIRTH.
I WAS... BLOWN AWAY BY GOD'S MIRACLE.
YEAH, MY GIRL HAD A KID BEFORE BATU BALAN OFFED HER.
FUUUUCK... HOW DO YOU GET OVER THAT?
DIDN'T THINK I COULD. THEN LOVE FOUND ME AGAIN. HAPPENS SOMETIMES.
LOOK, I APPRECIATE THE ADVICE, AND I'M LOOKING INTO SOME GIRLS WHO MIGHT--
NOT TALKIN' ABOUT YOU, MATE. TALKIN' ABOUT ME.
THINK I'M IN LOVE.
IN LOVE WITH WH--
OH, NO. LOOK, THAT'S-- REALLY NOT A GOOD IDEA.
DON'T SWEAT IT... SEEMS I'M NOT HER TYPE.

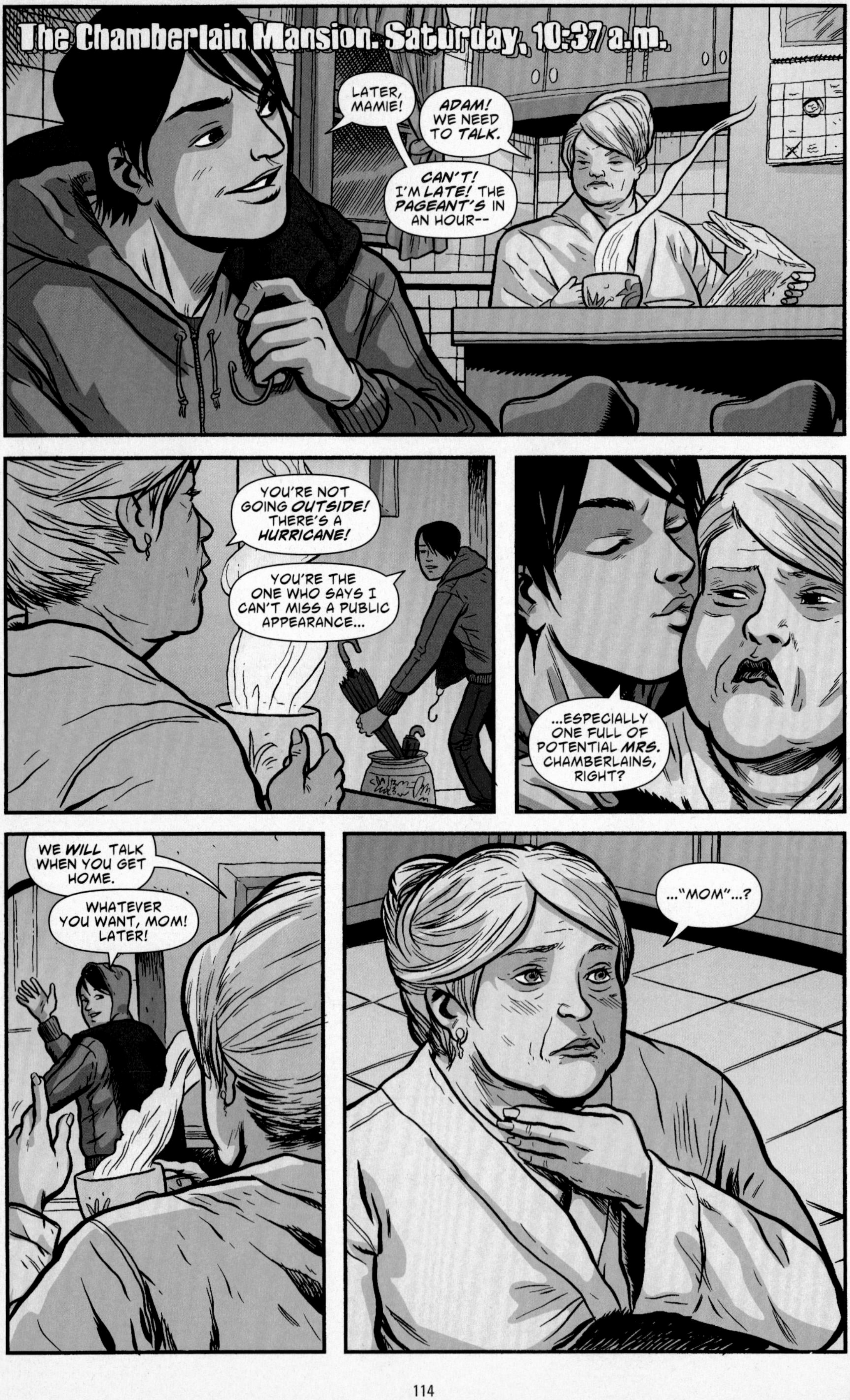
The Chamberlain Mansion. Saturday, 10:37 a.m.
LATER, MAMIE!
ADAM! WE NEED TO TALK.
CAN'T! I'M LATE! THE PAGEANT'S IN AN HOUR--
YOU'RE NOT GOING OUTSIDE! THERE'S A HURRICANE!
YOU'RE THE ONE WHO SAYS I CAN'T MISS A PUBLIC APPEARANCE...
...ESPECIALLY ONE FULL OF POTENTIAL MRS. CHAMBERLAINS, RIGHT?
WE WILL TALK WHEN YOU GET HOME.
WHATEVER YOU WANT, MOM! LATER!
..."MOM"...?

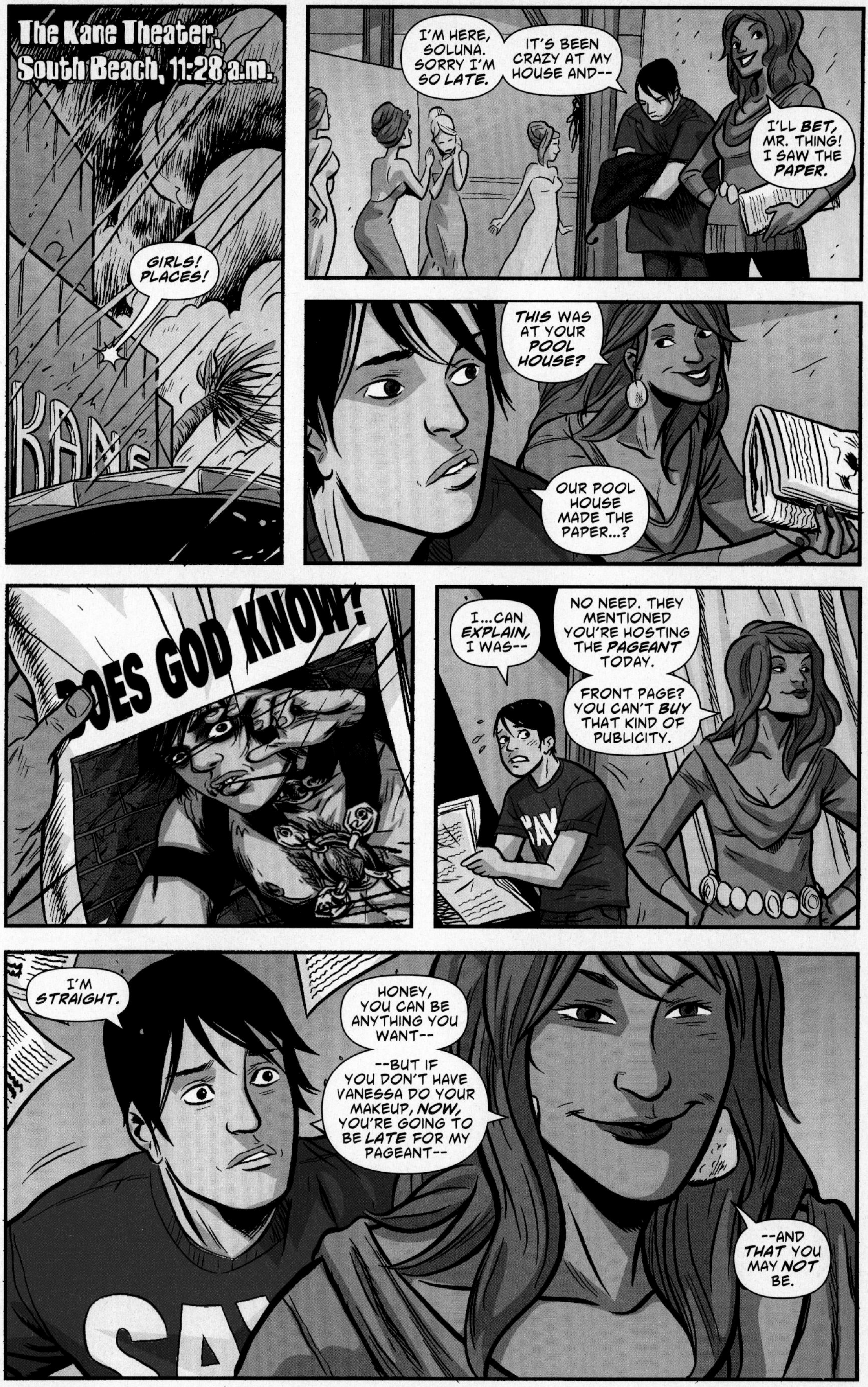

The Kane Theater, South Beach, 11:28 a.m.
GIRLS! PLACES!
I'M HERE, SOLUNA. SORRY I'M SO LATE.
IT'S BEEN CRAZY AT MY HOUSE AND--
I'LL BET, MR. THING! I SAW THE PAPER.
THIS WAS AT YOUR POOL HOUSE?
OUR POOL HOUSE MADE THE PAPER...?
DOES GOD KNOW?
I...CAN EXPLAIN, I WAS--
NO NEED. THEY MENTIONED YOU'RE HOSTING THE PAGEANT TODAY.
FRONT PAGE? YOU CAN'T BUY THAT KIND OF PUBLICITY.
I'M STRAIGHT.
HONEY, YOU CAN BE ANYTHING YOU WANT--
--BUT IF YOU DON'T HAVE VANESSA DO YOUR MAKEUP, NOW, YOU'RE GOING TO BE LATE FOR MY PAGEANT--
--AND THAT YOU MAY NOT BE.

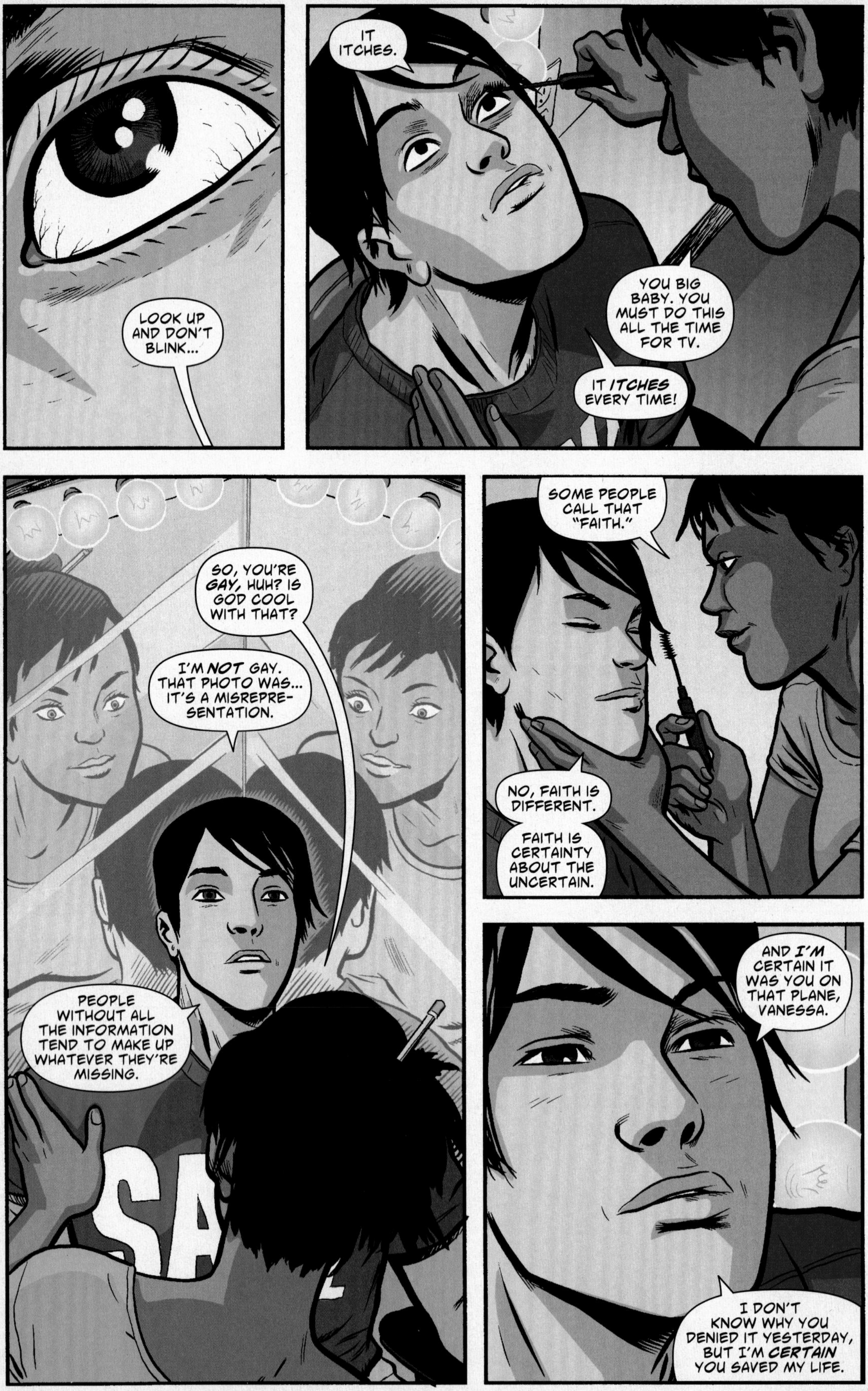
LOOK UP AND DON'T BLINK...
IT ITCHES.
YOU BIG BABY. YOU MUST DO THIS ALL THE TIME FOR TV.
IT ITCHES EVERY TIME!
SO, YOU'RE GAY, HUH? IS GOD COOL WITH THAT?
I'M NOT GAY. THAT PHOTO WAS... IT'S A MISREPRESENTATION.
PEOPLE WITHOUT ALL THE INFORMATION TEND TO MAKE UP WHATEVER THEY'RE MISSING.
SOME PEOPLE CALL THAT "FAITH."
NO, FAITH IS DIFFERENT.
FAITH IS CERTAINTY ABOUT THE UNCERTAIN.
AND I'M CERTAIN IT WAS YOU ON THAT PLANE, VANESSA.
I DON'T KNOW WHY YOU DENIED IT YESTERDAY, BUT I'M CERTAIN YOU SAVED MY LIFE.

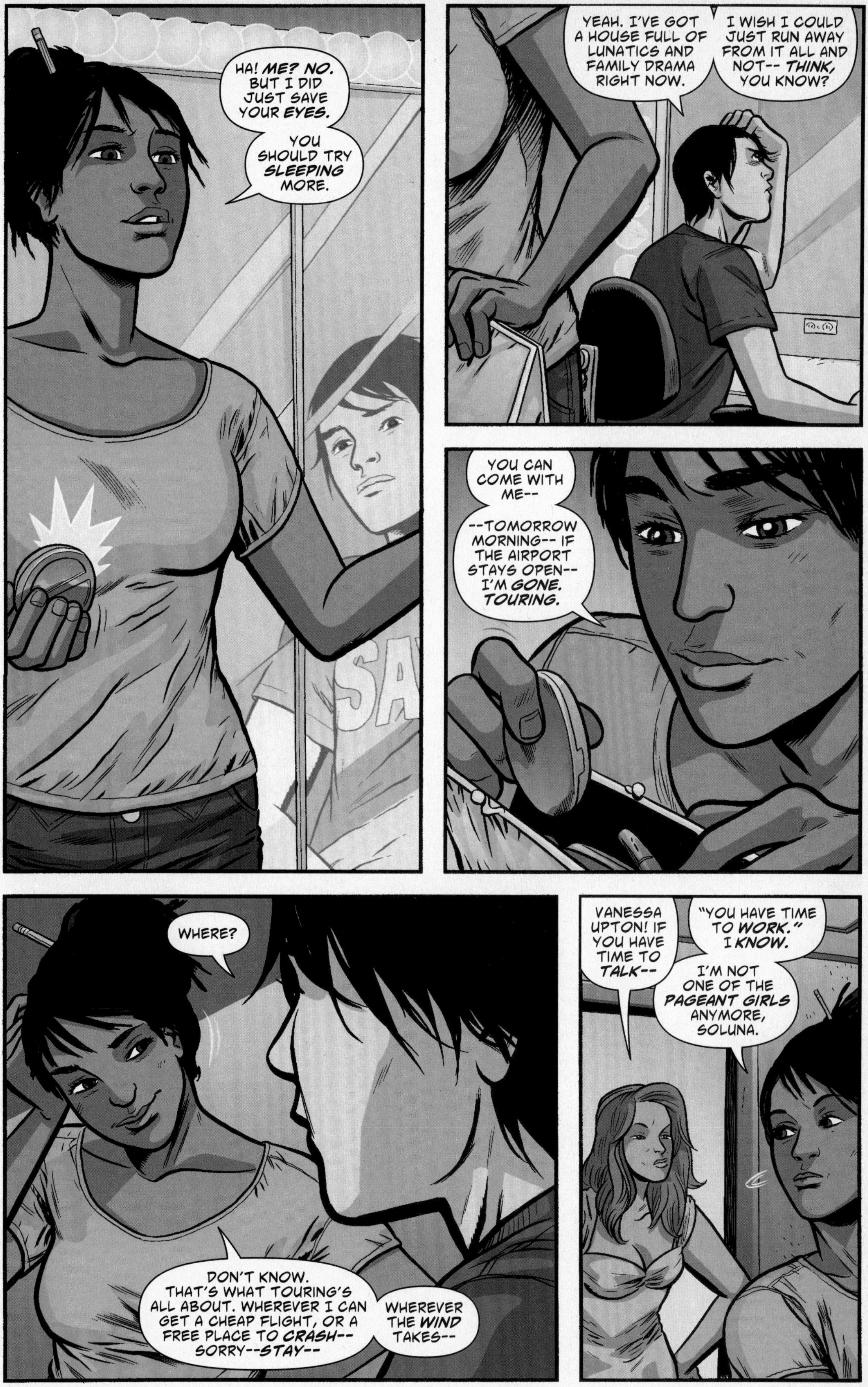
HA! ME? NO. BUT I DID JUST SAVE YOUR EYES.
YOU SHOULD TRY SLEEPING MORE.
YEAH. I'VE GOT A HOUSE FULL OF LUNATICS AND FAMILY DRAMA RIGHT NOW.
I WISH I COULD JUST RUN AWAY FROM IT ALL AND NOT-- THINK, YOU KNOW?
YOU CAN COME WITH ME--
--TOMORROW MORNING-- IF THE AIRPORT STAYS OPEN-- I'M GONE. TOURING.
WHERE?
DON'T KNOW. THAT'S WHAT TOURING'S ALL ABOUT. WHEREVER I CAN GET A CHEAP FLIGHT, OR A FREE PLACE TO CRASH-- SORRY--STAY--
WHEREVER THE WIND TAKES--
VANESSA UPTON! IF YOU HAVE TIME TO TALK--
"YOU HAVE TIME TO WORK." I KNOW.
I'M NOT ONE OF THE PAGEANT GIRLS ANYMORE, SOLUNA.

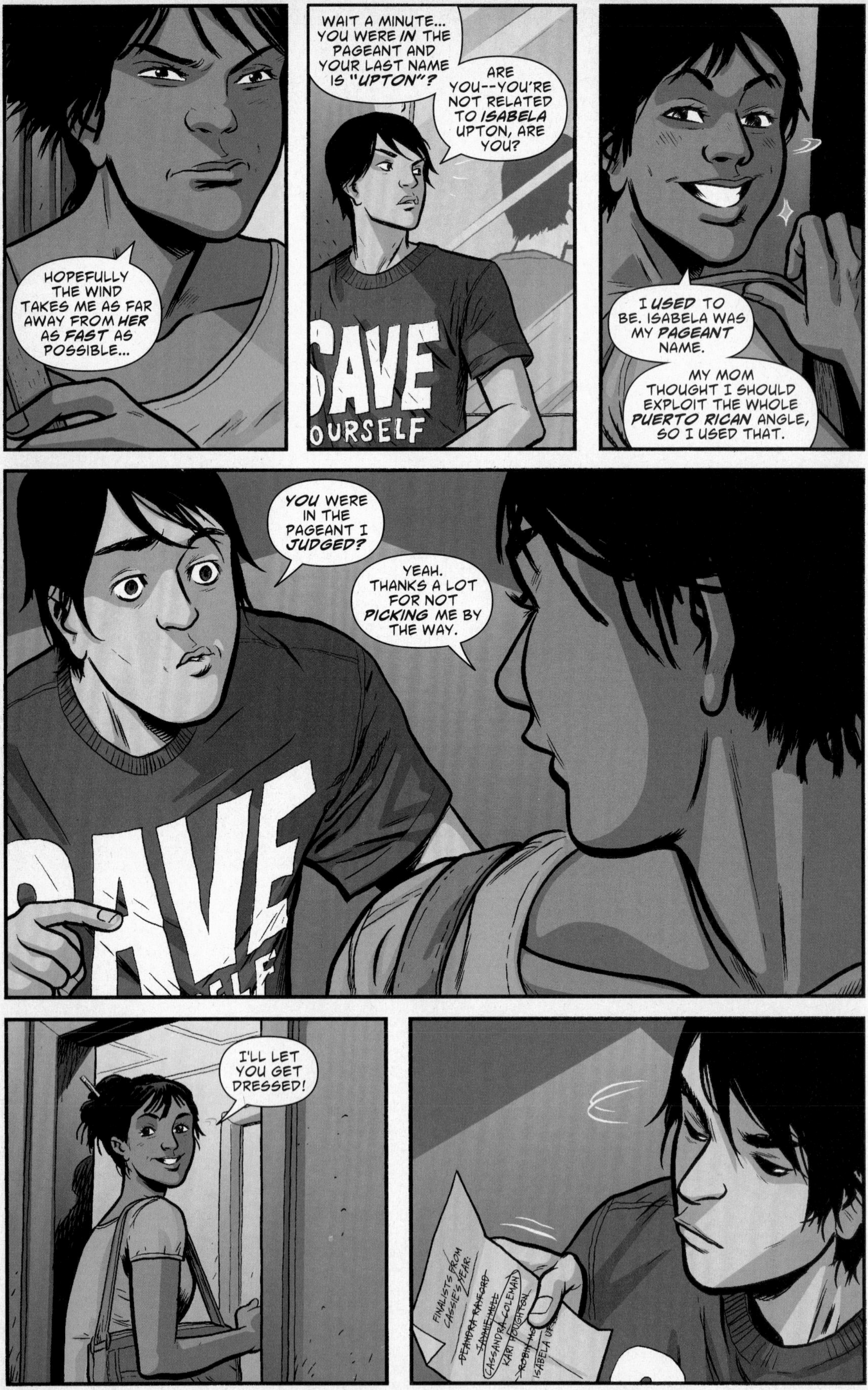
HOPEFULLY THE WIND TAKES ME AS FAR AWAY FROM HER AS FAST AS POSSIBLE...
WAIT A MINUTE... YOU WERE IN THE PAGEANT AND YOUR LAST NAME IS "UPTON"?
ARE YOU--YOU'RE NOT RELATED TO ISABELA UPTON, ARE YOU?
SAVE YOURSELF
I USED TO BE. ISABELA WAS MY PAGEANT NAME.
MY MOM THOUGHT I SHOULD EXPLOIT THE WHOLE PUERTO RICAN ANGLE, SO I USED THAT.
YOU WERE IN THE PAGEANT I JUDGED?
YEAH. THANKS A LOT FOR NOT PICKING ME BY THE WAY.
I'LL LET YOU GET DRESSED!
FINALISTS FROM CASSIE'S YEAR:
DEANDRA RAYFORD
JAMIE HULL
CASSANDRA COLEMAN
KARI HOUGHTON

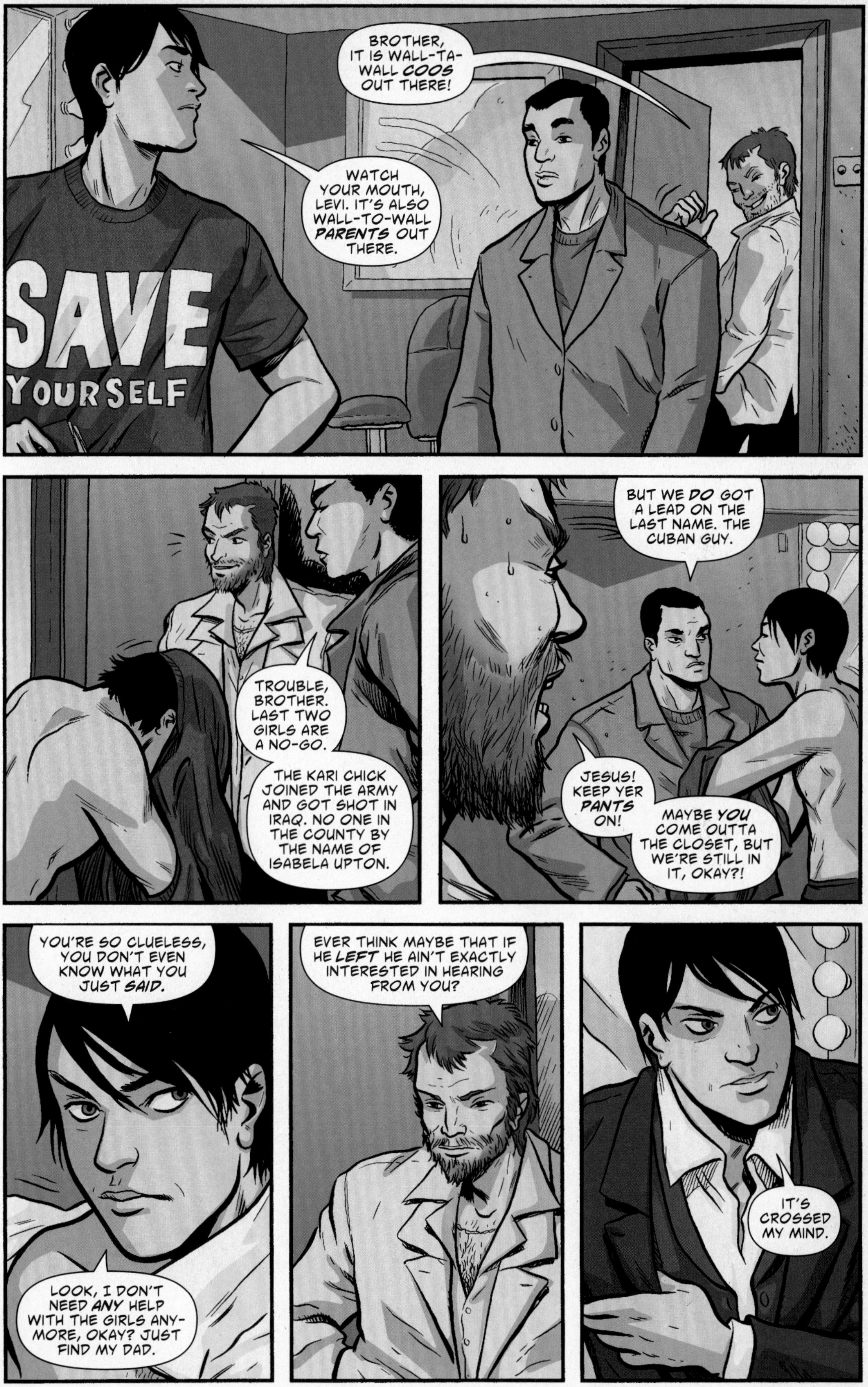
BROTHER, IT IS WALL-TA-WALL COOS OUT THERE!
WATCH YOUR MOUTH, LEVI. IT'S ALSO WALL-TO-WALL PARENTS OUT THERE.
SAVE YOURSELF
TROUBLE, BROTHER. LAST TWO GIRLS ARE A NO-GO.
THE KARI CHICK JOINED THE ARMY AND GOT SHOT IN IRAQ. NO ONE IN THE COUNTY BY THE NAME OF ISABELA UPTON.
BUT WE DO GOT A LEAD ON THE LAST NAME. THE CUBAN GUY.
JESUS! KEEP YER PANTS ON!
MAYBE YOU COME OUTTA THE CLOSET, BUT WE'RE STILL IN IT, OKAY?!
YOU'RE SO CLUELESS, YOU DON'T EVEN KNOW WHAT YOU JUST SAID.
LOOK, I DON'T NEED ANY HELP WITH THE GIRLS ANY-MORE, OKAY? JUST FIND MY DAD.
EVER THINK MAYBE THAT IF HE LEFT HE AIN'T EXACTLY INTERESTED IN HEARING FROM YOU?
IT'S CROSSED MY MIND.

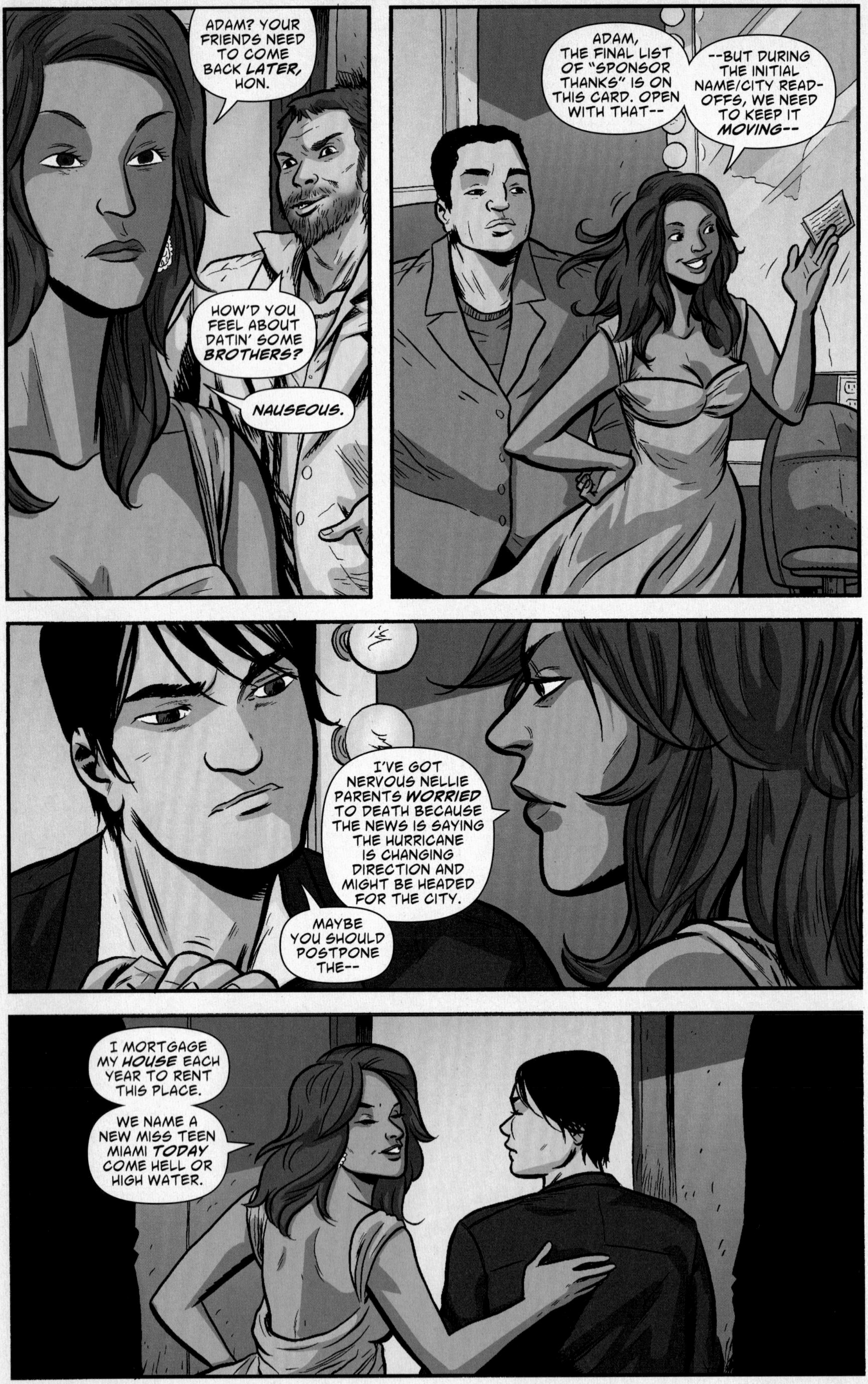
ADAM? YOUR FRIENDS NEED TO COME BACK LATER, HON.
HOW'D YOU FEEL ABOUT DATIN' SOME BROTHERS?
NAUSEOUS.
ADAM, THE FINAL LIST OF "SPONSOR THANKS" IS ON THIS CARD. OPEN WITH THAT--
--BUT DURING THE INITIAL NAME/CITY READ-OFFS, WE NEED TO KEEP IT MOVING--
I'VE GOT NERVOUS NELLIE PARENTS WORRIED TO DEATH BECAUSE THE NEWS IS SAYING THE HURRICANE IS CHANGING DIRECTION AND MIGHT BE HEADED FOR THE CITY.
MAYBE YOU SHOULD POSTPONE THE--
I MORTGAGE MY HOUSE EACH YEAR TO RENT THIS PLACE.
WE NAME A NEW MISS TEEN MIAMI TODAY COME HELL OR HIGH WATER.

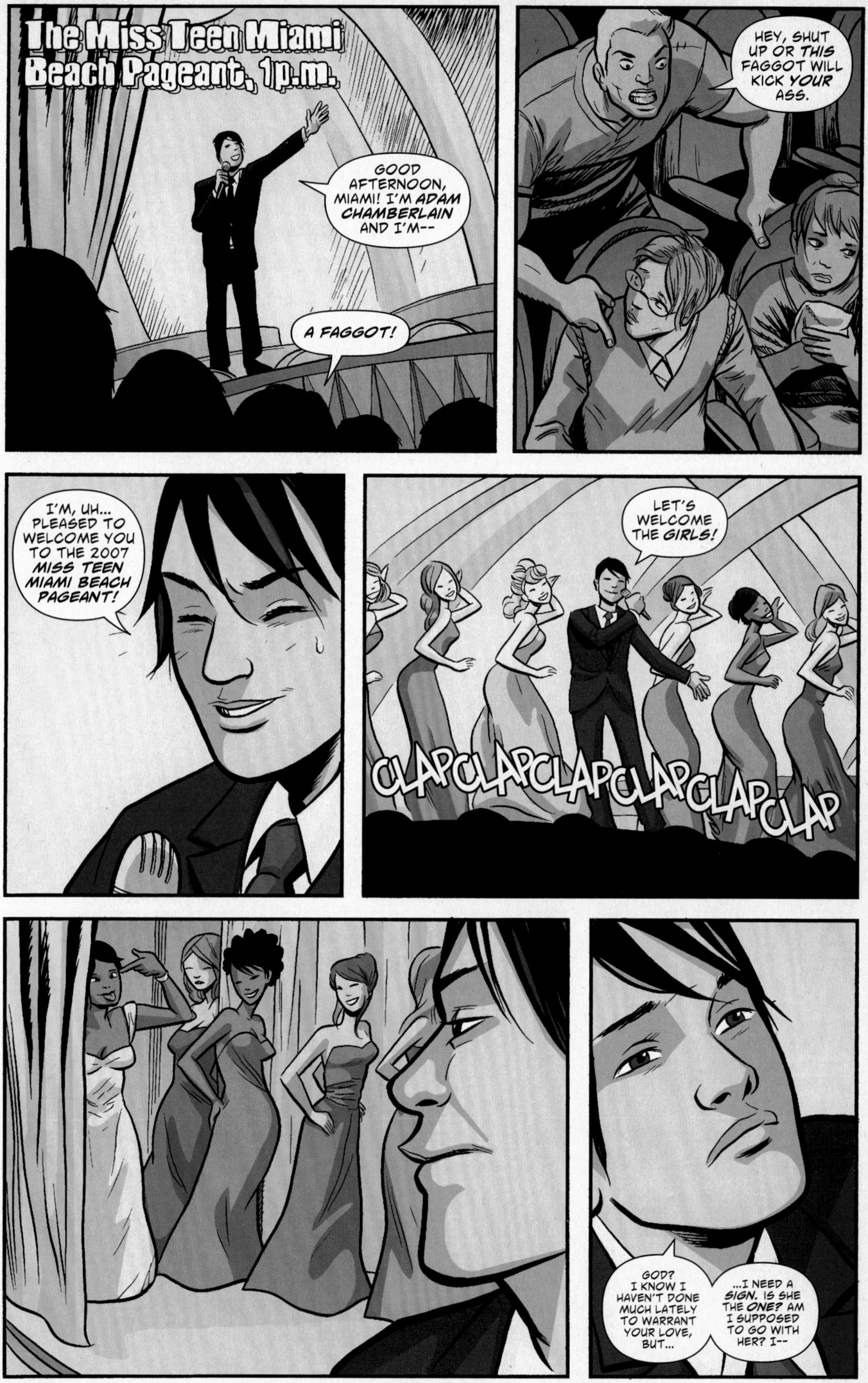
The Miss Teen Miami Beach Pageant, 1p.m.
GOOD AFTERNOON, MIAMI! I'M ADAM CHAMBERLAIN AND I'M--
A FAGGOT!
HEY, SHUT UP OR THIS FAGGOT WILL KICK YOUR ASS.
I'M, UH... PLEASED TO WELCOME YOU TO THE 2007 MISS TEEN MIAMI BEACH PAGEANT!
LET'S WELCOME THE GIRLS!
CLAPCLAPCLAPCLAPCLAPCLAP
GOD? I KNOW I HAVEN'T DONE MUCH LATELY TO WARRANT YOUR LOVE, BUT...
...I NEED A SIGN. IS SHE THE ONE? AM I SUPPOSED TO GO WITH HER? I--

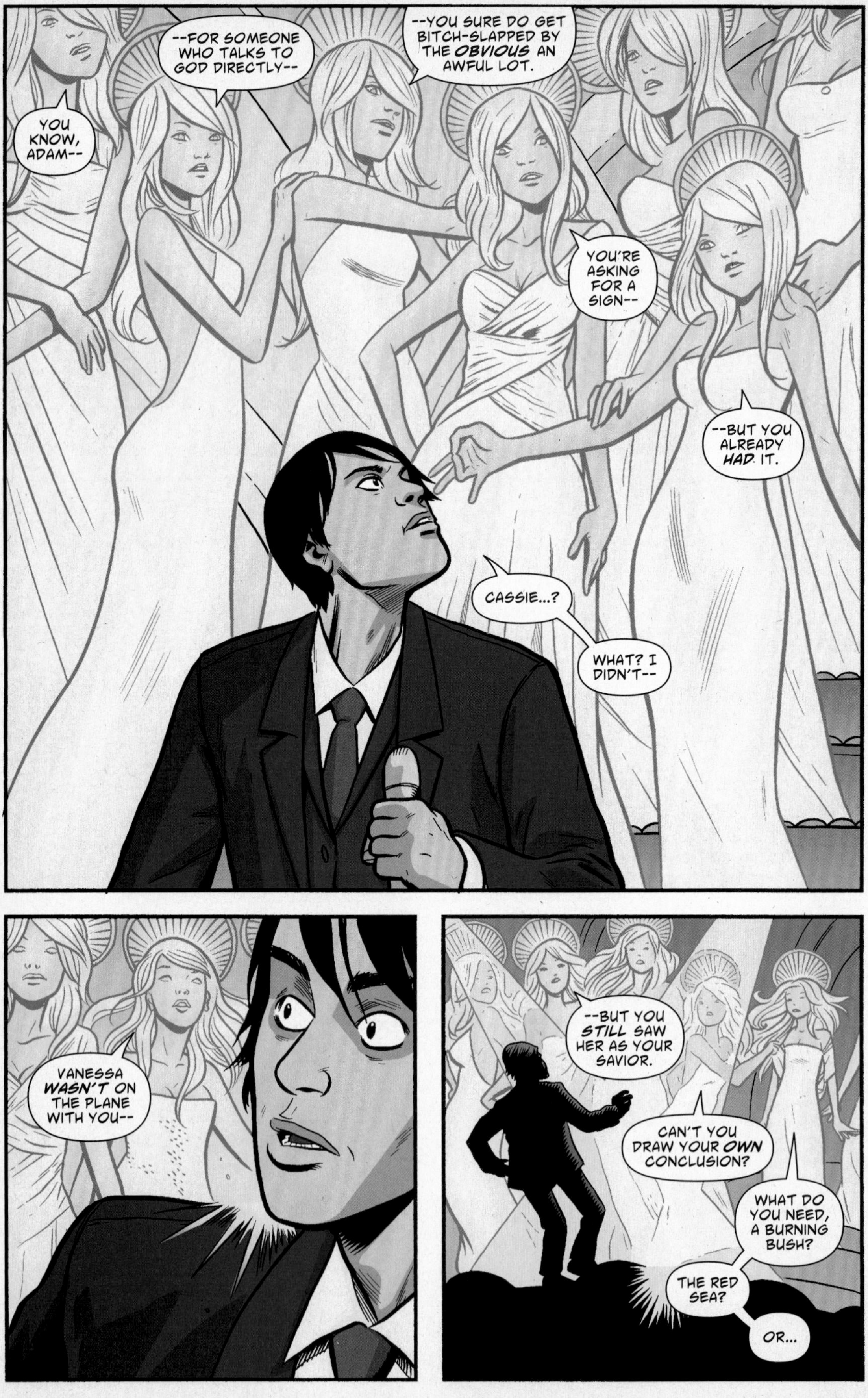
YOU KNOW, ADAM--
--FOR SOMEONE WHO TALKS TO GOD DIRECTLY--
--YOU SURE DO GET BITCH-SLAPPED BY THE OBVIOUS AN AWFUL LOT.
YOU'RE ASKING FOR A SIGN--
--BUT YOU ALREADY HAD IT.
CASSIE...?
WHAT? I DIDN'T--
VANESSA WASN'T ON THE PLANE WITH YOU--
--BUT YOU STILL SAW HER AS YOUR SAVIOR.
CAN'T YOU DRAW YOUR OWN CONCLUSION?
WHAT DO YOU NEED, A BURNING BUSH?
THE RED SEA?
OR...

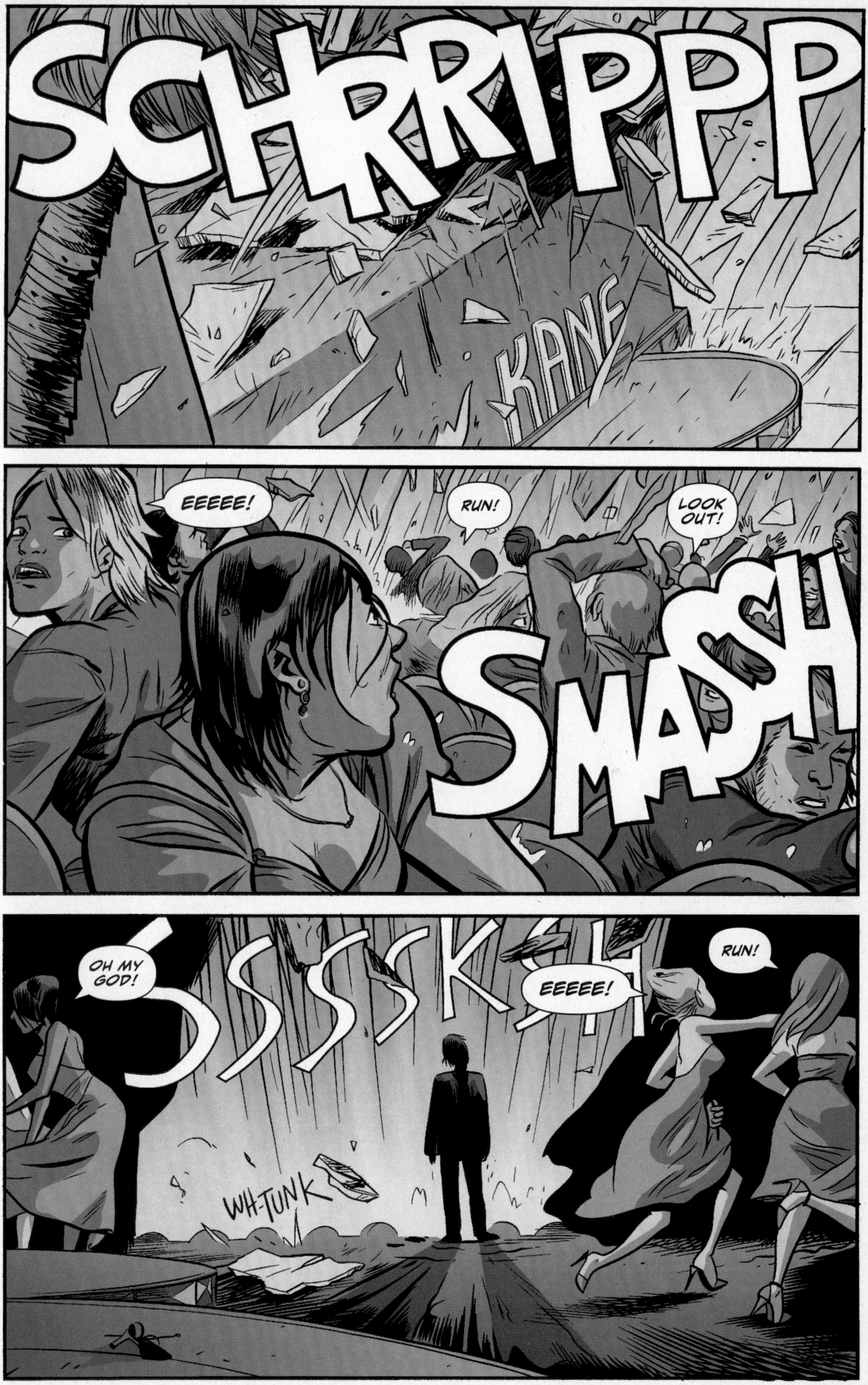
SCHRRIPPP
KANE
EEEEE!
RUN!
LOOK OUT!
SMASH
OH MY GOD!
SSSSKSH
EEEEE!
RUN!
WH-TUNK

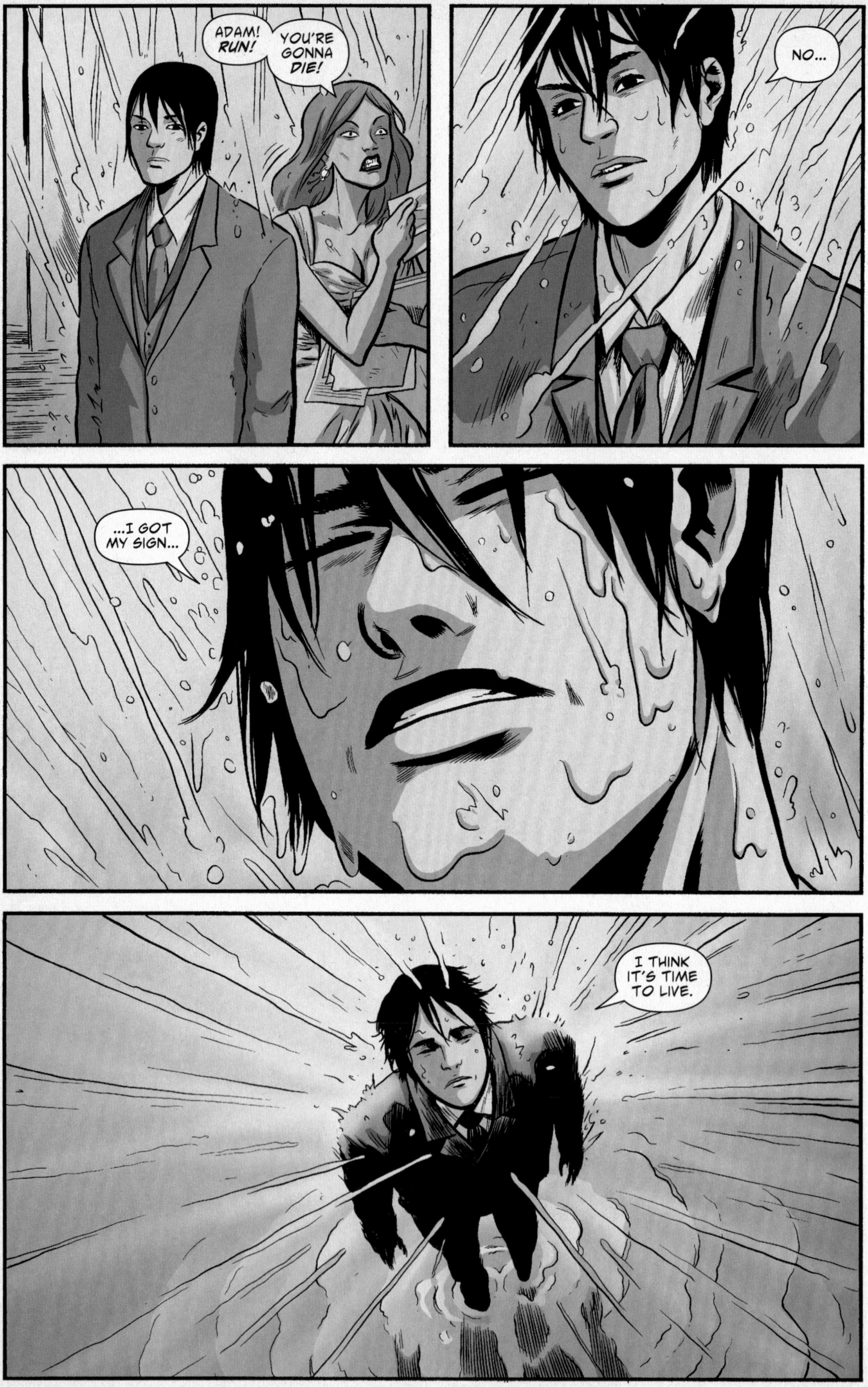
ADAM! RUN!
YOU'RE GONNA DIE!
NO...
...I GOT MY SIGN...
I THINK IT'S TIME TO LIVE.

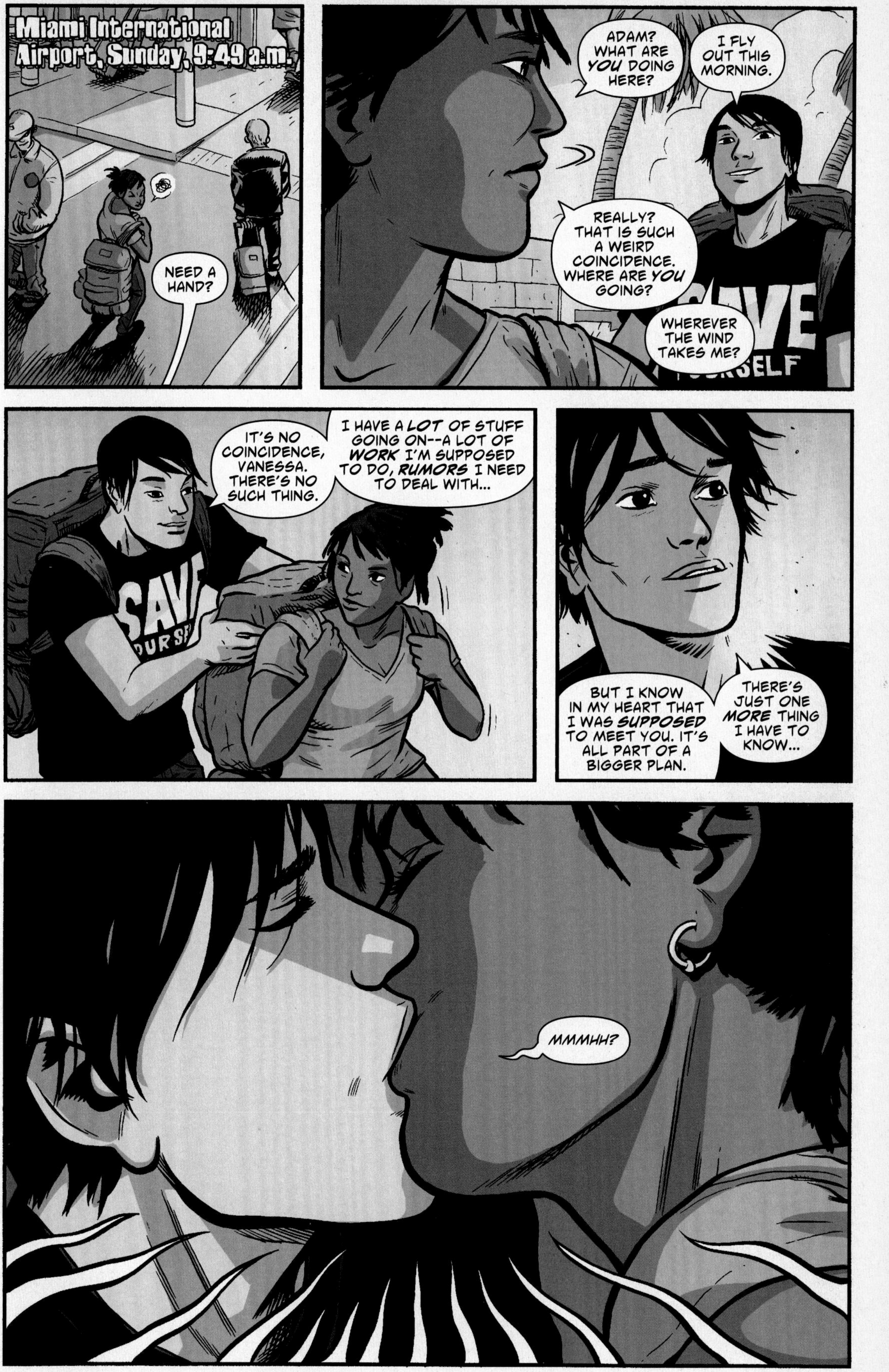
Miami International Airport, Sunday, 9:49 a.m.
NEED A HAND?
ADAM? WHAT ARE YOU DOING HERE?
I FLY OUT THIS MORNING.
REALLY? THAT IS SUCH A WEIRD COINCIDENCE. WHERE ARE YOU GOING?
WHEREVER THE WIND TAKES ME?
SAVE YOURSELF
IT'S NO COINCIDENCE, VANESSA. THERE'S NO SUCH THING.
I HAVE A LOT OF STUFF GOING ON--A LOT OF WORK I'M SUPPOSED TO DO, RUMORS I NEED TO DEAL WITH...
BUT I KNOW IN MY HEART THAT I WAS SUPPOSED TO MEET YOU. IT'S ALL PART OF A BIGGER PLAN.
THERE'S JUST ONE MORE THING I HAVE TO KNOW...
MMMHH?

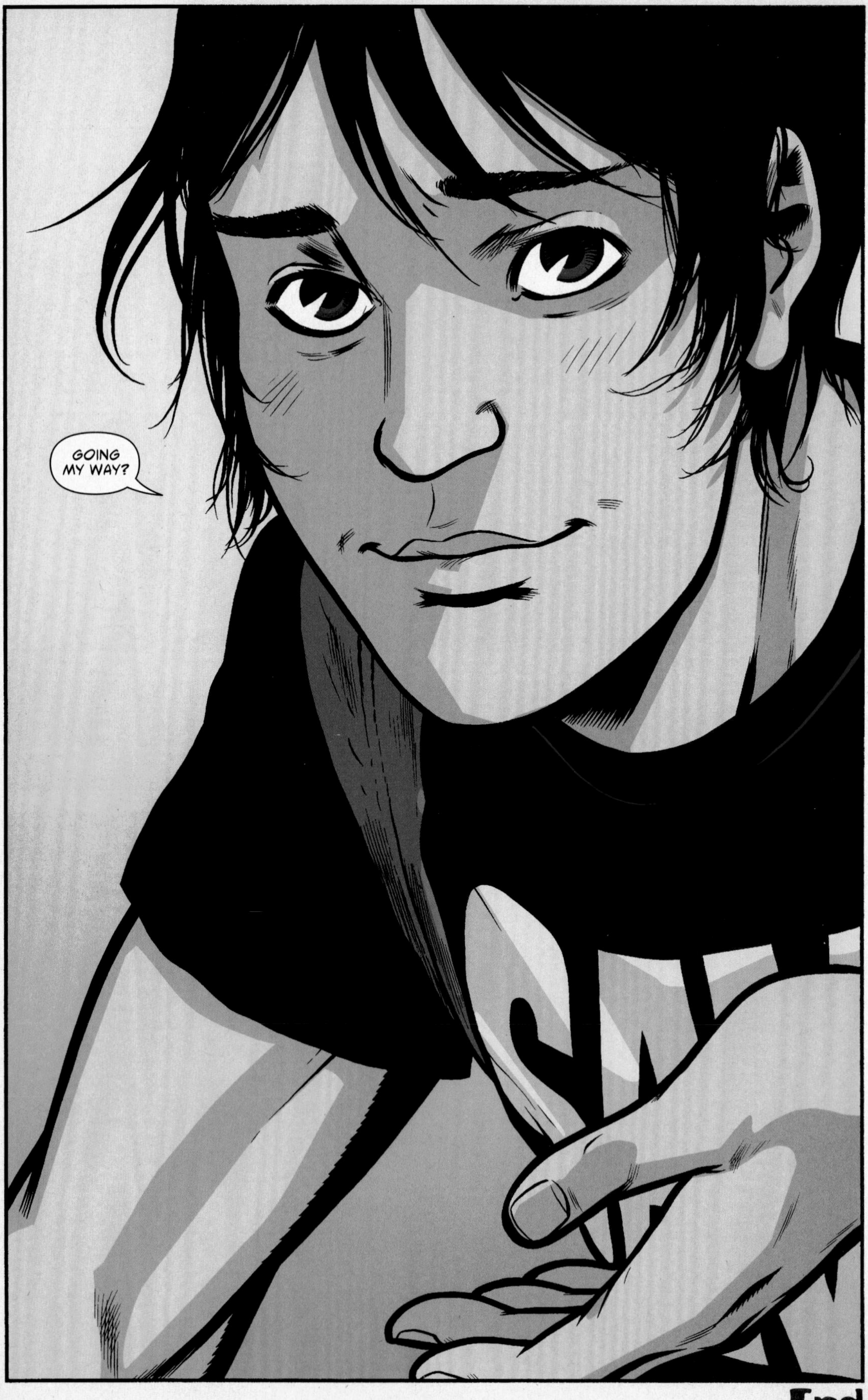
GOING MY WAY?

End

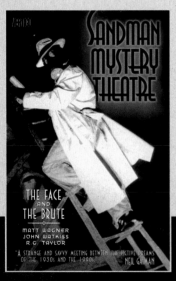

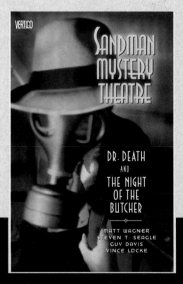